A READER OF
CLASSICAL ARABIC LITERATURE

RESOURCES IN ARABIC
AND ISLAMIC STUDIES

series editors

Joseph E. Lowry
Devin J. Stewart
Shawkat M. Toorawa

Number 1
A Reader of Classical Arabic Literature

A READER OF CLASSICAL ARABIC LITERATURE

annotated and edited by

S. A. Bonebakker
and
Michael Fishbein

LOCKWOOD PRESS
Atlanta, Georgia
2012

First published in 1995 by Cafoscarina, Università Ca' Foscari di Venezia,
Dipartimento di Scienze Storico-Archeologiche e Orientalistiche
as volume 1 of Quaderni di Studi Arabi. Studi e testi.

This edition published under license from the Istituto per l'Oriente, Rome, Italy.

ISBN: 978-1-937040-03-1

Library of Congress Control Number: 2012933525

Cover image: The first page of an annotated manuscript copy of the *Maqāmāt* of al-Ḥarīrī.

Printed in the United States of America on acid-free paper.

Contents

Preface to the First Printing

This reader is based in large part on lecture notes by Dr. Bonebakker. In the course of its preparation we added a few selections that had not been previously used in our classes, but most selections have been tried out more than once.

In keeping with the purpose of the Reader as stated in the Introduction, these notes have been considerably enlarged not only with grammatical and lexicographic references, but also with information gathered from handbooks such as the second edition of the *Encyclopaedia of Islam*, the first edition with its Supplement, biographical dictionaries in Arabic, monographs such as Jacob's *Altarabisches Beduinenleben*, C. Brockelmann's *Geschichte der arabischen Literatur*, and F. Sezgins's *Geschichte des arabischen Schrifttums*; but in doing so we did not—and due to limitations of space could not—aim at doing justice to the enormous growth of important publications that had appeared, especially after the Second World War. Many readers therefore will miss references to publications they feel should have been included in the introductions and notes to the individual selections.

A work of this kind written with a didactic purpose in mind, though modest in size, could not be put together by a single teacher, however experienced. A thorough critical revision of the notes by a younger scholar, and, in some cases, a fresh trial before a classroom audience was imperative. Dr. Fishbein charged himself with this task, correcting and sometimes rewriting entries in the glossaries and making additions where necessary. Moreover, Dr. Fishbein undertook the task of typing the glossaries in Arabic and English and, last but not least, correcting the style of notes and introductions.

We both owe a large debt of gratitude to the editors of *Quaderni di Studi Arabi* who accepted this Reader for publication. We also thank our students at the University of California at Los Angeles and, for a shorter period, students at the Palazzo Capello in Venice for their patience and suggestions.

S. A. Bonebakker
Michael Fishbein

Preface to the Reprint Edition

When *A Reader of Classical Arabic Literature* appeared in 1995,[1] it joined a very small group of resources in English for the teaching of intermediate and advanced level classical Arabic.[2] The *Reader* was based on the lecture notes of the late Seeger Bonebakker, who was aware that "a single teacher, however experienced" needed the assistance of "a younger scholar, and, in some cases, a fresh trial before a classroom audience." Professor Bonebakker accordingly asked Dr Michael Fishbein to be his collaborator. The result was a truly valuable reader, one that we use in our own teaching and which colleagues across the Atlantic use too. Indeed, the book was first published in Italy by the discerning editors of the journal, *Quaderni di Studi Arabi*.[3]

When we decided to launch 'Resources in Arabic and Islamic Studies,' one of the first questions we asked ourselves was: What should our first publication be? Given that Arabic grammars do not get students to the point of actually reading texts, and given the focus in many modern textbooks on media and modern Arabic, we agreed that we would try and get permission to reprint *A Reader of Classical Arabic Literature*, a work that was becoming increasingly hard to find. We are very grateful to our School of 'Abbasid Studies colleague, Professor Antonella Ghersetti, and to Professors Giovanni Canova and Claudio Lo Jacono at l'Istituto per l'Oriente C. A. Nallino in Rome, with whom she put us in touch, for permission to reprint the *Reader*. It is a pleasure to make available a work that has been described

1. *A Reader of Classical Arabic Literature*, annotated and edited by Seeger A. Bonebakker and Michael Fishbein (Venice: Cafoscarina: Università Ca' Foscari di Venezia, 1995), p. iii.

2. See also Rudolf-Ernst Brünnow and August Fischer, *Chrestomathy of Arabic Prose Literature*, 8th revised edition by Lutz Edzard and Amund Bjørsnøs (Wiesbaden: Harrassowitz, 2008). The paucity of such teaching materials is described by Bonebakker and Fishbein in their Introduction below.

3. The Italian publication of the work is described by Roger Allen, in his review of the *Reader* in the *Middle East Studies Association Bulletin* 33/2 (Winter 1999), pp. 170–171, as "a telling commentary on the priorities of a market-driven publishing industry in the English-speaking world" (171).

as "well thought-out and thorough," and one in which "the apparatuses ... are stunning, providing a rich resource guide for students embarking on their adventures in Arabic medieval texts."[4]

By virtue of the fact that we are reprinting the original edition, we have not been able to make formatting or font changes, but we did contact Dr. Fishbein to ask whether he had any corrections, and he very kindly shared some with us. We include these, together with our own, in the Addenda and Corrigenda.

We would like to express our gratitude to Ian Stevens for introducing us to Billie Jean Collins of Lockwood Press. Her enthusiasm about the Resources in Arabic and Islamic Studies series has been unflagging: indeed, it is thanks to her perseverance that this wonderful resource has found its way into print again.

Joseph E. Lowry
Devin J. Stewart
Shawkat M. Toorawa

4. Clarissa Burt, in *Journal of Arabic Literature* 29/2 (1998), pp. 85–90.

Introduction

This reader was put together with a view to helping those students who intend to study Arabic prose texts on their own. In the course of many years of teaching I have often heard the complaint that there exist no easily accessible texts which would help the beginning Arabist during the summer, when it is not always possible to attend a summer school or to find a tutor. Others may find that courses offered at the university have to emphasize grammar at the expense of offering the necessary routine. With this in mind, I have collected some texts which I hope will not only be useful to the beginner, but will also offer interesting, sometimes amusing, reading. Another consideration was the relatively limited number of other chrestomathies available to students. The famous readers by R. A. Nicholson in English and by A. Fischer in German have been out of print for many years and are often found too difficult for self-study. Other chrestomathies have appeared since that time; I am thinking in particular of R. Blachère and H. Darmaun, *Géographes arabes du Moyen Age,* Paris, 1957; and H. Pérès and P. Mangion, *Les mille et une nuits,* Algiers, n.d.; but, with the exception of the attractive *Elementary Classical Arabic Reader* by M. C. Lyons, Cambridge, 1962, there are not too many works of this kind in English. I therefore felt that an additional reader might be welcome. I do not pretend that I am doing more than follow the footsteps of my predecessors, except that the texts offered here have, as far as I know, not yet been presented in this form in other chrestomathies.

Again with a view to helping students work on their own, I have included some texts that exist in reliable translations. I have not aimed at offering a collection that represents all genres; this would have been difficult under any circumstances.[1] Instead, I have chosen to limit myself to those genres with which I was most familiar. Thus the reader will find many selections from so-called adab works,[2] a term which has been widely adopted, although it has never been properly

---

[1] For historical and medical texts see C. H. M. Versteegh, *Werkschriften van het Instituut voor talen en culturen van het Midden Oosten*, nos. 3–4 (in Dutch), privately printed, Nijmegen, 1977–78.

[2] The term seems to be a modern invention; I know of only two cases in medieval texts where there is question of *kutub adabiyya*. In other places where the term appears in medieval documents, the context does not suggest that *adab* has to be understood as a genre. On the other hand, it is difficult to avoid using a term that has been common for at least half a century, even though there is no agreement on the way it should be understood. I would suggest taking what usually goes under the name of "*adab* book" as: col-

defined, and which I would suggest should be understood in the sense of collections of quotations in poetry and prose considered to have literary merit and reflecting the cultural, esthetic, educational, and moral traditions of the Arabs.

I did not hesitate to add some passages of which the correct reading and interpretation are not always clear. In my opinion, it makes little sense to limit oneself to 'easy' passages, or to 'grade' the selection. This conflicts with the realities of engaging in a relatively young discipline which does not have completely adequate tools at its disposal. For the same reason I have chosen not to follow the solution adopted in some readers of changing the wording of difficult sentences. I have chosen instead to provide very ample annotation without (as a rule) repeating information given earlier. By attempting to determine which selections are 'difficult' and which are not, one risks finding that what is 'difficult' for some may be 'easy' for others. On the other hand, I feel that it makes sense to bring together selections from poetry and rhymed prose in a separate volume provided with an apparatus for prosody.

I have attached short biographies to each selection without attempting to bring anything original, but offering, I hope, some references that will help the reader find his way in the literature about the author. That I am much indebted to the *Encyclopedia of Islam*, F. Sezgin's *GAS*, and to a lesser extent, C. Brockelmann's *GAL* goes without saying. Since these handbooks invariably offer both Muslim and Christian dates, and since tables of corresponding Christian dates are easily available, I have limited myself to dates of the Muslim calendar.

The glossary is not intended to make the use of dictionaries unnecessary, but rather, especially in the earlier pieces, to avoid making the interpretation of the text an endless exercise in hunting for the English equivalent of difficult or not easily identifiable terms. Grammatical references are almost exclusively to Wright's famous grammar, which, although in some respects outdated, is still an excellent work of reference and probably for this reason has been regularly reprinted. Other Arabic grammars in English have the handicap that they are too elementary. However, I did not hesitate to refer to some grammars in French, German, and Italian when I felt that these foreign grammars offered some advantages over the

---

lections of prose and poetry of artistic merit, and, at the same time educational in the sense that they embody the old Arab traditions in the widest sense: moral, religious, ethical, and stylistic. *Adab* also appears in the more limited sense of 'linguistics,' 'philology.' Some scholars may include texts written for amusement only, but often requiring a solid background in history, and probably created by the 'professional secretaries' (*kuttāb*). See S. A. Bonebakker, "Early Arabic Literature and the Term *Adab*," in *Jerusalem Studies in Arabic and Islam*, 5 (1984), 398–421, and the literature quoted there.

explanation on a given subject offered by Wright. I also did not hesitate to offer translations of an entire phrase and to leave the explanation of the syntax of that particular phrase to a later selection in order not to overload the glossaries at the beginning of the book with grammatical references. In selecting translations for difficult terms, i.e., translations for which no support was found in any dictionary or glossary, a certain subjectivity could not be avoided, especially in passages from Ibn Jubayr dealing with architecture.

A word must be said here about the problems of Arabic lexicography. We have the Arabic-Latin dictionary by G.W. Freytag, which is no longer in use, even though it has been reprinted. We also have the small, but fairly reliable dictionaries by A. de Biberstein Kazimirski, J.-B. Bélot (French), and J. G. Hava (English). The large and detailed dictionary by R. Blachère *et al.* is still in progress and has not yet reached beyond the sixth letter of the Arabic alphabet. There is an excellent tool for contemporary literary Arabic by H. Wehr[3] as well as a famous collection of additions to Freytag and Lane by Dozy, entitled *Supplément aux dictionnaires arabes,* based in large part on texts coming from Spain, but also incorporating texts from other areas and relatively late periods. The monumental dictionary by E. W. Lane[4] unfortunately was incomplete when the author died (beginning with the letter *qāf* it offers only fragmentary information); moreover it is basically a translation of a large number of native dictionaries which Lane had to consult in manuscript. With few exceptions, these native dictionaries neglect historical, geographical, and scientific texts, and do not reach beyond the 2nd/8th century, not to speak of other deficiencies which one would expect to find in medieval lexicons. This means that all Arabic texts (as far as they represent original work, not digests of earlier texts) still have to be examined or reexamined before we can consider any dictionary for the medieval period to be complete. A comprehensive dictionary should also make use of the glossaries appended by some editors to their text editions. Since the works of many medieval authors survive only in manuscript and new manuscripts are still being discovered, the situation of Arabic lexicography, even if limited to

---

3 *A Dictionary of Modern Written Arabic*, ed. (i.e., translated) by J. M. Cowan (several reprints). The latest edition, Wiesbaden, 1985 (*Arabisches Wörterbuch für die Schriftsprache der Gegenwart*) has not yet been translated. The vowelings in Wehr's dictionary are reliable; those in Hava are correct in most cases. Whenever it is essential to avoid mistakes, Wehr or Hava should be consulted.

4 *An Arabic-English Lexicon*, London, 1863–93, 8 vols., several facsimile reprints. See below, Arabic Grammars.

the classical period, can only be characterized as very precarious.[5] A large step forward was taken by the *Wörterbuch der klassischen arabischen Sprache* now being prepared by M. Ullmann, which took up where Lane ended, that is at the letter *kāf*, following the letter *qāf*, where Lane's dictionary begins to be deficient; but the lack of proper dictionaries can be expected to remain a serious problem for many years to come.[6] The dictionary by Freytag now is seldom used; the dictionary by Lane is to be preferred, in spite of its limitations, of which Lane himself was well aware. All this leads to the conclusion that much is left to the reliance of the student of Arabic texts on (and his thorough familiarity with) the semantic spectrum of the forms of the verb, of certain nominal forms, certain forms of the broken plural, and, last but not least, his reliance on his intuition.

The following may be observed with regards to the grammars listed: Wright's Grammar, itself the almost completely rewritten translation of an early 19th-century German work by a certain Caspari, dates from 1852-1856, and, in its present form, from 1896. Wright's translation, as well as the revision by de Goeje, often used phrases which the two authors had collected during their long careers as editors of medieval texts. The work leans heavily on native medieval authorities. In many ways this is an advantage: Wright mentions much, but not all, of the terminology of medieval grammar, such as one finds it in commentary literature, thereby making it easier for the student to use the often valuable clarifications by ancient grammarians and philologists. Unfortunately, Wright's indexes to both Arabic and English terminology are incomplete.

An essential supplement to Wright are the two books by Reckendorf, which are based on hundreds of observations collected by the author and explained in a way that does not take medieval syntax as a point of departure, though it does not fail to refer to it wherever possible. Nevertheless, the book's usefulness is limited: Reckendorf concentrates on the syntax of early Arabic literature; indexes are almost non-existent, and it is often easier to use the table of contents.

The grammar by Gaudefroy Denombynes has some original observations on grammar and syntax and is therefore worth studying. Unfortunately, it also contains some inaccuracies and cannot completely replace Wright's grammar.

---

[5] A good example is the term *iqlīm*, 'clime,' which, according to Yāqūt, who died in 626, was used in Spain in the classical period in the sense of "large and populous village" (Fr. *bourgade*; see W. Jwaideh, *The Introductory Chapters of Yāqūt's Mu'jam al-Buldān*, Leiden, 1959, p. 40).

[6] The above is no more than a very concise picture of the problem; for a detailed discussion see, for instance, the introductions in the dictionaries by Dozy and Ullmann.

The grammar by Brockelmann is an ideal textbook for those who have already mastered the essentials of Arabic grammar. Those who have mastered one or two Semitic languages can even use it as a beginner's grammar. In only 209 small pages it carries the student far beyond the information offered by the common textbooks used at American universities. A bibliography, unfortunately omitted in modern reprints, offers the reader an introduction to some of the most famous older editions of texts, grammars, and dictionaries, many of which are still used today, sometimes in facsimile reproductions. Brockelmann also adds a small chrestomathy. An English translation would be welcomed by many.[7]

The *Grammatica teorico-pratica* by L. Vaccia Vaglieri is a learner's grammar that does not keep grammar and syntax separated; yet it probably contains as much information as Wright's grammar. In some places it even gives more detailed information, e.g., in the (unfortunately dispersed) rules for the use of *hamza.* It offers also many original and balanced observations (e.g., II, 219–26). An English translation would again be most desirable.

The grammar by Haywood and Nahmad is, in the opinion of this writer, to be preferred over the textbooks currently used (Michigan Reader, etc.). In any case, it is a good grammar for the beginner to consult when he feels the need to brush up his elementary grammar and syntax without the help of a teacher. For those familiar with German, the *Einführung* by Ambros is to be preferred, even though it introduces itself as a grammar on contemporary Arabic. In this case again an English translation would be very desirable.

The *Traité* by Fleisch is a fascinating study of grammar from the point of view of the contemporary student of language, as well as for those who are interested in medieval grammatical studies. To a more limited extent it offers insights in the study of Arabic in relation to other Semitic languages and dialectology. There is, as far as I know, no book that does more justice to the outstanding achievements of medieval scholars. In *L'Arabe classique,* Fleisch made a very successful attempt to digest some of the material offered in his larger work. One should not buy the first edition.

The grammars by Beeston and Wickens are serious and interesting attempts to present Arabic grammar in ways different from those of the older grammars. Unfortunately, neither of the two offers sufficient information to be considered a complete introductory grammar. In spite of this, students who study grammar for its

[7] To what extent the grammar by W. Fischer (not on the list) replaces Brockelmann I have not attempted to establish.

own sake or who find it profitable to consult several grammars on a given problem (this writer is one of them) will find it worthwhile to consult these two books. Particularly rewarding is the introduction of Wickens, which emphasizes the effort needed to become a good Arabist.

Finally, the *Adminiculum* of Ullmann, the author of the *WKAS*, one of the truly outstanding Arabists of this century, is a small but precious collection of examples illustrating difficult points of grammar. At a more advanced stage, no Arabist should, after a visit to his bookseller, return home without it.

Many other grammars could be mentioned; and there may be many useful books, not to speak of articles and monographs, that cannot be mentioned here or that are not of much practical use in the context of an elementary reader.[8]

The present Reader refers, almost without exception, to Wright's *Grammar*, despite its venerable age and the clear intent of the authors to put together an advanced and comprehensive work, mentioning details that are of little importance to a beginning Arabist. At this time the writer knows of no handbook in English that is more easily accessible.[9]

---

8 See M. H. Bakalla, *Arabic Linguistics: An Introduction and Bibliography*, 2nd ed., London, 1983.

9 This writer has not hesitated to paraphrase Wright's grammar and occasionally some other grammars. On purpose he has also taken over some of Wright's examples, not only because of their usefulness or simplicity, but also because looking up the references to Wright and recognizing these examples facilitates committing them to memory.

Arabic Grammars

W. Wright, *A Grammar of the Arabic Language,* 3rd ed., 2 vols. (Cambridge, 1896). Facsimile reprints and a paperback edition available.

H. Gaudefroy-Demombynes and R. Blachère, *Grammaire de l'arabe classique* (Paris, 1937).

C. Brockelmann, *Arabische Grammatik* (Leipzig, 1948). Facsimile reprints available.

L. Veccia Vaglieri, *Grammatica teorico-pratica della lingua araba,* 2 vols. (Rome, 1959–61).

Haywood and Nahmad, *A New Arabic Grammar of the Written Language* (London, 1982; key, London, 1983).

H. Reckendorf, *Die syntaktischen Verhältnisse des Arabischen* (Leiden, 1898). Reprint available.

__________, *Arabische Syntax* (Heidelberg, 1921). Reprint available.

H. Fleisch, *L'Arabe classique: esquisse d'une structure linguistique,* 2nd ed. (Beirut, 1968).

__________, *Traité de philologie arabe,* 2 vols. (Beirut, 1961–70).

A. F. L. Beeston, *Written Arabic: an Approach to the Basic Structures* (Cambridge, 1968).

G. M. Wickens, *Arabic Grammar: a First Workbook* (Cambridge, 1980).

M. Ullmann, *Adminiculum zur Grammatik des klassischen Arabisch* (Wiesbaden: Otto Harrassowitz, 1989).

A. A. Ambros, *Einführung in die moderne arabische Schriftsprache,* (München: Hüber Verlag, 1969).

Dictionaries

E. W. Lane, *An Arabic-English Lexicon,* 8 vols., London, 1863–93. Reprints New York, 1955–56; Beirut, 1968; London, 1984.

R. Dozy, *Supplément aux dictionnnaires arabes,* 2nd ed., 2 vols., Leiden-Paris, 1927. Reprint Beirut, 1968.

J. Kraemer, *Th. Nöldecke's Belegwörterbuch zur klassischen arabischen Sprache, Erste Lieferung,* Berlin, 1952. Letter *alif* only; includes translations in English.

J. Kraemer, H. Gätje, M. Ullmann, *Wörterbuch der klassischen arabischen Sprache,* vol. 1, Wiesbaden, 1970; vol. 2, Wiesbaden, 1972. Letters *kāf* and part of *lām;* includes translations in English.

R. Blachère, M. Chouémi, C. Denizeau, Ch. Pellat, *Dictionnaire Arabe-Français-Anglais (Langue classique et moderne),* I–III, Paris 1967–76; IV, Paris, 1978. Letters *alif-jīm* and part of *ḥā'.*

A. de Biberstein-Kazimirski, *Dictionnaire arabe-français,* 2 vols., Paris, 1860.

J. B. Bélot, *Vocabulaire arabe-français,* 10th ed., Beirut, 1911 (Arabic title, *Al-Farā'id al-durriyah*).

J. G. Hava, *Al-Faraid Arabic-English Dictionary,* Beirut, 1964. Frequent reprints.

H. Wehr, *A Dictionary of Modern Written Arabic,* ed. J. Milton Cowan, 4th ed., Wiesbaden, 1979. Paperback edition Ithaca, N.Y., 1994.

Abbreviations

Admin.: M. Ullmann, *Adminiculum zur Grammatik des klassischen Arabisch* (Wiesbaden: Otto Harrassowitz, 1989).

Aghānī: Abū 'l-Faraj al-Iṣfahānī, *K. al-Aghānī* (Cairo, 1345–94/1927–74).

Amari, *Storia*: Amari, M. *Storia dei Musulmani di Sicilia,* 2nd ed., 3 vols. (Catania 1933–39).

Ar. Syntax: H. Reckendorf, *Arabische Syntax* (Heidelberg, 1921). Reprint available.

Baghdad: Le Strange, *Baghdad during the Abbasid Caliphate* (Oxford 1900), reprint.

Bl : H. Blachère: Gaudefroy-Demonbynes and R. Blachère, *Grammaire de l'Arabe classique* (Paris, 1937).

Bro.: C. Brockelmann, *Arabische Grammatik* (Leipzig, 1948). Reprints available.

Dozy: R. Dozy, *Supplément aux dictionnaires arabes* (Leiden, 1881). Reprint Leiden/Paris, 1927.

Ed. Wright–de Goeje: Ibn Jubayr, *Riḥla=Tadhkira bi-'l-akhbār 'an itifāqāt al-asfār,* ed. W. Wright, revised by M. J. de Goeje (Leiden 1907).

*EI*1: M. Th. Houtsma *et al., The Encyclopaedia of Islam,* 4 vols. and Supplement (Leiden/London, 1913–38).

*EI*2: (English ed.) H. A. R. Gibb *et al., The Encyclopaedia of Islam: New Edition,* 8– vols. (Leiden/London, 1960–), Supplement (1981–83), Indexes I–VII (1993).

Fihrist: Ibn al-Nadīm, *Fihrist,* ed. G. Flügel (Leipzig 1871–72), reprint, n.d.

GAL: C. Brockelmann, *Geschichte der arabischen Literatur,* G[rundband] I–II (revised ed., Leiden, 1943–44), S[upplementband] I–III (Leiden, 1937–42).

GAS: F. Sezgin, *Geschichte des arabischen Schrifttums* II (Leiden, 1975), VIII (1982), IX (1984).

Glossarium: Separate vol. of al-Ṭabarī, Muḥ. b. Jarīr, *Annales: Introductio, Glossarium, Addenda et Emendenda*, ed. M. J. de Goeje, et al. (Leiden 1897–1901), reprint. This volume dated 1965.

Glossary: Ibn Jubayr, *The Travels,* ed. W. Wright, 2nd ed. by M. J. de Goeje, Leyden 1907, pp. 25–51.

Inbāh: Ibn al-Qifṭī, *Inbāh al-ruwāt 'alā anbāh al-nuḥāt,* 4 vols. (Cairo 1396–93).

Irshād: Yāqūt, *The Irshād al-arīb ilā ma'rifat al-adīb or Dictionary of Learned Men,* ed. D. S. Margoliouth (Leiden, 1907–31).

Isl. Dyn.: C. E. Bosworth, *The Islamic Dynasties,* Islamic Surveys 5, (Edinburgh, 1967).

K: Kitāb.

L: E. W. Lane, *An Arabic-English Lexicon* (London, 1863–93). Reprints available.

Lands: Le Strange, G. *The Lands of the Eastern Caliphate* (Cambridge 1930).

Lisānaddīn: Lisānaddīn b. al-Khaṭīb, *al-Qism al-thālith min K. A'māl al-a'lām*, apud A. M. al-'Abbādī, *Ta'rīkh al-Maghrib al-'Arabī fī 'l-'aṣr al-wasīṭ* (Casablanca 1964).

Passion: Massignon, L., *La passion de Ḥallāj* (Paris 1975).

Pellegrini: G. B. Pellegrini, "Terninologia geografica araba in Sicilia" in *Annali dell'Istituto orientale di Napoli,* sez. ling. 3 (1961).

Rawḍ: al-Ḥimyarī, *K. al-Rawḍ al-mi'ṭār fī khabar al-aqṭār*, ed. I 'Abbās (Beirut 1975).

Sicilia: Touring Club Italiano,*Guida Italia del TCI: Sicilia* (Milano 1968).

Ta'r. Bagh.: al-Ṭabarī, Muḥ. b. Jarīr, *Annales*: ed. M. J. de Goeje, et al. (Leiden 1897–1901), reprint.

Vagl.: L. Veccia Vaglieri, *Grammatica teorico-pratica della lingua araba,* 2 vols. (Rome, 1959–61).

Vizirat: D. Sourdel, *Le vizirat 'abbaside de 749 à 863* (Damascus 1959–60).

W: Wright, *A Grammar of the Arabic Language,* 3rd ed., 2 vols. (Cambridge, 1896). Reprints available.

Wafayāt: Ibn Khallikān, *Wafayāt al-a'yān*, ed. I 'Abbās, 7 vols. (Beirut 1968–71).

Wāfī: al-Ṣafadī, Ṣalāḥaddīn Khalīl b. Aybak, *al-Wāfī bi-'l-wafayāt,* ed. H. Ritter, S. Dedering, *et. al.* (Leipzig/Wiesbaden, 1931–).

WKAS: M. Ullmann et. al, *Wörterbuch der klassischen arabischen Sprache*, Harrassowitz Wiesbaden 1970–91; I: *kāf*, II, 1–2: *lām-l-ml-m.*

Wuzarā': Hilāl b. Muḥassin al-Ṣābī, *Ta'rīkh al-wuzarā* '(The Historical Remains of Hilāl al-Ṣābī), ed. H. F. Amedroz (Leiden 1904).

Yāqūt: *Mu'jam al-buldān,* 5 vols. (Beirut, 1955–57).

b.: ibn
d.: died
fem.: feminine
lit.: literally
masc.: masculine
plur.: plural
sing.: singular

The abbreviations for periodicals are those common in the *Index Islamicus* of J. D. Pearson, *et. al.* (Cambridge 1958), and the *EI2*.

I. Al-Silafī, *Mu'jam al-safar*

Al-Silafī, whose full name is Abū Ṭāhir Aḥmad b. Muḥammad b. Aḥmad b. Muḥammad b. Ibrāhīm Silafah, was born in 492 or 478 and died in 576. His *nisba*[1] is said to derive from the nickname of his ancestor *silafah* (which is interpreted as a Persian term for "hare lip") or from Silafah, a village in the eastern half of the Islamic world. The *Ansāb* of al-Sam'ānī,[2] though mentioning Silafī, does not inform us about the origin of the *nisba*. Nor does the *Mu'jam al-buldān* mention a village by the name of Silafah.

Al-Silafī established himself as a scholar of Tradition before he had finished his own studies. His career as a student began inauspiciously: he had to lean instead of sitting straight, which drew a gross insult from his teacher, and Silafī had to explain that he was suffering from pustules *(damāmīl)*.

Al-Silafī traveled all over the eastern half of the Islamic world and left his writings in several places. He finally settled in Alexandria, where he married a rich woman. He gave up his plans to return to his home town, Iṣfahān (or rather Jarāwā'ān or Jarwān, a village nearby). Alexandria offered him many advantages: a *madrasa* especially built for him and frequent visits of scholars from all over the Islamic world. He seems to have been primarily a Tradition scholar, though we find among his teachers also the famous philologist al-Tibrīzī (died 502). He also wrote some poems.

The *Mu'jam al-safar* survives in two manuscripts, neither of which is complete. It may be that al-Silafī himself did not finish the work (see, however, *Wāfī* VII, 352, lines 17–18, where a book with this title is said to contain two thousand biographies). The editor therefore decided to limit himself to biographies of scholars from Spain, rather than attempt to edit the whole text, hoping that at some time a complete manuscript of the text would show up, which would make an

---

1 Part of a Muslim's name ending on *-iyyun*. The *nisba* frequently refers to the tribal affiliation or birthplace of a person, or to the locality where he is known to have lived; but it may also refer to the affiliation of his father, grandfather, etc., thereby becoming a family name. Frequently also it is derived from the name of the grandfather himself. However, the *nisba* is not restricted to this function, but may refer to someone's legal affiliation (e.g., al-Shāfi'ī, one who follows the legal school of al-Shāfi'ī) or profession (e.g., al-Qindīlī, the maker of candles). For grammatical details see W I, 149C–165B, as well as various medieval texts on the subject, one of the most practical of which is Ibn al-Athīr, 'Izzaddīn 'Alī, *al-Lubāb fī tahdhīb al-ansāb,* Cairo 1357, 3 vols. See also J. Sublet, *Le voile du nom*, Paris (Presses universitaires de France) 1991, pp. 95–113 and *passim.*

2 See below, VI, Handbooks on Spelling.

edition of the whole text meaningful. The book deals with biographies of scholars who were not from Iṣfahān or from Baghdad, since the author had already dealt with scholars from these two cities in previous writings.

Al-Silafī died in 576, which makes 492 the more acceptable date for his birth. For further information, see the Introduction of the edition by I. 'Abbās (*Akhbār wa-tarājim Andalusiyya... li-'l-Silafī,* Beirut, 1963) and the references quoted there, to which one may add Ibn al-Jazarī, Abū 'l-Khayr Muḥammad, *Ghāyat al-nihāya,* ed. G. Bergsträsser, Cairo 1351/1932–1352/1932, I, 102–3; and al-Ṣafadī, *al-Wāfī bi-'l-wafayāt,* ed. H. Ritter, S. Dedering, *et al.,* Leipzig/Wiesbaden (1931–), VII, 351–56 (curious observations on good manners to be observed during lectures on *ḥadīth*); and *GAL*, G I, 365, S I, 624.

From: *Akhbār wa-tarājim Andalusiyyah mustakhrajah min Mu'jam al-Safar li-l-Silafī,* ed. Iḥsān 'Abbās, Beirut 1963, p. 126.

سمعت مكيّة بنت عمر بن هانئ التجيبيّ الأندلسيّ بالإسْكَنْدَرِيّة تقول: سمعت الحكيم أبا عبد الله الأشقر الطبيب بالمريّة من مدن الأندلس يقول: من أكل الخبز بالزبيب لم يحتج أبداً إلى طبيب.

مكيّة هذه امرأة صالحة كبيرة السنّ، قدمت الإسكندريّة راغبة في الحجّ، وكانت تأوي عندنا إلى أن توجّهت إلى الحجاز، وانقطع عنّا خبرها، ثمّ بلغنا أنّها حجّت وتوفّيت بعد قفولها من الحجاز بمدينة قوص من الصعيد الأعلى.

Notes

مَكِّيَّةُ name of a woman.

سَمِعْتُ . . . تَقولُ I heard [her] saying.

عُمَرُ ، هانِئٌ proper names of men.

التُجِيبيّ الأَنْدَلُسيّ the man from the tribe of Tujīb, the Andalusian.

حَكيم scientist, philosopher, physician; see *EI*2, s.v.

طَبيب physician.

أَبو عبد الله strictly speaking, a *kunya* (surname or agnomen—i.e., أَبو for a man, or أُمّ for a woman, followed by the name of the person's son or some other element, e.g., Abū Shāma, "the man with the birth mark"); people are often better known by their *kunyas* than by their proper names—e.g., the poet Abū Nuwās, whose name (*ism*) was al-Ḥasan ibn Hāni'. See *EI*2, s.v. KUNYA.

الأَشْقَرُ a nickname *(laqab)*—'the Red-Haired.'

المَرِيَّة Almería.

مِن مُدُنِ الأَنْدَلُس [which is] one of the cities of Spain.

زَبِيب raisins.

اِحْتَاجَ إلى to need.

الإِسْكَنْدَرِيَّة Alexandria.

رَغِبَ في to desire, to plan (see W II, 155D); cf. رَغِبَ عَنْ to hate (see W II, 141A).

أَوَى literally, to take refuge with; here, 'to stay with [a trusted family].' She was apparently traveling without the company of male relatives.

تَوَجَّهَ to set out.

الحِجاز the Ḥijāz.

بَلَغَهُ the [news] reached him.

حَجَّ to perform a pilgrimage to Mecca.

تُوُفِّيَتْ she died. From وَفاة, 'accomplishment, fulfillment': تُوُفِّيَ is the passive of تَوَفَّاهُ اللهُ 'God brought to its close his foreordained period'—i.e., made him die. See W I, 37C-D on examples of Form V verbs in which the idea of reflexiveness is not very prominent and which are connected with an accusative. See also *EI*2, s.v. MAWT.

قَفَلَ to return.

قُوص a city on the Nile; see *EI*2, s.v. ḲŪṢ.

مِن الصَعيد الأعْلَى in [part of] Upper Egypt.

* * *

From: *Akhbār wa-tarājim Andalusiyyah mustakhrajah min Mu'jam al-Safar li-l-Silafī*, ed. Iḥsān 'Abbās, Beirut 1963, p. 126.

سمعت الفقيه أبا الحسن عدل بن محمّد بن عدل الغافقيّ الأندلسيّ بالإسكندريّة يقول: كتب ابن الأغلب صاحب ميرقة إلى ابن رَشيقٍ القيروانيّ يستدعيه في البحر فأجابه بهذين البيتين:

أمرتني بركوبِ البحرِ مغترراً
عليك غيرِيَ فأْمُرْهُ بذا الراء

ما أنت نُوحٌ فتنجيني سفينَتُهُ
ولستُ عيسى أنا أَمشي على الماءِ

Notes

فَقيه scholar specializing in Islamic law (*fiqh*)—see *EI* 2, s. vv.

أَبا الحَسَنِ *kunya.*

عَدْل . . . مُحَمَّد proper names.

الغافِقِيّ a man belonging to the clan of Ghāfiq; the index to *EI*2 lists several scholars bearing this *nisba* [term *nisba* in biography Silafī]. Members of this clan had settled in Spain, see *EI*2, II, 744a.

الأَنْدَلُسِي the man from al-Andalus, Islamic Spain.[3]

الأَغْلَب (المُرْتَضَى) or ابن الأَغْلَب governor of Majorca (428-36) on behalf of al-Mujāhid, ruler of Denia and the Balearics. See Zambaur, *Manuel de généalogie et de chronologie*, reprint Bad Pyrmont 1955, p. 57; see also *EI*2, svv. MAYŪRḲA, 926b, and MUDJĀHID.

صاحِبُ مَيُرْقَة the ruler of Majorca.[4]

ابن رشِيق القَيْرَوانِي (390-456 or 463) poet and author of *al-'Umda fī maḥāsin al-shi'r wa-ādābih*, "The Pillar Dealing with Good Poetry and the Skills Pertaining to It," an outstanding work on literary theory and criticism.[5]

إسْتَدْعَى to call somebody; to ask somebody to present himself, to summon—see L, Dozy.

في البَحْرِ [traveling] on the sea/by boat.

أَمَرَ بِ to order to [do something]; here probably 'to invite,' 'to urge.'

---

3 Recently and rather convincingly derived from *landa-hlauts*, 'land-lot,' the Gothic equivalent of the very common Latin *Gothica sors*. See H. Halm, "Al-Andalus and Gothica Sors," in *Der Islam* LXVI (1989), 252-63.

4 The cultural importance of Majorca in this period has been extensively discussed by D. Urvoy, "La Vie intellectuelle et spirituelle dans les Baléares Musulmanes," in *Al-Andalus* XXVII, (1972), 87-132.

5 See *EI*2, s.v. For a good edition of this work, see below, XIII, 333, note on al-Akhṭal. The invitation may not have been addressed to Ibn Rashīq, who would not have answered in these terms. Nor is he the only poet to whom the following lines are attributed. There is no room to discuss this intricate question. It may well be that Ibn Rashīq addressed these lines to a friend who had asked him to join him in a trip to Majorca or mainland Spain. Ibn Rashīq's career as a court poet began in Qayrawān (hence the *nisba* al-Qayrawānī) and al-Mahdiyya. Later he fled to Mazara in Sicily where he died.

اِغْتَرَّ to be inexperienced, to be heedless [of the dangers].

عَلَيْكَ غَيْرِي lit. "it is upon you [as a duty, as an advice, to take] somebody else," "choose somebody else"—W II, 78B; and cf. also W II, 172D; غَيْرِي for غَيْرِي is a poetic form here adopted for the sake of the meter. See below, XIV, second poem.

فَأْمُرْ the imperative مُرْ of أَمَرَ frequently recovers the first radical after وَ or فَ —see W I, 76C-D.[6]

بِذَا الرَّاءِ The *i* is pronounced long, see below, XIV, Arabic Metrics. The meaning of this phrase is uncertain as long as we do not have the support of an authoritative commentary or find a similar expression in a similar context. In some collections quoting the poem we find the variant بِذَا الدَّاءِ, "[order him to engage in/venture into] this disaster." This reading, which is easier to understand, shows that the reading in our text was not understood and was therefore changed by a scribe or by the author of a collection of poems into بِذَا الدَّاءِ. In spite of this, the reading بِذَا الرَّاءِ, should not be rejected: to conform to the rhyme, رَأْي 'plan, idea, proposal,' may have been changed into راء.[7] راء may also stand for 'foam of the sea.'[8] Finally راء could allude to the ر as beginning letter and end letter of ركوب البحر or to the sequence of ر's in the first half of the line. The translation would then be: "You urged me to

---

6 The metrical scheme of the poem is *basīṭ*. One could argue that *'alayka ghayriya* is placed at the beginning of the sentence for emphasis' sake; in such cases *fa-* is often used: *bali 'llāha fa-'bud*; and even *fa-kadhālika fa-'f'alū binā*—see *Ar. Syntax*, pp. 318-19. But one could as well take *'alayka ghayriya* in the sense of "take somebody else and then. . ."

7 Having *rā'* instead of *ra'y* seems to be common. One could explain this form in the following way: substituting *ā* for *a'* is accepted as a poetic licence (see W II, 376B-C). *Yā'* is then changed into *hamza* (as in *irḍā'un*, the *if'āl* pattern of the root *r-ḍ-y*; see Vagl. I, 163, parag. 315; Bro., p. 24 (parag. 13c); cf. W I, 93D).

8 The dictionaries fail to quote an example and limit themselves to an example

travel by sea risking [my life]. Find somebody else to urge [to accept] that idea/ to urge [to accept to venture on] that foam/to urge [upon him: "Take] that letter (those letters) ر !" Yet this may not exhaust the translations that could be suggested. Note also the variant فَاخْصُصْهُ بِذَا الرَّاءِ , "choose him for/select him for. . ." which would make the interpretation easier.

نوح Noah; for Noah and the ark see Koran 29:14-15, and Genesis 6-8 in the Old Testament.

تُنْجِي imperfect of أَنْجَى (root *n-j-w*) to save; see Koran 29:15 where the same verb is used. فَ in the sense of 'so that' should be followed by a subjunctive (see W II, 30C-31D), but this rule is frequently violated in poetry (see W II, 389A-C).

لَسْتُ I am not, from لَيْسَ . *Laysa* is one of the "sisters of *kāna*"—see W II, 101D, 102 B.

أنا the pronoun of the first person is already implied in لَسْتُ , but is made explicit to contrast أنا with أَنْتَ .

عِيسَى (same in all cases) Jesus; for the story see the gospels of St Matthew 14:25 and St Mark 6:48.

أَمْشِي imperfect of مَشَى (root *m-sh-y*) 'walking.'

---

of *rā'* in the sense of 'foam on a horse's mouth'.

II. Ibn al-Qifṭī, *Inbāh al-ruwat ʿalā anbāh al-nuḥāt*

Not much of interest can be said about the biography of Ibn al-Qifṭī, Abū ʾl-Ḥasan ʿAli b. Yūsuf al-Shaybānī. As his *nisba* indicates, he was born in Qifṭ in Upper Egypt. The date is given as 568. He was educated in Cairo and moved with his father to Jerusalem in 583. His father was the deputy of al-Qāḍī al-Fāḍil, a man of letters in the service of Saladin, famous for his correspondence, which is considered a model. Upon the death of Saladin in 590, he moved to Aleppo, where the Atabeg, al-Malik al-Ẓāhir, put him in charge of the Dīwān of Finances. From 633 till his death in 646, he served as vizier under al-Malik al-ʿAzīz. He never married, but seems to have held at least one slave girl.

Perhaps the most important episode in Ibn al-Qifṭī's life was his encounter with the geographer and biographer Yāqūt al-Rūmī (d. 626), to whom he offered shelter in Aleppo when Yāqūt had to flee from the Mongols and who later offered a very detailed biography of his host, including a few charming anecdotes.

Ibn al-Qifṭī began collecting materials for his publications when he was still a student. He also built up a valuable collection of books, which became famous in his days. The *Inbāh al-ruwāt,* from which the following two selections are taken, is the best known of his own works and has been published in an excellent edition by the Dār al-Kutub al-Miṣriyya in four volumes (Cairo, 1369–93). This edition has the merit of listing in the footnotes references to other collections of biographies where an entry on the personality in question occurs. Ibn al-Qifṭī's *K. Ikhbār al-ʿulamāʾ bi-akhbār al-ḥukamāʾ* has not come down in its complete form and exists only in an unreliable edition by J. Lippert, Leipzig, 1903. This is the more regrettable since it contains information that cannot be found elsewhere.

For further information see *EI* 2, s.v.; *GAS,* S I, 325; *Irshād* V, 497–94; *Wāfī* XXII, 378–79 (with further references to collections of biographies).

From: Ibn al-Qiftī, *Inbāh al-ruwāt ʻalā anbāh al-nuḥāt*, ed. M. Ibrāhīm, Cairo 1369 [1949-50], Vol. 3, pp. 190-91.

٦٨٩ – محمّد أبو بكر بن عليّ بن الحسن بن البِرّ اللغويّ الصَّقَليّ التميميّ الغوْثيّ

فاضل كامل. ولد بصِقِلّيّة، ورحل عنها في طلب العلم إلى جهة المشرق، وروى كثيرا من اللغة، ثم اسطوطن صِقِلّيّة، وصحب ابن متكود صاحب مازَر من مدن صِقِلّيّة، فقربّه وأدناه، وأكرم محلّه وأجلّ مَثْواه، وكان ابن متكود هذا على غاية من الصيانة والدين والزهد، وبلغه عن ابن البِرّ أنه يشرب الخمر سِرًّا، فعزّ عليه ذلك وسيّر إليه: إننا إنما أردناك لعلمك ودينك، وأردنا منك الصيانة، وإذا كان ولا بدّ من شرب الخمر فهذا النوع ببَلَرْم كثير، وربما يعزّ وجوده ههنا. فخجل من قوله وارتحل إلى بَلَرْم، وهي مدينة من مدن صِقِلّيّة، وأقام بها للإفادة، وكان موجودا هناك إلى سنة خمسين وأربعمائة.

وممن أخذ عنه وأكثر تلميذُه عليّ بن جعفر بن عليّ السَّعديّ المعروف بابن القطّاع اللغويّ الصَّقَليّ نزيل مصر. وكتاب «الصِّحاح» بمصر لا يُرْوى إلّا من طريق ابن البِرّ هذا. والله أعلم بصحة هذا الطريق.

أنبأنا أبو طاهر السِّلفيّ قال: سمعت علي بن عبد الجبّار بن سلامة الهذليّ اللغويّ التونسيّ بالإسكندريّة يقول: رأيت أبا بكر محمد بن علي بن البرّ الغوْثيّ اللغوي بمدينة مازَر من جزيرة صِقِلّيّة، وكنت على أن أقرأ عليه لما اشتهر من فَضْله

وتبحّره في اللغة، فاتصل بابن مَتْكُود صاحب البلد أنه يشرب الخمر – وكان يكرمه– فشقّ عليه وصار يكرهه، وأنفذ إليه وقال: المدينة أكبر، والشراب بها أكثر. فأحوجته الضرورة إلى الخروج منها، ولم أقرأ عليه شيئا.

Notes

أبو بَكْرٍ here apparently used as a *kunya*, though Abū Bakr is also quite frequently used as a 'first name.'

عَلِيٌّ ، الحَسَنُ proper names.

اللُّغَوِيّ the scholar of lexicography; see *EI*2, s.v. IBN AL-BIRR.

الصَقَلّيّ the Sicilian, also vocalized الصِقِلّيّ. According to Yāqūt's *Mu'jam al-buldān*, s.v., the Sicilians pronounced the name of their island as Ṣaqallīya, while others used the form Ṣiqillīya.

التَميمي a member of the tribe of Tamīm.

الغَوْثي there is no reference for this *nisba* in the handbooks. Perhaps one should think of "al-Taymī al-Ghawthī"; see Ibn Ḥazm, *Jamharat ansāb al-'Arab* (Beirut 1402/1983), pp. 454-55.

فاضِل كامِل an outstanding and accomplished [scholar].

طَلَب العِلْم the quest for knowledge ('knowledge' to be understood as study of *ḥadīth* and other disciplines connected with Islam).

رَوَى literally, to transmit; here, 'to learn,' 'become a scholar versed in. . . .'

لُغَة here meaning 'lexicography'; but see *EI*2, s.v. LUGHA for the complex history of the term.

ابن متكود also known as Ibn Mankūd; see *EI*2, s.v. IBN AL-BIRR.

صاحب often to be taken in the sense of 'ruler', 'governor,' but also used in a variety of other meanings—e.g., 'master,' 'friend,' 'author [of a book].' See Lane, s.v.

مازَر Mazara del Vallo. See *Sicilia*, pp. 311-15.

قَرَّبَهُ وأَدْناهُ probably to be taken as a hendiadys: "he made him part of his entourage."

أَكْرَمَ مَحَلَّهُ وأَجَلَّ مَثْناهُ again a hendiadys: "considered him an honored guest." Note the rhyme in these two sentences.

عَلَى engaged in, following; see W II, 169C-170B. Cf. الناسُ على دينِ مُلوكِهِم 'people follow the religion of their kings.'

على غايةٍ من الصِيانة والدِين والزُهْد "[he was a man] who avoided sin to the utmost extent, following the precepts of religion, and living the life of an ascetic." For *zuhd* 'asceticism,' see *EI*1, s.v., and L. Kinberg, "What Is Meant by *Zuhd*," in *Studia Islamica* LXI, 27-44.

عَنْ concerning; see W II, 140B-C.

عَزَّ على be difficult [to accept] for someone.

سَيَّرَ إلى to send [a message] to.

إنَّنا "(truly) we. . ." "we (actually). . ."

إنَّما 'only'; *innamā*, originally a corroborative particle, stresses the end of the sentence; see W II, 335B-D.

أَرَدْناك we wanted you [to take up residence].

وَإذا كانَ ولا بُدَّ مِنْ شُرْبِ الخَمْرِ 'if you cannot avoid drinking wine.' لا بُدَّ 'necessarily' (literally, 'there is no avoiding it'—see W I, 289C), usually appears as a parenthesis, e.g. إن كُنْتَ هذا الدَّهْرَ لا بُدَّ شاكِراً "If, at this time, you are—there being no avoiding it—grateful" (*Ar. Syntax*, p. 121). لا بُدَّ is, moreover, often construed with مِنْ. The وَ here appears to introduce a *ḥāl* clause; see W II, 330B-331A. The idiom is difficult to translate literally; one could suggest: "when there is [in you an urge]—while there is no avoiding it—to drink."

نَوْع 'type [of drink],' "this item on the table."

بَلَرْم Palermo.

رُبَّما 'often,' 'sometimes,' 'perhaps'; according to Vagl. II, 150-51, the two last meanings are more common than the first.

عَزَّ to be difficult [to find], expensive.

إفادة teaching, see Dozy II, 292a-b.

وكان مَوْجوداً هُناك إلى . . . he was found there till, was [known to] have lived there till. . . .

ومِمَّنْ 'and among those who. . .' مَنْ can have the function of an antecedent and relative pronoun together; see W II, 319A.

أخَذَ عَنْهُ وأكْثَرَ literally, "he took from him and did it much," i.e., he learned from him a good deal.

جَعْفَر proper name.

السَّعْديّ *nisba* referring to Sa'd, which is the name of several tribes.

المَعْروف بِابن القطّاع [commonly/better] known as Ibn al-Qaṭṭā' (433 to beginning of 6th century); see *EI*2, s.v. IBN AL-ḲAṬṬĀ'.

نَزِيل مِصْر settled in Egypt.

كتاب الصحاح voweled *Ṣiḥāḥ* as well as *Ṣaḥāḥ*, a dictionary by al-Jawharī (4th century); see *EI*2, s.v. DJAWHARĪ.

لا يُرْوَى إلّا من طَرِيق . . . [the book] is only handed down in this way, i.e., relying for the accuracy of the text only on Ibn al-Birr.

اللهُ أَعْلَمُ بِ 'God knows best about. . .' The elative uses the same preposition as the verb to which it corresponds (cf. عَلِمَ بِ); see W II, 72A-C.

صِحَّة correctness, authenticity [of the text]. Ibn al-Birr must at times have been intoxicated.

أَنْبَأَنا he informed us (a term frequently used in dealing with Traditions).

حَدَّثَنِي قال/ حَدَّثَنا or أَنْبَأَنا. . . قال he informed us, told us/me. . . saying.

عبد الجَبّار ، سَلامة proper names.

الهُذَلِيّ *nisba* referring to the tribe of Hudhayl, famous for its tribal *dīwān* (collection of poetry), the only collection of its kind to have survived. In forming *nisba*s, the long vowel *ī* and the diphthong *ay* are often replaced by the vowel *a*—e.g., قُرَشِيّ from قُرَيْش , جَزَرِيّ from الجَزِيرة , but تَمِيمِيّ from تَمِيم; see W I, 154B-155B.

التونِسِيّ *nisba* referring to Tūnis.

كُنْتُ على أَنْ . . . I was about to. . .; see W II, 170A.

قَرَأَ على study under [somebody], the student reading the text, and the teacher verifying the accuracy of the student's text and the student's understanding of it.

لِـمَا اشْتَهَرَ مِن because of/on account of that which was known of. . ., because of the. . . for which he was known; see W II, 137D.

اتَّصَلَ ب to reach (literally, to be connected with).

بَلَد often means 'town.' See note on بلدة, p. 202.

شَقَّ على synonym of عَزَّ على.

صار يَكْرَهُهُ he turned to disliking him, he began to dislike him.

يُكرمه . . . يكرهه ، أكبر . . . أكثر note the alliterations!

المدينة i.e., Palermo.

أَنْفَذَ a synonym of سَيَّرَ.

أَحْوَجَتْهُ الضرورةُ إلى necessity (i.e., the need to take Ibn Matkūd seriously) forced him to. . . .

Arabic Biographical Dictionaries

The biographical dictionary is a genre in which the Arabs were prolific. Typically, many biographies give little attention to the scholarly personality of the subject, except in an indirect way. In the above biography, Ibn al-Birr's reliability is questioned. This is done implicitly by quoting two versions of a story about his habit of wine drinking where one would have sufficed, and explicitly by warning the reader not to rely too heavily on the text of the *Ṣiḥāḥ* of Jawharī as transmitted by Ibn al-Birr. But we learn nothing about Ibn al-Birr's merits as a philologist.

Other biographies often limit themselves to a list of the teachers and students of their subject, a short statement about his reliability when it comes to the transmission of *ḥadīth* or lexicographical information, details about his career, and a list of his books ('books' in early times are sometimes to be understood as the contents of series of lectures which the scholar's students noted down and the authenticity of which the scholar in question then confirmed), frequently without more than a hint of their contents or no indication whatsoever. The biographers also take care to note the year and date of the death of their subject and of his birth, if known (hence the use of the term *wafayāt,* 'deaths' as a near synonym of 'biography'). If one takes the term 'literature' in a narrow sense, then only the anecdotes merit to be considered as literature, and many biographies are interesting only as historical documents, though their value in this sense is not always sufficiently appreciated. The anecdote in the following selection is more attractive than what we have seen in the two previous biographies.

To what has been said here there are a few exceptions in the sense that the biographer appears to have structured his biography.

Main Types of Biographical Dictionaries

The following is intended to give an impression of the variety of biographical literature in Arabic. It is not intended to single out the most important among the hundreds of collections of biographies that are useful in one way or another.[1] Since there is, to the best of our knowledge, no easily accessible history of biographical literature, reference is made to H. A. R. Gibb, *Arabic Literature: An Introduction*

[1] For a complete list of all biographical dictionaries known to exist in print or in manuscript, one has to consult the relevant chapters in C. Brockelmann's *Geschichte der arabischen Literatur* (Leiden, 1937–49) or F. Sezgin's *Geschichte des arabischen Schrifttums* (Leiden 1967–), e.g., the introductory chapters in volumes VIII and IX.

(Clarendon, Oxford, 1963), which offers examples of the most common genres.[2] Even though it is out of print at this time, this short but useful history may well be rewritten in the not too distant future, and is in any case available in many libraries.

Most of the texts listed here exist in several editions and have a complicated publication history; offering a complete bibliography would be beyond the scope of this Reader.[3] We offer the names in the abbreviated form in which they are found in Gibb's book and in the *EI2*.

A. General:

Ibn Khallikān (d. 681), *Wafayāt al-a'yān*	Gibb, p. 133
al-Dhahabī (d. 748), *Ta'rīkh al-Islām*	Gibb, p. 144
al-Ṣafadī (d. 764), *al-Wāfī bi-'l-wafayāt*	Gibb, p. 144

B. Personalities connected with a particular city or area:

al-Khaṭīb al-Baghdādī (d. 463), *Ta'rīkh Baghdād*	Gibb, p. 96
Ibn 'Asākir (d. 519), *Ta'rīkh Dimashq*	Gibb, p. 134

C. Annals that give almost no attention to historical events, but mention under each year the scholars who died in that year and then proceed to give their biographies, i.e., best characterized as chronologically arranged biographical dictionaries:

Ibn al-Jawzī (d. 597), *al-Muntaẓam fī ta'rīkh al-mulūk wa-'l-umam* Gibb, p. 126[4]

---

[2] The 'Onomasticon Arabicum' based at the CNRS in Paris aims at composing a computerized list of names and biographical details taken from Arabic biographical dictionaries. It has published a mimeographed *Liste de sources biographiques* (arranged alphabetically); it does not aim, at this time, to bring out a history of biographical literature. Other publications of this international organization include P. Brichard-Bréaud et al., *Nouveaux documents sur la mise en ordinateur des données biographiques* (Éditions du Centre National de la Recherche Scientifique, Paris, 1973), which has a list of works useful in determining the orthography of names; and a periodical *Cahiers d'onomastique arabe* (Paris, 1971–). The *EI2* has, so far, no entry for biographical literature, but lists individual authors; cf. *Index of Subjects to Volumes I–VI* (P.J. Bearman), pp. 48–49.

[3] See below, Introduction to XII.

[4] A more detailed description in B. Lewis and P. M. Holt, *Historians of the Middle East* (Oxford University Press, London, 1964), pp. 62–63.

D. Collections of biographies of certain categories of people:

Transmitters of *ḥadīth:*
Dhahabī (d. 748), *Mīzān al-iʻtidāl fī naqd al-rijāl*
EI2, s.v., al-Dhahabī (without details)

Scholars of the various *madhhabs*, e.g., the *madhhab* of al-Shāfiʻī:
al-Subkī, Tāj al-Dīn (d.771), *Ṭabaqāt al-Shāfiʻiyya*

Philologists:
Yāqūt al-Rūmī (d. 626), *Irshād al-arīb ilā maʻrifat al-adīb* (=Dict. of Learned Men) Gibb, pp. 127–28
Ibn al-Qifṭī (d. 646), *Inbāh al-ruwāt ʻalā anbāh al-nuḥāt*

Ṣūfīs:
Shaʻrānī (d. 973), *Lawāqiḥ al-anwār fī ṭabaqāt al-akhyār*
Gibb, p. 156

Poets:
Abū 'l-Faraj al-Iṣfahānī (d. 356 or 357), *Kitāb al-aghānī*
Gibb, pp. 25, 97
Taʻālibi (d. 430), *Yatīmat al-dahr* Gibb, p. 103

Scientists, physicians, and philosophers:
al-Mubashshir b. Fātik (5th century), *Mukhtār al-ḥikam,*
EI2, s.v.
Ibn al-Qifṭī (d. 646), *Ta'rīkh al-ḥukamā'* Gibb, p. 134
Ibn Abī Uṣaybiʻa (d. 668), *ʻUyūn al-anbā' fī ṭabaqāt al-aṭibbā'*
Gibb, p. 134

The blind:
al-Ṣafadī (d. 764), *Nakt al-himyān fī nukat al-ʻumyān*

Martyrs of love:
Mughulṭāy (sic) (d. 762), *al-Wāḍiḥ al-mubīn fī man ustushhida min al-muḥibbīn*

From: Ibn al-Qifṭī, *Inbāh al-ruwāt ʿalā anbāh al-nuḥāt*, ed. M. Ibrāhīm, Cairo 1369 [1949-50], Vol. 2, pp. 95-97.

٣١٢ – طاهر بن أحمد بن بابشاذ أبو الحسن النحويّ المصريّ

العلامة المشهور المذكور. أصلُه من العراق، وكان جدّه أو أبوه قدم مِصْرَ تاجرا. وكان جوهريّا فيما قيل.

وطاهر هذا ممن ظهر ذكره؛ وسارت تصانيفُه؛ مثل «المقدِّمة» في النحو وشرحها، وشرح «الجُمَل» للزَّجّاجيّ؛ سار كل منهما مسيرَ الشمس.

وقد كان يتولى تحرير الكتب الصادرة عن ديوان الإنشاء في دولة القصرية بالديار المِصْريّة إلى الأطراف؛ ليُصلِح ما لعلّه يجد بها من لَحْن خفيّ. وكان له على ذلك رزق سنيّ؛ مع رزقه على التصدّر للإقراء في جامع عمرو بن العاص. واشتمل على العبادة والمطالعة.

وجَمَع في حالةِ انقطاعه تعليقة كبيرة في النحو؛ قيل لنا: لو بُيِّضَتْ قاربت خمسة عشر مجلّدا، وسمّاها النحاة بعده الذين وصلت إليهم «تعليق الغُرْفة». وانتقلت هذه التّعليقة إلى تلميذه أبي عبد الله محمّد بن بركات السعيديّ النحويّ اللغويّ المتصدّر بموضعه والمتولّي للتحرير. ثم انتقلت بعد ابن البركات المذكور إلى صاحبه أبي محمّد عبد الله بن بَرِّيّ النحويّ المتصدّر في موضعه والمتولّي للتحرير. ثم انتقلت بعده إلى صاحبه الشيخ أبي الحُسَيْن النحويّ المنبوز بثَلْت الفيل، المتصدّر

في موضعه.

وقيل إن كل واحد من هؤلاء كان يَهَبُها لتلميذه المذكور، ويعْهَد إليه بحفظِها. ولقد اجتهد جماعة من طَلَبة الأدب في انتساخها، فلم يُمْكِن.

ولما توفّي أبو الحسين النحويّ المقدّم ذكره، وبلغني ذلك وأنا مقيم بحلَب أرسلت مَنْ أثق به، وسألته تحصيل «تعليق الغرفة» بأيّ ثمن بلغت، وكتاب «التذكِرة» لأبي عليّ. فلما عاد ذكر أن الكتابين وصلا إلى ملك مصر الكامل محمّد بن العادِل أبي بكر بن نَجْم الدين أيّوب، فإنه يرغب في النحو وغريب ما صُنِّف فيه.

وذُكِر أن سبب تزهُّد طاهر بن بابشاذ — رحمه الله — أنه كان له قِطّ قد أنس به وربّاه أحسنَ تربية، فكان طاهر الخُلُق، لا يخطَف شيئا، ولا يؤذي على عادة القطط. وأنه يوما اختطف من يديه فَرْخَ حمام مَشْويّ، فعجِب له، ثم عاد بعد أن غاب ساعة، فاختطف فَرْخا آخر وذهب؛ فتتبّعه الشيخُ إلى خَرْق في البيت، فرآه قد دخل الخَرْق، وقفز منه إلى سطح قريب، وقد وضع الفَرْخ بين يدي قِطّ هناك. فتأمّله الشيخ فإذا القطّ أعمى مفلوج لا يقدر على الانبعاث. فتعجَّب، وحضَره قلبه، وقال: مَنْ لم يقطعْ بهذا القطّ — وقد سخّر له غيره يأتيه برزقه، ويَخرج عن عادته المعهودة منه لإيصال الراحة إليه — لَجدير ألّا يَقْطَعَ بي!

وأجمع رأيه على التخلّي والانفراد بعبادة الله. وضمّ أطرافه وباع ما حوله، وأبقى ما لا بدّ من الحاجة إليه، وانقطع في غرفة بجامع عمرو، وأقام على ذلك مدّة.

ثم خرج ليلةً من الغرفة إلى سطح الجامع، فزلّتْ رجلُه من بعض الطاقات المؤدّية للضوء إلى الجامع، فسقط وأصبح ميتا قد رُزق الشهادة – رحمه الله. قيل: وكان ذلك في سنة أربع وخمسين وأربعمائة، وقيل بعد ذلك. والله أعلم.

Notes

بابَشاذ ، أَحْمَد ، طاهِر proper names. For Bābashādh see F. Justi, *Iranisches Namenbuch*, reprint Hildesheim (G. Olms), 1963, p. 55.

أَبو الحَسَن the *kunya* belongs to Ṭāhir.

النَحْوِيّ 'the grammarian,' see *GAL*, G I, 301, S I, 529; *GAS* IX, 84, 89, 212, 239, and the references in the footnotes by the editor, especially *Wafayāt* I, 235; *Irshād* IV, 274; *Wāfī*, XVI, 390; and *EI*, s.v. *Naḥw*: the term means 'grammar' in the wider sense, and 'syntax' in the narrower sense.

عَلاّمة most learned, see W I, 139 C: the adjective of the type *fa''āl*, already an intensive adjective, can be further strenthened by the addition of a feminine ending.

مَشْهور مَذْكور hendiadys: 'well-known,' 'famous.'

أَصْلُهُ his country of origin.

فيما قيل "according to what was said," "he was said to be a. . . ."

ظَهَرَ ذِكْرُهُ lit.: his mention was apparent, "he was frequently mentioned." See Dozy II, 86b: *ẓahara*, 'se faire connaître,' 'se faire un renom.'

سارت lit.: traveled. "Were found everywhere," cf. *mathal sā'ir*, "well-known / current proverb."

مُقَدِّمة prolegomena, introduction.

الزَجَّاجِيّ d. 377, see *GAS*, IX, 88-95; the *K. al-Jumal* deals with grammar.

سار . . . مَسِيرَ الشَمْسِ see above, under *sārat*. 'It traveled the traveling of the sun'—a verbal noun in the accusative as absolute object (مفعول مطلق) can be specified by a following genitive with which it forms a construct phrase; see W II, 54B.

تَحْرِير to correct, to revise, see Dozy I, 262a, and *Irshād*. See also *EI*2, s.v. INSHĀ', and the references quoted there.

تَوَلَّى to be in charge.

صَدَرَ to come forth, to be given out.

ديوان here: office. For other meanings see L.

ديوان الإِنْشاء 'Chancellery of State'—see *EI*2, 328b, and passim; see also Index I-VII, s.v.

الدَّوْلة القَصْريّة the Fatimid State, this appears from two other passages in this text: *Inbāh*, I, 317, and II, 95, 238.

إلى الأطراف complement to صَدَرَ عَنْ.

الأطراف according to the dictionaries 'nobles,' but it is more likely that 'extremities,' 'all the regions' is intended here.

خَفِيّ hidden, not immediately apparent.

لَحْن grammatical errors, see J. Fück, *'Arabiyya*, trad. C. Denizeau, Paris, 1955, Index.

على ذلك on the basis of that, in compensation of that; see W II, 171A.

خَفِيّ. . . سَنِيّ note the rhyme.

تَصَدَّرَ لِلإِقْراء to set oneself up as a teacher, to hold a professorship; examples in Dozy, s.v. *taṣaddara.*

جامِع عَمْرِو بن العاص the [Friday] Mosque of 'Amr b. al-'Āṣ. For al-'Āṣ, which can also be written with a short ending: al-'Āṣi (العاصِ) but read as al-'Āṣī, see W I, 10A-B; for 'Amr b. al-'Āṣ (d. 41 or 52), see *EI*2, s.v.

اِشْتَغَلَ على to devote oneself entirely to.

مُطالَعة study.

جَمَعَ here: to write.

اِنْقَطَعَ to isolate oneself.

تَعْليقة treatise, supplement, scholia (not clear which of these several meanings is intended here); تعليق later in this paragraph is used in the same sense.

بَيَّضَ to make a fair copy.

مُجَلَّدات sing. مُجَلَّد verbal adjective of *jallada,* see W I, 33A: Form II is used to indicate 'to occupy onself with,' in this case a skin, *jild,* in the sense of 'flogging' or 'using leather for binding a volume'; *mujallad* is 'a bound [volume].' Passive participles used as substantives use the sound fem. plural; see W I, 199A; see also J. Pedersen, *The Arabic Book,* Princeton 1984 (translated by G. French, but unfortunately not updated), pp. 101-12.

نُحاة grammarians; see W I 208B-C.

بَعْدَهُ after [his death], see W II, 187A.

وَصَلَ إلى come into the hands of.

تعليق الغرفة the... [composed in the well-known/famous] room; see below, the next-to-last paragraph of the biography.

اِنْتَقَلَ to move, come into the hands of.

تِلْمِيذ pupil.

بَرَكَات proper name.

سَعِيدِيّ *nisba;* there are many tribes by the name of Saʿīd.

بِمَوْضِعه in his [master's] place.

صَاحِب here: friend, colleague.

اِبن بَرِّيّ Ibn Barrī, d. 582; see *EI2,* s.v.

نَبَزَ ب to nickname (often in an unfavorable sense).

ثَلْط thin dung. See L.

فِيل elephant (I have not succeeded in tracing the origin of this nickname).

صَاحِب here: pupil.

عَهِدَ إِليه بِحِفْظه he exacted from him the promise to keep it to himself.

طَلَبَة الأَدَب students of philology; for the difficult term *adab,* see Introduction to
this Reader, note.

فِي *fī* may indicate the subject, the purpose, or the reason for an activity; see W II,
155A-D.

اِنْتَسَخَ to copy; cf. نُسْخَة, 'copy,' 'manuscript.'

الْمُقَدَّم ذِكْرُه 'the above mentioned.' Interpret as a relative clause; see W II, 283B-
284D, Bro. 190-91, and *Ar. Syntax,* 421-23. Interpret the phrase as though the
article were a relative pronoun, and substitute the finite verb for the passive

participle, i.e., الذي قُدِّمَ ذِكْرُهُ. In this type of sentence, the case of the adjective follows that of the antecedent, while the gender of the adjective follows the gender of the subject of the (implied) relative clause—e.g., رأيتُ امْرَأَةً حَسَنًا وَجْهُها.

وأنا مُقيمٌ بِحَلَبَ parenthetical; حَلَبُ is Aleppo.

أَرْسَلْتُ introduces the main clause.

مَنْ 'somebody whom. . .'; see W II, 319A-B. مَن means 'one who. . .,' 'he who. . .,' and can also introduce a clause implying a condition—e.g., مَنْ جَدَّ وَجَدَ, "whoever exerts himself (i.e., seeks), finds."

وَثِقَ يَثِقُ see W I, 78B: eight initial-*wāw* verbs of the type *fa'ila, yaf'ilu* lose their first radical in the imperfect.

تَحْصيل here: to buy.

بَلَغَتْ "[price] it would reach"; the subject (to be understood) is probably تعليقة (for تعليق), hence the feminine ending on the verb.

كتاب التَّذْكِرة For the *Tadhkira* see *Inbāh* III, 334; IV, 168; and *GAS* IX, 108. The book seems to have dealt with difficult lines of poetry. For *taf'ila*, one of the verbal nouns of Form II, see W I, 115B.

لِأَبي عليٍّ by the grammarian Abū 'Alī al-Fārisī, d. 377; see *EI*2, s.v. al-Fārisī; *GAL*, G I, 116, S I, 175.

الكامِل . . . أَيُّوب the Ayyūbid ruler of Egypt (615-35); see *Isl. Dyn.*, p. 59, and *EI*2, s.v al-KĀMIL.

نَجْم الدِّينِ 'the Star of [this] Religion,' honorific title; see *EI*2, s.v. LAḲAB, 621b.

غريبِ ما صُنِّفَ فيه uncommon / unconventional writings about this subject (lit.: the strange of that which was written about the subject).

تَزَهَّدَ to adopt *zuhd* as a way of life. The fifth form of the verb may be used to indicate 'to adopt [a religion or way of life]'; see W I, 36D-37A.

رَحِمَهُ الله May God have mercy on him.

قِطَط sing. قِطّ ، قِطّة cat.

رَبّاهُ أَحْسَنَ تَرْبِيَةٍ he had raised it in the best possible way.

طاهِر الخُلُق pure / blameless in character.

خَطَفَ to snatch.

آذَى to hurt, molest (root *'-dh-y*).

على عادةِ القِطَطِ as cats so often do.

فَرْخ chick, young bird.

شَوَى to roast.

عَجِبَ له he was amazed on account of it; this amazed him.

تَتَبَّعَ probably: to follow step by step, cautiously; see again W I, 37C.

خَرْق crack, hole.

فرآه قد دخل *qad dakhala* is the second object to *ra'āhu*.

قفز to jump.

قد وضع 'and unexpectedly, or surprisingly he put. . . .' The particle قد has many meanings, some of which are not listed in most grammars and dictionaries. The best discussions are in *Ar. Syntax*, pp. 300-303, and *Adminiculum* (see Index). In this context قد can also be left untranslated (as in the preceding قد

دخل), since we often find قد before perfects without being able to find a proper equivalent in English.

بَيْنَ يَدَيْ in front of; frequent idiom, literally 'between the two hands of.' See W II, 181B. Also used in the sense of 'before,' 'preceding.'

تَأَمَّلَ to examine, look carefully at..

فإذا and lo and behold. See W I, 283, II, 157, 345; *Ar. Syntax*, 308, and Index.

أَعْمَى مَفْلوج blind and half-paralyzed.

لا يَقْدِرُ على الانْبِعاث here: unable to get up.

حَضَرَهُ قَلْبُهُ his heart was there, his heart spoke to him (see *EI*2, s.v. ḲALB); "he took to self-admonition" (?).

مَنْ whoever (the reference is to God).

قَطَعَ ب to cut off [the means of subsistence]; see Dozy II, 368b.

سَخَّرَ put at somebody's service.

يأتيه برِزْقِه relative clause to غَيْرَهُ: "who brings him / to bring him the food he needs."

يَخْرُجُ عَنْ عادَتِه المَعْهودة gives up his habit, his customary behavior (lit., 'behavior of his that is known').

إِيصال verbal noun of أَوْصَلَ.

راحة relief.

جَدِيرٌ أَنْ here: is likely to, can be expected to.

أَجْمَعَ رَأْيَهُ على to decide (أجمع على has the same sense).

التَّخَلّي والانْفِراد hendiadys: to live by himself, to live in isolation.

فانْقَطَعَ في غُرْفَةٍ بجامعِ عَمْرٍو and he lived in isolation in a room in the mosque of 'Amr b. al-'Āṣ.

ضَمَّ أطْرافَهُ "he took stock of his possessions" (?).

ما حَوْلَهُ his household.

أَبْقَى to save.

لا بُدَّ مِنْهُ it is unavoidable.

ما لا بُدَّ مِنَ الحاجةِ إليه what he could not possibly do without.

أَقامَ على ذلك مُدَّةً he lived that way for a while; for على see W II, 169C-170B, and Index.

طاقات sing. طاقة apparently: windows in the roofed section of the mosque.

أَدَّى to convey.

ضَوْء light, daylight.

وقد رُزِقَ الشَّهادةَ "having been granted martyrdom"—رزق is often used in speaking of gifts by God.

شَهادة 'martyrdom'; see *EI*, s.v. SHAHĪD. This term, as well as the term شهادة are often used when speaking of a tragic death.

وقيلَ بَعْدَ ذلك "but some say [that it happened] after that date."

واللهُ أَعْلَم "but God knows best."

IV. Abū 'l-Faraj al-Mu'āfā b. Zakariyyā b. Yaḥyā al-Nahrawānī al-Jarīrī, *K. al-Jalīs al-ṣāliḥ al-kāfī wa-'l-anīs al-nāṣiḥ al-shāfī*

The full name of the author of the following selection is Abū 'l-Faraj al-Mu'āfā b. Zakariyyā b.Yaḥyā al-Nahrawānī, variously known as al-Mu'āfā, al-Nahrawānī, and al-Nahrawānī al-Jarīrī. The *nisba* Nahrawānī derives from Nahrawān near Baghdad; the *nisba* Jarīrī he owes to his having been an adherent of the short-lived school of law (*madhhab*) of Muḥammad b. Jarīr al-Ṭabarī (d. 463), the well-known historian. Several anecdotes testify to al-Mu'āfā's encyclopedic knowledge. The *K. al-Jalīs al-ṣāliḥ al-kāfī wa-'l-anīs al-nāṣiḥ al-shāfī*,[1] from which the following selections were taken, is a curious mixture of serious discussions on juridical and philological questions alternating with stories. The *Fihrist* of Ibn al-Nadīm, ed. G. Flügel, Leipzig 1871–72, p. 236, characterizes al-Mu'āfā's *Jalīs* as containing, besides stories, all kinds of useful knowledge.

Al-Mu'āfā lived from 303 or 305 to 390. For his biography, see *GAS*, I, 522–33, and the references quoted there, especially *Ta'r. Bagh.* XIII, 230–31, *Irshād*, VII, 162–64, and A. Dietrich in *ZDMG* C V (1955), 271–86, and *Orientalia Suecania* XXX–XXXV (1984–86), 241–56. A curious anecdote in Dhahabī's biography of al-Mu'āfā will be quoted in this reader.

The following two selections are taken from the edition by M. M. al-Khūlī and I. 'Abbās, 4 vols., Beirut 1981–93, II, 370 and 336.

[1] Not to be confused with *al-Jalīs al-ṣāliḥ wa-'l-anīs al-nāṣiḥ* of Sibṭ Ibn al-Jawzī, which is a work of a totally different character.

From: Abū al-Faraj al-Muʿāfā b. Zakariyyā al-Nahrawānī al-Jarīrī, *Kitāb al-Jalīs al-ṣāliḥ al-kāfī wa-ʾl-anīs al-nāṣiḥ al-shāfī*, ed. Muḥammad Mursī al-Khūlī, Beirut 1981-93, Vol. 2, p. 370.

شكرٌ وردٌّ عليه

حَدَّثَنا مُحَمَّدُ بْنُ الحَسَنِ بْنِ زِيادٍ المُقْرِي، قال: حدّثنا أبو خَلِيفَةَ قال: أَخْبَرَني القاضي محمّد بن الفَتْح السَّيَّارِيّ.

قال: اجْتَزْتُ بالكُوفةِ في بعض شوارعِها، فأَخَذَني بَطْني فَلَمْ أَدْرِ ما أَصْنَعُ، إذ رأيتُ خَصِيًّا على باب كبير، فقلت: أَصْلَحَكَ اللهُ، هل من مَوْضِعٍ أَبولُ فيه؟ فقال لي: أُدْخُل، فدخلتُ فإذا دار كبيرة قَوْراء، في وسطها بُسْتانٌ، فرأيت عَيْناً من ثُقْبٍ في السَّتَارة، ووجهاً لا ينبغي أن يكون أحسن منه، فلمّا قَضَيْتُ حاجتي، قلتُ في نفسي: إن كان مع هذا الوجهِ الحَسَنِ براعةُ لِسانٍ فهو غايةٌ، فقلت وأنا خارج لأُسْمِعَها: أحسن اللهُ لكم، وباركَ عليكم، وتولَّى مكافأتَكم بالحُسْنى، فقالت مُسْرِعَةً: وأنت، فبارك الله عليك وأحسن إليك، فما رأينا خَارِئاً أشكرَ منك، فأفْحَمَتْني.

Notes

حَدَّثَنا 'has told us,' the usual formula introducing a *ḥadīth,* but also used to introduce 'profane stories,' as well as scholarly information of any kind.

محمّد بن . . . المُقْري subject of حَدَّثَنا.

زِياد proper name.

المُقْري from أَقْرَأَ in the sense of 'to make read' [the Koran], to teach the different readings of the Koran, to teach Koran interpretation.

أبو خَلِيفة ، محمّد بن الفَتْح السَيّاري proper names.

أَخْبَرَني considered less formal than حَدَّثَني or حَدَّثَنا, though in practice often a synonym.

اِجْتازَ (root جوز) pass through, walk along.

الكوفة place name in Iraq.

أَخَذَني بَطْني 'my belly gripped me,' 'I felt a need to relieve myself.'

لم أَدْرِ root دري.

إِذْ 'at that moment'; it can also be used in the sense of 'lo,' 'behold' (after بَيْنَما 'while'—see W I, 283D-284B), and in the sense of 'since,' 'because,' (see W I, 291D). Here إِذْ refers to the situation described in اِجْتَزْتُ . . . ما أَصْنَعُ. See also *Ar. Syntax*, pp. 473-74, 482; and Index.

خَصِيٌّ eunuch (root خصي).

على here 'at.'

أَصْلَحَكَ اللهُ (frequently used blessing) "May God keep you in good health/bless you."

هل مِنْ مَوْضِعٍ "Is there a place. . . ?" The phrase من موضع is the subject of the sentence: cf. French *Est-ce qu'il y a du lait?* —see W II, 135C-D.

فَإِذا lo and behold, there I saw.

دار usually fem; occasionally masc.; see W I, 180C.

قَوْراءُ (fem. of أَقْوَرُ) دار قَوْراء a house with a spacious interior.

مِنْ [looking] from behind, [looking] through.

ثَقْبٌ or ثُقْبٌ hole (both vowelings are acceptable).

سِتارة = سِتْر, curtain closing off women's quarters.

لا يَنْبَغي أنْ يكونَ 'to be suitable/proper'[3]—here, 'it was not possible/one could not imagine that there existed. . . .'

قَضَى حاجَتَهُ 'to fulfill one's need'; common expression for 'to relieve oneself.'

مع with, in addition to.

بَراعةُ لِسانٍ virtuosity of tongue, eloquence.

غاية root غيي.

فهو غايةٌ "then that is the utmost," "then one cannot think of anything more enchanting, more amazing, etc." If the second part of a conditional sentence is a nominal sentence, فَ introduces this nominal sentence—see W II, 15C-D, 345A-D.

فقلتُ وأنا خارجٌ "therefore/thereupon/and so I said while leaving." فَ allows several translations—see W II, 330A-B; also W I, 290D-291A.

لِأُسْمِعَها "with the purpose of making her hear, in such a way that she could hear it."

وتَوَلّى مُكافأتَكُمْ بالحُسْنَى "and may He [God] take it upon Himself to requite you with good / with blessing." See L., s.v. حُسْن and حُسْنَى, 'what is good, best; حَسْناءُ is often used in the sense of 'beautiful woman.'

---

3 A poet by the name of Abū al-Yanbaghī (unidentified) finds himself in prison. To a visitor he declares: أنا أبو اليَنْبَغي ، فَعَلْتُ ما لا يَنْبَغي ، فحُبِسْتُ حَيْثُ يَنْبَغي .

أَسْرَعَ to hasten, to do quickly.

وأنت فَبَارَكَ اللهُ عَلَيْكَ Sentence within a sentence: "And you, may God bless you!" Take أنتَ as the subject and فبارك الله عليك (which by itself is a sentence) as the predicate. See W II, 256A-B.

فما رأينا here فَ is best translated 'for': "for we never saw..."

خَرِئَ to defecate.

أَشْكَرُ مِنْكَ more grateful (elative of شاكِرٌ) than you.

أَفْحَمَ to snub, squash [somebody], make him unable to find an answer.

* * *

From: Abū al-Faraj al-Mu'āfā b. Zakariyyā al-Nahrawānī al-Jarīrī, *Kitāb al-Jalīs al-ṣāliḥ al-kāfī wa-'l-anīs al-nāṣiḥ al-shāfī*, ed. Muḥammad Mursī al-Khūlī, Beirut 1981-93, Vol. 2, pp. 336-41.

حيلة عراقي في أخذ جارية ابن جعفر

حدثنا أبو النضر العقيلي، قال: حدثني عبد الله بن أحمد بن حمدون النديم، عن أبي بكر العجلي، عن جماعة من مشايخ قُرَيْش من أهل المدينة، قالوا:

كانت عند عبد الله بن جعفر جاريةٌ مُغنّية يقال لها عمارة، وكان يَجِدُ بها وجداً شديداً، وكان لها منه مكانٌ لم يكن لأحدٍ من جواريه، فلما وفد عبد الله بن جعفر على معاوية خرج بها معه، فزاره يَزِيدُ ذات يوم فأخرجها إليه، فلما نظر إليها وسمع غناءها وقعتْ في نفسه، فأخذَهُ عليها ما لا يملكه، وجعل لا يمنعه من أن يبوح بما يجد بها إلّا

مكان أبيه مع يأسه من الظفر بها.

ولم يزل يكاتمُ الناس أمرها إلى أن مات معاوية وأفضى الأمر إليه، فاستشار بعض من قَدِم عليه من أهل المدينة وعامةَ من يثق به في أمرها وكيف الحيلة فيها، فقيل له: إن أمر عبد الله بن جعفر لا يُرام، ومنزلته من الخاصة والعامة ومنك ما قد علمت، وأنت لا تستجيزُ إكراهه، وهو لا يبيعها بشيء أبداً، وليس يُغني في هذا إلا الحيلة.

فقال: انظروا لي رجلاً عراقياً له أدبٌ وظَرْفٌ ومعرفة، فطلبوه فأتوه به، فلما دخل رأى بياناً وحلاوة وفَهْماً، فقال يزيد: إني دعوتُك لأمر إن ظفرت به فهو حُظْوَتُك آخر الدهر، ويدٌ أكافئك عليها إن شاء الله، ثم أخبره بأمره فقال له: إن عبد الله بن جعفر ليس يُرام ما قِبَلَهُ إلا بالخديعة، ولن يقدر أحدٌ على ما سألت، وأرجو أن أكونه والقوّة بالله، فأَعِنِّي بالمال، قال: خذ ما أحببت، فأخذ من طُرَف الشام وثياب مصر واشترى متاعاً للتجارة من رقيقٍ ودوابّ وغير ذلك، ثم شخص إلى المدينة فأناخ بعَرْصَة عبد الله بن جعفر، واكترى منزلاً إلى جانبه ثم توسّل إليه، وقال: رجلٌ من أهل العراق قدمتُ بتجارة وأحببت أن أكون في عزّ جوارك وكنفك إلى أن أبيع ما جئت به.

فبعث عبد الله إلى قهرمانه أن أكرم الرجل ووسِّع عليه في نُزُله، فلما اطمأنّ العراقيُّ سلّم عليه أياماً وعرفه نفسه وهيّأ له بغلة فارهة وثياباً من ثياب العراق وألطافاً، فبعث بها إليه وكتب معها: إني يا سيّدي رجلٌ تاجر ونعمة الله تعالى عليَّ سابغة، وقد بعثت إليك بشيء من لَطَفٍ وكذا وكذا من الثياب والعطر، وبعثت ببغلة خفيفة العنان

وطيئة الظهر فاتخذها لرجلك، فأنا أسألك بقرابتك من رسول الله (صلى الله عليه وسلم) إلا قبلت هديّتي، ولا توحشني بردّها، فإني أدين لله تعالى بمحبتك وحبّ أهل بيتك، فإن أعظم أملي في سفرتي هذه أن أستفيد الأنس بك والتحرّم بمواصلتك.

فأمر عبد الله بقبض هديته وخرج إلى الصلاة، فلما رجع مرّ بالعراقيّ في منزله فقام إليه وقبّل يده واستكثر منه، فرأى أدباً وظَرفاً وفصاحةً فأُعجب به وسُرَّ بنزوله عليه، فجعل العراقيُّ في كلّ يوم يبعث إلى عبد الله بلَطَف وطُرَفٍ، فقال عبد الله: جزى اللهُ ضيفَنَا هذا خيراً، فقد مَلأنا شكراً وما نقدر على مكافأته، فإنه لكذلك إلى أن دعاه عبد الله ودعا عمارة وجواريه، فلما طاب لهما المجلس وسمع غناء عمارة تعجّب وجعل يزيد في عجبه، فلما رأى ذلك عبد الله سُرَّ به إلى أن قال له: هل رأيت مثل عمارة؟ قال: لا والله يا سيدي، ما رأيت مثلها ولا تصلح إلا لك، وما ظننت أنه يكون في الدنيا مثل هذه الجارية حسن وجه وحسن غناء، قال: وكم تساوي عندك؟ قال: ما لها ثمن إلا الخلافة، قال: تقول هذا لتزيّن لي رأيي فيها وتجتلب سروري؟ قال له: يا سيدي والله إني لأحب سرورك، وما قلت لك إلا الجد، وبعد فإني تاجر أجمع الدرهم إلى الدرهم طلباً للربح، ولو أعطيتها بعشرة آلاف دينار لأخذتها، فقال له عبد الله عشرة آلاف دينار؟ قال: نعم، ولم يكن في ذلك الزمان جارية تُعرف بهذا الثمن، فقال له عبد الله: أنا أبيعكها بعشرة آلاف دينار، قال: وقد أخذتها، قال: هي لك، قال: قد وجب البيع، فانصرف العراقي.

فلما أصبح عبد الله لم يشعر إلا بالمال قد وافى به، فقيل لعبد الله: قد بعث العراقي بعشرة آلاف دينار، وقال: هذا ثمن عمارة فردّها وكتب إليه: إنما كنت أمزح معك، ومما أعلمك أن مثلي لا يبيع مثلها، فقال له: جُعلتُ فداك، إن الجِدَّ والهَزْل في البيع سواء، فقال له عبد الله: ويحك! ما أعلم جاريةً تساوي ما بذلت، ولو كنت بائعها من أحدٍ لآثرتُك، ولكني كنت مازحاً، وما أبيعها بملك الدنيا لحُرْمتها بي وموضِعها من قلبي، فقال العراقي: إن كنت مازحاً فإني كنت جادًّا، وما اطَّلَعْتُ على ما في نفسك، وقد ملكت الجارية وبعثت إليك بثمنها، وليست تَحِلُّ لك وما لي من أخذها من بدّ.

فمانعه إيّاها، فقال له: ليست لي بيِّنة، ولكني أستحلفك عند قبر رسول الله (صلى الله عليه وسلم) ومنبره، فلما رأى عبد الله الجِدَّ قال: بئس الضيف أنت، ما طرقنا طارق ولا نَزَل بنا نازل أعظم علينا بَلِيَّةً منك، تحلِّفُني فيقول الناس اضطهد عبد الله ضيفه وقهره فألجأه إلى أن استحلفه، أما والله ليعلمنّ الله جل ذكره أني سائله في هذا الأمر الصبر وحسن العزاء، ثم أمر قهرمانه بقبض المال منه وتجهيز الجارية بما يشبهها من الثياب والخدم والطيب، فجُهّزت بنحو من ثلاثة آلاف دينار، وقال: هذا لك ولها عوضاً مما ألطفتنا، والله المستعان.

فقبض العراقي الجارية وخرج بها، فلما برز من المدينة قال لها: يا عمارة! إني والله ما ملكتُك قط، ولا أنت لي، ولا مثلي يشتري جارية بعشرة آلاف دينار، وما كنت

لأقدم على ابن عم رسول الله (صلى الله عليه وسلم)، فأستلبه أحبَّ الناس إليه لنفسي، ولكنني دسيسٌ من يزيد بن معاوية وأنت له، وفي طلبك بعث بي فاستتري منّي، وإن داخلني الشيطانُ في أمرك وتاقت نفسي إليك فامتنعي.

ثم مضى بها حتى ورد دمشق فتلقّاه الناس بجنازة يزيد، وقد استُخْلِف ابنه معاوية بن يزيد، فأقام الرجل أياماً ثم تلطّف للدخول عليه فشرح له القصة – وروي أنه لم يكن أحدٌ من بني أمية يُعدَل بمعاوية بن يزيد في زمانه نُبْلا ونُسكا – فلما أخبره قال: هي لك، وكل ما دفعه إليك في أمرها فهو لك، وارحل من يومك فلا أسمع من خبرك في بلاد الشام، فرحل العراقي، ثم قال للجارية: إني قلت لك ما قلت حين خرجتُ بكِ من المدينة، وأخبرتُكِ أنك ليزيد وقد صرت لي، وأنا أُشهد الله أنك لعبد الله بن جعفر، فإني قد رددتك عليه فاستتري مني، ثم خرج بها حتى قدم المدينة فنزل قريباً من عبد الله بن جعفر، فدخل عليه بعض خدمه، فقال له: هذا العراقي، ضيفُك الذي صنع بنا ما صنع وقد نزل العَرْصَة لا حيّاه الله.

فقال عبد الله: مه! أنزلوا الرجل وأكرموه.

فلما استقرّ به، بعث إلى عبد الله: جُعلت فِداك، إن رأيت أن تأذَنَ لي أَذْنة خفيفة لأشَافهك بشيء فعلتَ.

فأذن له، فلما دخل سلّم عليه وقبّل يده وقرّبه عبد الله ثم اقتصّ عليه القصة حتى فرغ، ثم قال: قد – والله – وهبتُها لك قبل أن أراها أو أضع يدي عليها فهي لك،

ومَرْدُودة عليك، وقد علم الله جلّ وعزّ أني ما رأيت لها وجهاً إلا عندك، وبعث إليها فجاءت وجاءت بما جهّزها به موفّراً، فلما نظرت إلى عبد الله خَرَّتْ مغشيًّا عليها، وأهوى إليها عبد الله وضمّها إليه.

وخرج العراقي وتصايح أهل الدار: عمارة عمارة، فجعل عبد الله يقول ودموعه تجري: أحُلْمٌ هذا؟ أحقٌّ هذا؟ ما أصدّق هذا! فقال له العراقي: جعلت فداك، ردّها الله عليك بإيثارك الوفاء وصبرك على الحق، وانقيادك له، فقال عبد الله: الحمد لله، اللهم إنك تعلم أني صبرت عنها، وآثرتُ الوفاء وسلّمتُ لأمرك، فرددتَها عليَّ بمنّك، ولك الحمد.

ثم قال: يا أخا العراق! ما في الأرض أعظم مِنَّةً منك، وسيجازيك الله تعالى.

فأقام العراقيُّ أياماً، وباع عبد الله غنماً له بثلاثة عشر ألف دينار، وقال لقهرمانه: احملها إليه، وقل له: اعذر واعلم أني لو وصلتُكَ بكلِّ ما أملك لرأيتك أهلاً لأكثر منه.

Notes to Page 44

أبو النَضْر العُقَيْليّ proper name.

عبد الله بن أحمد بن حَمدون النَديم proper name; نديم means 'boon companion,' here of the caliphs al-Wāthiq (227-32) and al-Mutawakkil (232-247); see *Aghānī* VIII, 357-58, X, 231.

أبو بكر العِجْليّ proper name.

عَنْ on the authority of; see W II, 142B-D.

مَشايِخُ pl. of شَيْخٌ, see W I, 227B-D: one would expect مَشائِخُ. All plurals showing the vowel sequence *a-ā-i/ī*, as well as plurals ending in the fem. ending *ā'u* are diptote, except *fa'ālilatun;* seeW I, 226C-232D, 218D-219D, 213C-215D. For this term cf. also below, VIII, 100.

عبد الله بن جَعْفَر nephew of 'Alī b. Abī Ṭālib (died between 80 and 90).

غَنَّى to sing.

عَمَّارَةُ proper name.

وَجَدَ 'to find,' but also often 'to experience an emotion' (mostly love, but also ecstasy).

مِنْهُ 'in relation to him'; see W II, 132B-D: لَسْتَ مِنِّي, 'you stand in no relationship to me.'

جَوارٍ plur. of جارِيَةٌ root *j-r-y*, see W I, 214C-D, 247A-B: follows the irregular declension: nom./gen. جَوارٍ acc. جَوارِيَ.

مُعاوِيَةُ the caliph Mu'āwiya (ruled 41-60).

وَفَدَ على to come to [a ruler on a diplomatic mission], to pay a formal visit.

خَرَجَ بِها مَعَهُ see W II, 159B-C, 160B; *Ar. Syntax*, pp. 237-39: verbs of motion construed with بِ may often be translated as transitives: ذَهَبَ بِهِ, 'he took it away,' سَما بِهِ, 'he lifted it up.'

يَزِيدُ (ruled 60-64) successor of Mu'āwiya.

ذاتَ يَوْمٍ 'one day'; see W II, 110B for further examples of adverbs with ذات.

أَخْرَجَها إليه he [sc. 'Abdallāh] brought her out to him, showed her to him.

غِناءٌ singing (sometimes used in the sense of 'music').

وَقَعَتْ في نَفْسِهِ she made a [deep] impression on him, he fell in love with her.

فأَخَذَهُ عليها . . . See W II, 170 B; this sentence is quoted there. على may indicate cause or reason: lit. "because of her there seized him something he could not control."

وجَعَلَ the sentence beginning with لا يَمْنَعُ depends on جَعَلَ, which can be translated: 'he began to. . . ,' 'he came into a situation where. . . '; see W II, 108D-109B for verbs used in similar ways.

لا يَمْنَعُهُ . . . إلّا مكانُ أبيه the subject is مكانُ: 'not kept him from [i.e., nothing kept him from. . .] except the position of his father.'

ما يَجِدُ بها the emotions he experienced through her.

Notes to Page 45

مع [combined] with.

الظَفَر to get hold of; here, 'to acquire.'

زال 'to cease'; زال is one of the "sisters of كان," see W II, 101D-104A.

يُكاتِمُ The verb كاتم here has a double object; it fits into the category of verbs signifying 'to fill, satisfy, give, deprive, forbid, ask, entreat,' etc. mentioned W II, 47C-48C—e.g., أَطْعَمَهُ السيفَ, 'he made him taste the sword.' Form III of the verb may carry the notion of an effort; see W I, 32D-33A.

أمْرَها lit., "her situation [with regard to himself]"; i.e., the feelings and plans she had created in his mind.

الأمْر here: 'the government.'

اسْتَشار to consult, ask for an opinion.

بَعْض can mean 'some' or be equivalent to the indefinite article; see W II, 207A.

قَدِمَ عَلَيْهِ to arrive at his residence, to visit.

المَدِينة Medina in Arabia, where ʿAbdallāh b. Jaʿfar was residing.

وعامَّةَ مَن . . . take عامَّةَ as an object to اسْتَشارَ : "all those [whom he trusted]"; see W II, 206C-D.

في أمرِها 'in her case,'—i.e., for a solution to his infatuation with her.

كَيْفَ الحيلةُ فيها "how to find a way of acquiring her"; حيلة, plur. حِيَلٌ, is used in the sense of 'stratagem,' 'trick [to evade the letter of the precepts of Muslim Law],' and 'mechanical device.'

أَمْرُ عبدِ اللهِ . . . لا يُرامُ lit., "the affair of ʿAbdallāh b. Jaʿfar cannot be hoped for"; translate: " ʿAbdallāh b. Jaʿfar cannot be forced to do something against his will."

ومَنْزِلَتُهُ مِن . . . ومِنْكَ "his rank among. . . and his position in relation to you being. . ." (cf. above, p. 50, note on مِنْهُ).

لا تَسْتَجِيزُ "you cannot possibly allow yourself"; the so-called imperfect often expresses a potential something that could possibly happen; see *Ar. Syntax*, p. 14.

أَكْرَهَ to compel.

أَغْنَى to help, be of use.

انْظُروا لي "look out for me [till you find. . .]," "seek for me."

أدب see above, Introduction, p. 1, note 2; here either 'education' or 'skill.'

ظَرْفٌ here probably 'good manners.'

أَتَوْهُ بِهِ see above, p. 50 (note on خرج بها معه): 'they came to him (sc. Yazīd) with him,'—i.e., they brought Yazīd an Iraqi fitting these requirements.

فلمّا دَخَلَ رَأَى 'when he (sc. the Iraqi) entered, he (sc. Yazīd) noticed [that this man possessed. . .].'

بَيان here: 'eloquence,' 'subtlety in his way of expressing himself.'

حَلاوة probably: 'grace.'

حُظُوَتُكَ آخِرَ الدَهْرِ 'your fortune for the rest of your life' (i.e., it will make you a fortunate man).

ويَدٌ أُكافِئُكَ عليها [it will mean] that you have given me a [helping] hand for which I will reward you. يَدٌ as well as other parts of the body, especially those in pairs, are often fem.; see W I, 178C, 183B.

فقال له i.e., 'the Iraqi said to Yazīd.'

ما قِبَلَهُ W II, 180A: قِبَلَ is a near synonym of عِنْدَ ; "what he owns," "his household."

خَديعة trickery.

لَنْ with subjunctive, used in emphatic denials; see W II, 22C, 300C.

أَنْ أَكونَهُ "that I shall be he" [i.e., the person who accomplishes what you ask me]—though he has just stated that nobody can do it!

أَعِنّي Form IV imperative (+ object pronoun ني) from root عون ; to help, to support.

طُرَف الشام perhaps: 'the specialties of Syria.'

مَتاع لِلتِجارة goods suitable as merchandise.

مِنْ ‘consisting of,’ ‘such as’; مِن specifies مَتاع ; see W II, 137A-138A.

رَقيق slave, slaves (sing. and coll.).

دَوابُّ pl. of دابَّة (root دبب).

شَخَصَ to go out, to set out for.

أَناخَ to make [a camel] kneel, to make halt.

عَرْصَة open space between houses; here perhaps the square in front of the house of ‘Abdallāh b. Ja‘far or the square surrounded by houses belonging to ‘Abdallāh or to his clan.

تَوَسَّلَ إليه he approached him, asked him for an audience.

رَجُلٌ مِن أهل العراق nominal sentence without explicit subject: “[I am] a man from the inhabitants of Iraq.”

أَحْبَبْتُ أن أكونَ في عِزِّ جِوارِكَ وكَنَفِكَ “I wish to be under the might of your formal protection and defense,”—i.e., I hope to enjoy the protection and defense that your standing can provide me; I hope to become your client. جِوار is part of bedouin customary law; see *EI*2, s.v. <u>DJ</u>IWĀR.

إلى أَنْ أَبيعَ till I have finished selling. . . .

قَهْرَمان Iranian term: majordomo, steward, overseer.

أَنْ has here the same function as our quotation marks, see W I, 292C; *Ar. Syntax*, p. 405; e.g. ذَكَرْتَ أَنْ لا “you said no.”

أَكْرِمْ . . . ووَسِّعْ عَلَيْهِ the two imperatives appear to be near synonyms: “be very generous to him.”

اِطْمَأَنَّ Form IV of quadriliterals, root طمأن , see W I, 49B-C; in some dictionaries under طمن .

سَلَّمَ عَلَيْهِ (lit., to say السلامُ عليك) here: he paid his respects to him (?).

عَرَّفَهُ نَفْسَهُ (reading Form II) "he introduced himself," probably in the sense that ʿAbdallāh came to know him as a gentleman.

هَيَّأً to prepare (as a gift).

أَلْطاف plur. of لَطَف meaning obscure: 'present' as a general term is unlikely, after he has specified that he is giving him a mule and clothing; see, however, *WKAS*, s.v. (pp. 715a-176a), where, judging by the examples, we find the term used in the sense of small-sized niceties,' e.g., 715b, lines 8-10: *bi-alṭāfin min ṭībin wa-jawharin wa ghayri dhālika*; and (715a, lines 27-30) 'bakery specialties.' Dozy has *'friandises'* (delicacies). In the next sentence, لَطَف could have the sense of 'wine' (*WKAS*, p. 716a, line 44b, ff.); or it could be a misreading for الألطاف in the senses indicated earlier; or for لُطَف 'small gifts' (p. 716b, lines 25-39); or, finally, perhaps a misreading for طُرَف (the merchant had taken with him طُرَف from Syria). See also below, p. 46, لَطَف , where the correct reading is most likely لُطَف وطُرَف (see *WKAS*, p. 717b, lines 33-34). Cf. also below, p. 47, ما أَلْطَفْتَنا (and note).

بَعَثَ بِها إِليهِ he sent [someone] with these gifts.

نِعْمَةُ اللهِ عَلَيَّ سابِغة the favor(s) God. . . has bestowed on me have been abundant.

تَعالى 'God Almighty'; common parenthesis following God's name. Not to be taken as an optative, but assertory, i.e., 'God has made himself uplifted"; see W I, 39C-D.

خَفيفة العِنانِ light / easy to handle (عِنان 'bridle').

Notes to Page 46

وَطِيئَةُ الظَّهْرِ smooth to ride (وَطِيء 'smooth, even').

فاتَّخِذْها لِرِجْلِكَ take it for yourself in order to [save] your legs (or your feet) [from suffering fatigue].

بِقَرابَتِكَ مِن رَسولِ الله through, by, in the name of your close relationship to the Messenger of God.

إلّا 'except, unless' is used in oaths in the sense of: 'and the consequences of my oath will take effect unless. . . '; see W II, 339C-340A and note, and II 172C-D. Here: "I beseech you to accept my gift."

أَوْحَشَ to frighten, make unhappy.

أَدِينُ لله I do my duty / show my obedience to God.

أهل البيت

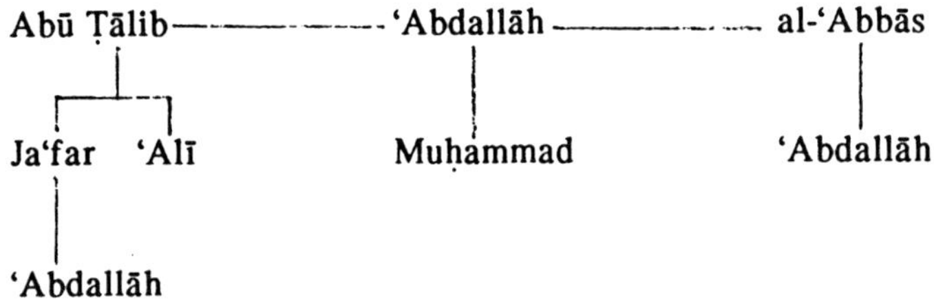

سَفْرَة journey.

أَنْ أَسْتَفِيدَ الأُنْسَ بِكَ "that I might win familiarity with you," "that I might become acquainted with you."

والتَّحَرُّمَ بِمُواصَلَتِكَ "and that I might feel protected by being in touch with you."

قام إليه "he stood up to meet him."

اسْتَكْثَرَ مِنْهُ "he gave much attention to him," "made clear his appreciation"; more examples in *WKAS*, s.v.

أَدَب ، ظَرْف see above, p. 46 (text) and p. 52 (notes).

فَصاحة eloquence; often a synonym of *balāgha*, but medieval literary theorists sometimes maintain that *faṣāḥa* relates to grammar or pronunciation, and *balāgha* to style.

أُعْجِبَ بِهِ he was pleased with him.

جَعَلَ see above, p. 44 (text), p. 51 (note).

لطف voweling uncertain, but *WKAS* confirms the combination طُرَف / لُطَف, translate: 'gifts and trinkets' (?).

جَزاهُ خَيْراً to reciprocate with good, to reward.

فإِنَّهُ لَكذلك W II, 79 A-B: *-hū* refers to the Iraqi; whenever the subject of *inna, fa-inna*, etc. comes first, the predicate may be introduced by the particle *la:* "and he was (i.e., continued to act) this way. . . ."

لَمّا طابَ لهما المَجْلِسُ when the meeting was pleasant for the two of them, when they both felt comfortable.

يَزِيدُ في عَجَبِهِ he (the Iraqi) began to add to his admiration; i.e., he more than once expressed his admiration.

إلى أَنْ قالَ "and this went so far that he said," "till he ventured to say."

أَنَّهُ يكونُ "that there would / could be"; the pronoun *-hū* anticipates the statement that follows: "that it was so that there could be"; see W II, 81 C.

حُسْنَ وَجْهٍ وحُسْنَ غِناءٍ W II, 122A-123B: the use of the so-called accusative here indicates in what respect something is the way it is, a specification.

ساوَى to be worth [in money].

عِنْدَكَ in your opinion; see W II, 179 C: عِنْدَهُ أَنَّ القرآنَ مَخْلوقٌ "he held that the Koran had been created," (i.e., had not been there from the beginning of time).

ما لها ثَمَنٌ إِلَّا الخِلافةُ she has no price but the caliphate, "she is worth a kingdom."

لِتُزَيِّنَ لي رَأْيي فيها "to embellish my opinion concerning her,"—i.e., to make her more beautiful in my eyes; لي is pleonastic.

اجْتَلَبَ to bring about.

جِدّ seriousness, a thing one means seriously.

وبَعْدُ فإِنِّي "and furthermore, I am. . .."; cf. W I, 292B: أَمَّا السفينة فكانت "as for the ship, it was. . ."; cf. also the formula أَمَّا بَعْدُ introducing the text of a letter after the formal greetings ('Now I wish to inform you of the following. . .,' 'I bring the following to your attention. . .').

أَجْمَعُ الدِرْهَمَ إلى الدرهمِ طَلَباً لِلرِّبْحِ "I add a dirham to a dirham,"—i.e., I know how to determine prices [so as to make a profit].

تُعْرَفُ بهذا الثَّمَن known to fetch this price.

أَبِيعُكَها for a double object expressed by two pronouns, see W I, 103A-B; the sequence must be first, second, third person.

قَدْ 'herewith'; particle used in formal statements.

وَجَبَ البَيْعُ "the sale has become binding." See *EI2*, s.v. BAY': the formalities of offer and acceptance required by Islamic law have been fulfilled.

Notes to Page 47

لَم يَشْعُرْ إِلاَّ بِـ "before he knew it, there was. . . ." See *Admin.*, pp. 63-65, nos. 566-82.

قد وافَى به "which he (i.e., the Iraqi) had [already] delivered [to him] in full"; قد is also used to indicate something that has happened in accordance with, or contrary to what was expected; see W I, 286B-C, II, 3C-6A; *Ar. Synt.*, p. 301.

رُدَّها deliver her, W I, 70B-C: vocalize رُدُّها , though رُدَّها and رُدِّها are also possible W I, 70B-C.

ومِمَّا أُعْلِمُكَ "among that which I [should like to] let you know is [the fact that. . .]"—i.e., I should like to let you know [once and for all]. . . .

جُعِلْتُ فِداكَ "may I be made your ransom,"—i.e., I would give my life for yours; frequently used polite formula, cf.W II, 162A-B: (فُدِيتَ) بأَبي وأُمّي , '[may you be ransomed] by my father and my mother.'

إِنَّ الجِدَّ والهَزْلَ في البَيْعِ سَوَاءٌ "when it comes to a sales contract, [whether one speaks in] jest or earnest makes no difference" (i.e., no written agreement is needed according to Islamic law).

وَيْحَكَ woe to you! [what are you doing?].

مِنْ أَحَدٍ 'to anybody'; see W II, 131C-D: مِن is used to indicate the debtor, also in a marriage contract, hence زَوَّجَ ابْنَتَهُ مِنِ ابْنِ أَخيهِ.

آثَرَ (Form IV) to prefer.

لِحُرْمَتِها بي "because of the high esteem in which I hold her."

مِن قَلْبي cf. above, p. 44 (text), p. 50 (note on مِنْهُ), and W II 132A-D: مِنْ indicates distance or closeness, literally as well as figuratively, e.g. دنا مني , and فإني

لستُ منك ولستَ مني, and هو مني مَناطَ الثُرَيَّا ('as far as the point where the Pleiades are hanging [in the sky]').

إنْ كُنْتَ مازِحاً فإني . . . "granted that you were joking. . . / you may well have been joking. . . , but I. . . ."

ما اطَّلَعْتُ على I did not inform myself [yesterday] of. . . .

في نَفْسِكَ in your soul, in your thoughts.

مَلَكَ to own [legally].

لَيْسَتْ تَحِلُّ لَكَ she is no longer legal to you (i.e., it is no longer legal for you to have her with you or to have sexual intercourse with her).

مِنْ بُدٍّ cf. above, II, p. 21 (text), p. 24 (note), and Index; مِن بُدٍّ is the subject of the sentence beginning with ما لي ; W II, D-136 B: after a negation, مِنْ + genit. expresses emphasis, e.g. ما جاءني من أحَدٍ , '[absolutely] nobody came to me.' مِن + genit. can also take the place of an object, e.g. إذ سَمِعْنا مِن مُنادٍ 'when we heard somebody calling.' See *Ar. Syntax*, pp. 267-68.

مانَعَ to contest, try to refuse; W I, 32D-33A: cf. above, p. 45, يُكاتِمُ ; for *iyyā*-marking an object or a second object, see W I, II, Index.

بَيِّنَة 'evidence,' 'testimony by a witness'; a written contract is not needed, see *EI*2, s. vv. BAY', BAYYINA. Dealing in a fair manner with the seller is recommended; see *EI*2, s.v. TIDJĀRA.

أَسْتَحْلِفُكَ عِنْدَ قَبْرِ رسول الله ومِنْبَرِهِ I will make you take an oath at the grave and the pulpit of the Messenger of God [here in Medina].

بِئْسَ الضَّيْفُ أنتَ what a bad guest you are! For نِعْمَ and بِئْسَ used in exclamations and considered as verbs, see W I, 97A-98A, 290A.

طَرَقَ lit., 'to knock at the door at night,' 'visit at night'; here a synonym of نزل ب /

نزل على, 'to take up lodgings with.'

بَلِيَّة *baliyya* specifies أَعْظَم مِن: greater than you in [bringing] disaster(s) upon us.

اِضْطَهَدَ to treat somebody unjustly.

تُحَلِّفُني... 'you are going to (or: you could) ask me to take an oath and then people will say: 'Abdallāh wronged his guest and forced him to have recourse to imposing an oath on him (i.e., 'Abdallāh).'

أَلْجَأَ to cause somebody to have recourse to.

أَما W II, 310B-C: exclamation strengthening واللهِ.

لَيَعْلَمَنَّ اللهُ the so-called Energetic (W I, 61A-C) here expresses a wish: 'May / Let God know,' or, more likely, an assertion: 'God should know,' see W II, 40D-41B.

صَبْر patience (especially in enduring hardship); considered a Muslim virtue, see *EI*2, s.v.

حُسْنُ العَزاءِ *ḥusn* + verbal noun is a frequent idiom: 'doing [something] well,' 'succeeding in [something],' here: 'consoling oneself in an exemplary manner,' 'finding consolation easily.'

أَشْبَهَ to be appropriate.

عِوَضاً مِنْ in exchange for.

ما أَلْطَفْتَنا what you (he means the Iraqi) bestowed upon us in presents.

المُسْتَعان lit.: the One who is asked for help.

ما مَلَكْتُكَ قَطُّ I never (by no means) [legally] acquired possession of you [when I bought you].

لا . . . ولا. . . *lā* is used to take up a previous negation; see W II, 303A-C.

ما كُنْتُ لِ W II, 266C: كان لِ , 'to be a person likely (or willing) [to do a thing].'

Notes to Page 48

أَقْدَمَ على to advance against, venture against.

اِسْتَلَبَ to rob, to carry away forcefully.

أَحَبَّ . . . إليه W II, 71D-72A: إلى following an *af'alu* form from a root signifying love or hatred indicates the person experiencing these sentiments.

لِنَفْسِي for myself.

دَسِيس secret agent.

في طَلَبِكِ in order to find [and acquire] you.

فاسْتَتِري مِنّي 'so veil yourself from me,' or perhaps: 'so conceal yourself from me.'

إِنْ داخَلَني الشَيْطانُ if Satan tries to snare me (lit. tries to enter me); cf. note on يُكاتِمُ above, p. 51.

في أَمْرِكِ when it comes to you (i.e., because I am now so close to you). Note the frequent and often ambiguous use of أمر .

تَاقَ إلى to desire.

تَلَقَّى بِ to meet [somebody] with.

جِنازة bier, funeral procession.

اِسْتَخْلَفَ to appoint as successor.

تَلَطَّفَ لِ to use a trick, use a stratagem.

شَرَحَ to explain (cf. شَرْحٌ, 'commentary').

رُوِيَ it has been transmitted (i.e., historians report).

بَنو أُمَيَّةَ the Umayyads.

عُدِلَ بِ to be considered the equal of.

نُبْلاً ونُسْكاً note the sequence of two terms of the same grammatical pattern, *fu'l*, and the alliteration in *nūn;* "in nobility of character and piety." For the accus., see the note on . . . حُسْنَ p. 57, above.

دَفَعَهُ presumably the subject is Yazīd. The verb دفع is often used in the sense of 'handing over a sum of money.'

في أَمْرِها 'for her sake,'—i.e., in order to bring her here.

فهو the use of فَ is understandable if one keeps in mind that he could have said "as for the money which he gave you," cf. note to وبعدُ فإني, p. 58, above.

وَارْحَلْ مِنْ يَوْمِكَ 'and depart today'; for the expression مِنْ يَوْمِكَ, 'today' (lit., 'as part of your day,' i.e., the day you are now passing through) see W II, 136C-D.

فلا أَسْمَعَ for فَ with subjunctive after an imperative, see W II, 30D, 32B.

مِن خَبَرِكَ (object to فلا أَسْمَعَ) see note on من بَعْدُ above, p. 60.

قُلْتُ لَكَ ما قُلْتُ I told you what I told you (i.e., remember what I told you).

وقد صِرْتِ لي and now (or 'as a matter of fact,' 'however'—see preceding notes on قد) you have become my property.

أُشْهِدُ اللهَ I ask God to witness.

فإني قد رَدَدْتُك عليه I have herewith given you back to him (ie., to 'Abdallāh)—cf. above قد وجب البيع, p. 46 (text), p. 58 (note).

بَعْضُ خَدَمِهِ one of his (i.e., 'Abdallāh's) servants [came before 'Abdallāh].

هذا العراقيُّ W II, 278 A-B: this word order, usually in the sense of 'this Iraqi,' sometimes has to be translated as 'this *is* the Iraqi,' '*here is* the Iraqi.' Cf. Qur'ān 4:119: ذٰلِكَ الْفَوْزُ الْعَظِيمُ "This is the Great Felicity."

لا حَيَّاهُ اللهُ 'May God not preserve him/help him.'

مَهْ 'never mind.'

اسْتَقَرَّ بِهِ he settled in it (i.e., in 'Abdallāh's home).

إنْ رَأَيْتَ أنْ. . . فَعَلْتَ "If you see fit. . . , do so [and I shall welcome the opportunity]."

أَذْنَة 'a single audience,' 'just one audience'; the اِسْمِ المَرَّة (verbal noun of single occurrence) of Form I always has the form فَعْلَة; it is not always noted in the dictionaries. See W I, 122D-123A.

خَفِيفَة the implication may be that this audience will not last long, or that it will not be cumbersome; the opposition ثقيل — خفيف is often used in speaking of boring or burdensome guests and pleasant guests.

قَرَّبَهُ to make somebody approach, sit nearby.

اقْتَصَّ على to tell a story to somebody (the common dictionaries do not mention على with اقتصّ, but given the state of Arabic lexicography, this is not uncommon).

قَبْلَ أنْ . . . عليها before I have seen her or put my hands on her (Mu'āwiya b. Yazīd had given her to the merchant).

Notes to Page 49

مَا رَأَيْتُ لَهَا وَجْهاً إِلَّا عِنْدَكَ 'that I never saw her face' (lit., 'a face belonging to her'); for this use of the possessive لِ, see W II, 149A; *Ar. Synt.*, pp. 228-29, 250, and cf. W II, addenda, p. xviii.

مُوَفَّراً in its entirety (referring to the jewelry, etc., that 'A. had provided when she left).

مَغْشِيًّا عَلَيْهَا derived from غُشِيَ عليه / عليها, 'a cover was thrown over him/her,' 'he/she lost conciousness'; hence: المَغْشِيُّ عليه / عليها, 'the man or woman who has lost consciousness. مَغْشِيًّا here used in the circumstantial accusative *(ḥāl)*: 'she fell down losing consciousness,' see W II, 268C.

أَهْوَى إلى to rush, to fall down upon.

تَصَايَحَ to shout to each other; see W I, 40A-B: Form VI may refer to the activity of a group or to a single body, cf. تَمَاسَكَ, 'to hold together.'

أَحُلْمٌ هذا is this a dream?

إِيثار from آثَرَ, 'to prefer.'

صَبْرِكَ على الحَقِّ your enduring with patience [the sorrows resulting from] the obligation [you had taken upon yourself].

انْقِيادُكَ لَهُ "your allowing yourself to be guided by it" (i.e., الحقّ); W I, 41B: Form VII sometimes indicates 'to allow something to be done', e.g. انهزم 'to let oneself be put to flight,' which therefore can even be used in the passive: اُنْهُزِمَ بَيْنَ يَدَيْهِ, 'there was a flight in front of him,' 'they fled before him.'

اَللّٰهُمَّ 'O God'; see W II, 89C-D and note.

صَبَرْتُ عَنْهَا 'I patiently suffered separation from her'; see W II, 141D-142C: عن often is used when a separation is expressed or implied, cf. the amusing example quoted by W 142B: لِي فِي طِلَابِ الْعِلْمِ غِنًى عَنْ غِنَاءِ الْغَانِيَاتِ , 'in the pursuit of scholarship there is for me [such pleasure] that I can do without the singing of beautiful maidens.'

سَلَّمَ لِأَمْرِهِ 'he obeyed his command.'

يا أَخا العراق The word أَخ sometimes is used in the sense of 'inhabitant,' 'member of a tribe.'

مِنَّة kindness.

لَ frequently introduces the main clause after لَوْ, see W II, 348D-349A.

أَهْلٌ لِ here: entitled to [receive as a reward].

VI. Al-Dhahabī, *Siyar a'lām al-nubalā'*

Al-Dhahabī, Shams al-Dīn, Abū 'Abdallāh Muḥammad b. Aḥmad [b. Aḥmad] b. 'Uthmān al-Dimashqī al-Shāfi'ī, was born in Damascus in 673, and died there in 748 or 753. He is best known as a historian and a scholar of Tradition, and is counted among the most important authorities in these two fields by Muslim scholars as well as contemporary Western scholars. As a historian he distinguished himself as the author of a *Ta'rīkh al-Islām* which differs from similar "histories" by the way it deals with the last four centuries: *Ta'rīkh* often means "collection of obituaries," instead of "history of political and social events," as one would expect. Typical examples are the *Ta'rīkh Baghdād* of al-Khaṭīb al-Baghdādī and the *Ta'rīkh Madīnat Dimashq* of Ibn 'Asākir; or *ta'rīkh* may mean "year-by-year history" with heavy emphasis on the obituaries and almost no information on political events. In the latter part of al-Dhahabī's history, however, we find that the author divides his work by periods and that he gives much more attention to what happened on the political and local scene than to obituaries of the scholars and other prominent personalities.

Al-Dhahabī also wrote works that are entirely devoted to biography, such as *al-Iṣāba fī ma'rifat al-ṣaḥāba* on the "Companions of the Prophet" (*ṣaḥāba*), and *Siyar a'lām al-nubalā'*, "Biographies of the leading personalities among prominent [men]." As early as 1881 a very useful handbook on proper punctuation and voweling of proper names was published in Leiden by P. J. de Jong under the title *al-Moschtabih auctore. . . ad-Dhahabī* (sic), reprinted with additions by 'A. M. al-Bijāwī, Cairo 1962 (with indexes).

For further information, see *GAL*, G II, 46-48, S II, 45–47; *EI*2, s.v. al-D̲h̲ahabī; F. Rosenthal, *A History of Muslim Historiography*, Leiden 1952, see index, p. 637*a* ; and the data collected by the editor of the *Siyar* I, 13–90. The *EI* does not draw up a list of references to the numerous medieval Arabic biographies of al-Dhahabī; two examples out of many: among his contemporaries we have Ṣafadī (d. 764), who gives his biography in *Wāfī* II, 163–68; a later work, *K. al-Dāris fī ta'rīkh al-madāris* of 'Abd al-Qādir b. Muḥ. al-Nu'aymī (d. 927), which is a voluminous monograph on educational institutions in Damascus, mentions him frequently (the references in the index cover an entire page).

The *Siyar* from which the following selection was taken has now apparently been published in its entirety. Volume XXIII published in Beirut 1413/1993 (indexes in volumes XXIV and XXV) reaches into the seventh century. Two undated volumes had been published earlier in Cairo.

From: al-Dhahabī, *Siyar a'lām al-nubalā'*, ed. Sh al-Arnā'ūṭ, Ḥ. al-Asad, and M. N. al-'Arqūsī, 2nd ed., Beirut 1402-3, XVI, 544-47.

المُعَافى

ابن زَكَرِيّا بن يَحْيَى بن حُمَيْدٍ، العلاَّمةُ، الفقيهُ الحافظُ القاضي المتفنِّن، عالم عصرِه، أبو الفَرَج النَّهرُوانيُّ الجريريُّ، نسبة إلى رأي ابن جَرير الطَّبَريّ، ويقال له: ابن طَرَارا.

سمع أبا القاسمِ البَغَويَّ، وأبا محمّد بن صاعدٍ، وأبا بَكْر بْنَ أبي داوُدَ، وأبا سعيدٍ العَدَويَّ، وأبا حامدٍ الحَضْرَميَّ، والقاضيَ المَحَامليَّ، وخلقاً كثيراً.

وتلا على ابن شَنَبُوذَ، وأبي مُزاحِم الخاقانيِّ.

قرأ عليه: القاضي أبو تَغْلِبَ المُلْحَميُّ، وأحمد بن مَسْرُور الخَبَّازُ، ومحمد بن عُمَرَ النِّهاوَنْديُّ، وطائفة.

وحدَّث عنه: أبو القاسم عُبيدُ الله الأزهَريُّ، والقاضي أبو الطَّيِّبِ الطَّبَريُّ، وأحمدُ بن عليّ التَّوَّزيُّ، وأحمد بن عُمَرَ بن رَوْحٍ، وأبو عَلِيّ محمد بن الحُسَيْنِ الجازِريُّ، وأبو الحُسَيْن محمد بن أحمد بن حَسْنُونٍ النَّرْسيِّ، وخلقٌ سواهم.

قال الخطيب: كان من أعلم الناس في وقته بالفقه، والنحو، واللُّغة، وأصناف الأدب، ولي القضاء بباب الطَّاق، وكان على مذهب ابن جرير، وبلغني عن أبي محمد البافيّ الفقيه، أنَّه كان يقول: إذا حضر القاضي أبو الفَرَج فقد حضرت العلومُ كلُّها.

قال الخطيب: وحدَّثني القاضي أبو حامدٍ الدَّلُويُّ، قال: كان أبو محمد البافيّ

يقول: لو أوصى رجلٌ بثلث ماله أن يُدفع إلى أعلم الناس لوجب أن يُدفع إلى المُعافى بن زكريا.

قال الخطيب: سألتُ البَرْقانيَّ عن المعافى، فقال: كان أعظم الناس، وكان ثقة، لم أسمع منه.

وحكى أبو حَيَّانٍ التَّوْحِيديُّ، قال: رأيت المعافَى بن زَكَرِيًّا قد نام مُستدبر الشَّمس ِ في جامع الرُّصافة في يوم شاتٍ، وبه من أثر الضُّر والفقر والبؤس أمرٌ عظيمٌ مع غزارة علمه.

قال أبو عبد الله محمد بن أبي نَصْر الحُمَيديّ: قرأتُ بخطِّ المُعَافى بن زكريّا، قال: حججتُ وكنتُ بمنى، فسمعت منادياً ينادي: يا أبا الفرج المعافى، قلت: مَن يُريدني؟ وهممتُ أن أجيبَه ثم نادى: يا أبا الفرج المُعافى بن زكريا النَّهرُواني، فقلت: ها أنا ذا، ما تريد؟ فقال: لعلَّك من نَهروان العراق، قلت: نعم، قال: نحن نُريد نهروان الغرب، قال: فعجِبتُ من هذا الاتِّفاق، وعلمتُ أن بالمغرب مكاناً يُسمَّى النهروان.

مات المعافى بالنهروان في ذي الحِجَّة سنةَ تسعينَ وثلاث مئة، وله خمسٌ وثمانون سنة.

وله تفسيرٌ كبيرٌ في ستِّ مجلّدات جمّ الفوائد، وله كتاب «الجليس والأنيس» في مجلّدين.

وكان من بحور العلم.

أخبرنا عُمَرُ بنُ عبد المُنْعِم، أخبرنا أبو اليُمْنِ الكِنْديّ، أخبرنا محمدُ بنُ عبد الباقِي، أخبرنا محمدُ بنُ أحمد النَّرْسي، أخبرنا المُعافى، حدثنا البَغَوِي، حدثنا وَهْبٌ، حدثنا خالِدٌ، عن الشَّيْبانيّ، عن عَوْنِ بْنِ عَبْدِ الله، عن أخيه عُبَيْدِ الله، عن أبي هريرةَ، عن النبيّ صلى الله عليه وسلم قال: «إنّ في الجُمُعَةِ لَساعَةً لا يَسْأَلُ اللهَ فيها عبدٌ مؤمنٌ شيئاً إلّا استجاب له».

Notes to Page 68

From here on the vocabulary will not note proper names, except in cases where the proper name is difficult to recognize. (The *isnāds* in this selection contain some famous names, but to identify them goes beyond the scope of this reader and would require too much space.) See the list of handbooks on names and their voweling below.

المُعافَى in some handbooks مُعافَى, without the article.

عَلاّمة for nouns of the type *fa"āla*, see above, p. 32 (note on عَلاّمة), and Index under Fem. endings.

فَقِيه scholar of Islamic jurisprudence (فِقْه).

حافِظ usually taken in the sense of 'one who has memorized the Koran'; in later times it becomes a title the meaning of which is not quite clear, perhaps 'most knowledgeable / most learned / outstanding scholar.'

النَّهْرُواني from Nahruwān or Nihrawān; the voweling Nahrawān seems to be the most common; see above, p. 40, and *EI*2, s.v.: site of a famous battle that took place in 38 A.H.

مُتَفَنِّن many-sided, versatile.

عالِمُ عَصْرِهِ the [best] scholar of his day, unsurpassed in his days.

أَبو الفَرَجِ النَّهْرُوانيّ الجَريريّ Dhahabī completes the name of his subject by adding the *kunya* (see above, pp. 14, 22) and two *nisbas*, one referring to his city of origin, the other explained in what follows.

نِسْبَةً one does not need a verbal sentence to allow the use of an adverbial accus., see W II, 116A-B; *Ar. Syntax*, p. 115.

رَأْي view, i.e., the views of the short-lived legal school of Muḥammad. b. Jarīr al-Ṭabarī (see above, Introduction to this selection).

ويُقالُ لَهُ and he is also called.

ابن طَرارا the name Ṭarār appears in Ibn Ḥajar al-ʻAsqalānī (see below, Handbooks on Spelling); the *Ta'r. Bagh.* XIII, 231, reads Ṭarāz.

سَمِعَ (what follows is a list of Mu'āfā's teachers). Cf. the term *samā'*, a certificate provided by a teacher to his pupil authorizing him to transmit a given text (or several texts) on the teacher's authority. It is often found at the beginning or the end of a manuscript. See *EI*2, s.v. ĪDJĀZA.

داوُد common spelling for داؤود; see W I, 18D.

وخَلْقاً كثيراً and many [other] people.

تَلا على (lit. he read [the Koran] to. . .) he studied Koran [and its variant readings] under. . . .

قَرَأَ على 'to study under. . .' (mostly in the sense that the student reads aloud a book to his teacher while the teacher corrects vowelings and makes certain that the student understands the text properly). What follows is a list of Mu'āfā's pupils.

عَلَيْهِ i.e., Mu'āfā.

النِّهَاوَنْدِيّ from Nihāwand, Nuhāwand, or Nahāwand, a city in Persia; see *EI*1, s.v., *EI*2, VIII, 23a-24a, and G. Le Strange, *The Lands of the Eastern Caliphate,* Cambridge 1930, pp. 196-97.

وطَائِفة and a group of [other] people, and several other [scholars].

حَدَّثَ عنه (what follows is a list of pupils who studied Tradition literature under Mu'āfā and presumably obtained the right to transmit the traditions they heard, quoting Mu'āfā as an authority).

سِواهُمْ besides, except; usually synonymous with غَيْر ; see W II, 209C-210A, 341C.

الخَطِيب al-Khaṭīb al-Baghdādī, the author of the *Ta'r. Bagh.*; see the Introduction to this selection and *Abbreviations*.

أَعْلَم بِ elative, from عَلِمَ بِ , 'to be well-versed in / to be an authority in.'

أَصْناف الأدب probably: 'various genres of literature'; see *Introduction* to this Reader, note 2.

وَلِيَ القَضاءَ he was in charge of the *qāḍī*ship.

باب الطاق an area in Baghdad. See G. Le Strange, *Baghdad during the Abbasid Caliphate,* Oxford 1900, pp. 218, 320, and Map V; see also J. Lassner, *The Topography of Baghdad in the Early Middle Ages,* Detroit 1970, pp. 172-76, 261, and index.

ابن جَرِير i.e., al-Ṭabarī.

بَلَغَنا عن . . . أَنَّهُ كان يقول [a story] reached us about Abū Muḥammad al-Bāfī that he..../ we were told that... used to say....

فَقَدْ This sequence of particles often introduces the second half of a conditional sentence; see W II, 346D. For *qad*, see above, p. 59, and Index.

حَضَرَ to be present.

Notes to Page 69

أَوْصَى بِ to make a testamental disposition for [something].

ثُلُث the relatives are entitled to 2/3 of the inheritance; only 1/3 can be earmarked for other purposes. See *EI*1-2, s.v. WAṢIYYA.

ثِقَة (root وثق) reliable scholar; term frequently used in biographies, especially of *ḥadīth* scholars, to indicate that they transmitted only *ḥadīth* that was well-documented.

لم أَسْمَعْ منه [but] I did not study with him; the expression is also used in the biography in the *Ta'r. Bagh.* Apparently al-Barqānī wishes to avoid giving the wrong impression: even though he was not among his students, he knows al-Mu'āfā to be reliable.

أَبو حَيَّان التَّوْحِيدي For Abū Ḥayyān al-Tawḥīdī (4th century) see *EI*2, s.v. Books and articles dealing with this famous littérateur and philosopher are too numerous to be listed here.

اِسْتَدْبَرَ to turn one's back to.

جامِع الرُّصافة the Friday mosque at Ruṣāfa, see Le Strange, *Baghdad*, p. 187, and Lassner, index; not to be confused with the castle of the Umayyad caliph Hishām b. 'Abd al-Malik, and two Ruṣāfas in Spain.

قَدْ نامَ the particle *qad* is best left untranslated; here it may express the amazement on the part of al-Tawḥīdī.

شات (root ش ت و) intensely cold.

ضُرّ ، بُؤْس need, misery, distress.

أَمْرٌ عَظِيمٌ 'something considerable,' 'a pitiful state'; the story is apparently intended to emphasize Mu'āfā's piety and ascetic tendencies: he may not have asked fees for lectures, or he may have given his salary to the poor.

مَعَ 'in spite of,' see W II, 164D.

غَزارة abundance, wealth, "wide extent."

بِخَطِّ المعافى in the handwriting of Mu'āfā.

مِنًى locality which is part of the pilgrimage, visited on 8-9 Dhū 'l-Ḥijja.

قُلْتُ I said [to myself].

أَراد here: to seek, look [for somebody].

نادَى to call out.

ها أنا ذا here I am! W I, 54D.

نَهْرَوان العِراقِ Nahrawān in Iraq; see *EI*1, s.v., and G. Le Strange, *Lands*, p. 61, and index: locality near Baghdad, near the site of the battle between 'Alī and the Khārijīs in 38 A.H.

نَهْروان الغَرْبِ Nahrawān in the West; probably a locality in the Maghrib or Spain; not found in any of the common handbooks; it may well have existed, cf. Ruṣāfa in Spain—and Cairo, Amsterdam, etc. in the USA!

اتِّفاق coincidence.

تَفْسِير [Koran] commentary.

مُجَلَّدات plur. of *mujallad*, see W I, 198D-199A.

جَمُّ الفَوائِدِ full of useful [scholarly] information.

بُحُور العِلْم 'sea' (بَحْر) is a common metaphor for a learned person. The term عِلْم is often limited to theology and the categories of scholarship connected with it.

Notes to Page 70

أَخْبَرَنا ، حَدَّثَنا see *EI*2, s.v. HADĪTH, p. 27b: various theories existed regarding the difference between the two terms.

عَنْ note that عن can mean 'on the authority of,' as well as 'of,' 'concerning' (e.g. the Prophet). See W II, 142C-D.

أَبو هُرَيْرَة one of the most frequently quoted Companions of the Prophet; the name is explained—wrongly—as deriving from his love for a kitten; Hurayra is also a woman's name.

الجُمُعة (usually vocalized الجُمْعة) Friday.

لا يَسْأَل . . . relative sentence to ساعة ; the subject is of يسأل is عَبْدٌ مُؤْمِنٌ , a [truly] believing servant [of God].

It is common for the biographer of a religious scholar to quote one or more traditions transmitted by this scholar.

The rest of this entry, on p. 547, only lists the names of a few scholars who died in the same year as Mu'āfā, and has therefore been omitted

A Few of the Most Common Handbooks on the Spelling of Names and *Nisbas*

al-Dhahabī, Muḥ. b. Aḥmad, *al-Mushtabih fī 'l-rijāl asmā'ihim wa-ansābihim*, ed. 'A. M. al-Bijāwī, Cairo 1962, 2 vols.

al-Sam'ānī, Abū Sa'd 'Abdalkarīm b. Muḥ. al-Tamīmī, *al-Ansāb,* ed. Muḥ. 'Abdalmu'īd Khān, Hyderabad 1962–78, 9 vols.

Ibn al-Athīr, 'Izzaddīn Abū 'l-Ḥasan 'Alī, *al-Lubāb fī tahdhīb al-ansāb,* Cairo 1357–69.

Ibn Durayd, Abū Bakr Muḥ. b. al-Ḥasan, *al-Ishtiqāq,* ed. 'A. M. Hārūn, Cairo 1378/1958.

Ibn Ḥajar al-'Asqalānī, *Tabṣīr al-muntabih bi-taḥrīr al-mushtabih,* ed. 'A. M. al-Bijāwī and M. al-Najjār, Cairo 1388/1964, 4 vols.

Yāqūt al-Rūmī, *Mu'jam al-buldān*, Beirut 1374/1955–1376/1957, 5 vols. Geographical dictionary from which the correct spelling of *nisbas* can sometimes be derived and which, in addition, often cites names and even biographies of famous scholars born in a particular town or village.

Ibn Manẓūr al-Ifrīqī, *Kitāb Lisān al-'Arab*, Būlāq 1300–1308, 20 vols.; Beirut 1955–56, 15 vols. Dictionary which often indicates the spelling of proper names.

Muḥ. Murtaḍā al-Zabīdī, *Tāj al-'arūs fī sharḥ al-qāmūs,* Cairo 1306–1307, 10 vols.; reprint in progress in Kuwait. Same characteristics as *Lisān al-'Arab.*

Ibn Khallikān, *Wafayāt al-a'yān,* ed. M. M. 'Abd al-Ḥamīd, Cairo 1367/1948, 6 vols.; *idem,* ed. I. 'Abbās, Beirut 1971, 8 vols.

VII. Al-Tanūkhī, *al-Faraj ba'd al-shidda*

Al-Tanūkhī belongs to the most famous story tellers in medieval Arabic literature, more famous even than al-Jāḥiẓ, even though in virtuosity of style and depth of understanding he never came anywhere close to his predecessor.[1] The popularity of al-Tanūkhī manifests itself in the survival of numerous manuscripts of his best-known story book, *al-Faraj ba'd al-shidda,* from which the following selection was taken. This proliferation of manuscripts is no doubt the principal reason why no critical edition has ever been undertaken; there are manuscripts in libraries that are not easily accessible or which do not provide microfilms; other manuscripts may exist in libraries of which no catalogues exist. The author of this chrestomathy once compared the oldest printed text to two texts in manuscripts and found that not all texts have the same stories.[2] Even if, in the distant future, it should be possible to identify and photograph all existing manuscript texts, the task of comparing these texts and establishing a genealogy (*stemma*) in order to eliminate the manuscripts that are copies of other manuscripts (*elimnatio codicorum*) may well take several months.

Abū 'Alī al-Muḥassin b. 'Alī al-Tanūkhī (327–84) was born in Basra as the son of a *qāḍī* who was famous enough to have found a place in several biographical dictionaries. He began his studies at the age of six, studying with his father and with the famous philologists Abū Bakr al-Ṣūlī and Abū 'l-Faraj al-Iṣfahānī, the author of the *Kitāb al-aghānī* (see below, XII). Thus he qualified not only as a scholar of *ḥadīth,* as one would expect from the son of a *qāḍī*, but also as a poet and a historian (*akhbārī*). Following in the footsteps of his father he held several government posts and ultimately became a *qāḍī* himself. Important for his intellectual career were his friendship with the vizier al-Muhallabī (vizier from 332 to 352), patron of Abū 'l-Faraj al-Iṣfahānī and the poet al-Mutanabbī, and his contacts with the Buyid 'Aḍuḍ al-Dawla during the years 367–70. As one can see from stories in *al-Faraj ba'd al-shidda,* many of the administrators of his days suffered periods of disgrace, and al-Tanūkhī himself was no exception.

The details of al-Tanūkhī's career have been outlined by R. Fakkar in his outstanding study *At-Tanûḫî et son livre: La délivrance après l'angoisse*, Cairo 1955. In the context of this reader it is important to know that there are three editions of

---

[1] Cf. Fakkar (see below), p. 36, who has the same opinion and wonders whether *al-Mustajād* is not an answer to al-Jāḥiẓ's "Book of the Misers [and Penny-pinchers]" (*Kitāb al-bukhalā'*).

[2] Cf. R. Fakkar (see below), p. 54.

al-Faraj ba'd al-shidda in existence: one dated Cairo 1903–4,[3] in two volumes; a second 1375/1955 which is not essentially different from the first; and a third abundantly annotated edition by 'A. al-Shāljī dated Beirut 1398/1978 in five volumes. This latest edition is based on five manuscripts, none of them older than the eighth century.[4]

Al-Tanūkhī has two other important books to his name, *Nishwār al-muḥāḍara,*[5] and *al-Mustajād min fa'alāt al-ajwād,*[6] both collections of anecdotes. The first of these was published in an expurgated edition by D. Margoliouth, and more recently in an edition based on several manuscripts by 'A. al-Shāljī, Beirut 1391/1971–1393/1973, in eight volumes. In the introduction to this work, al-Tanūkhī claims that in this work he has not copied anything from other texts, relying instead on oral communications. We do not have the complete text, and for this reason, the editor has added stories that he thinks might have belonged to the work in its original form (Intro. I, 11). To what extent this was a wise decision, I have not yet been able to determine. The second work is a collection of stories and sayings on generosity. It exists in a lithographed edition dating from 1939 and a more recent edition by M. Kurd 'Alī (Damascus 1946), who found discrepancies between the lithographed edition and the manuscript from Damascus which he used.

To give an account of the contents of *al-Faraj ba'd al-shidda* goes beyond the scope of this reader. The title of the book is derived from a well-known proverb, "Deliverance follows distress," i.e., "Do not give up hoping for a good outcome." This proverb is even presented in the form of a *ḥadīth* and became a genre in the sense that books on the same theme and with the same title existed before and after al-Tanūkhī's time. Keeping in mind how serious the plight of rejected lovers was taken by Muslim writers of all periods (there is even a book on the martyrs [*shuhadā'*], i.e., tragic victims, of love),[7] it is not surprising that al-Tanūkhī should have included a chapter on lovers saved *in extremis.*

Although no definitive editions of al-Tanūkhī's works exist, there is a rather extensive literature on the author and his work. In addition to the book by Fakkar,

---

[3] The absence of Islamic dates in this early edition is curious.

[4] It is hardly necessary to point out that a late manuscript may occasionally derive from a very old original and therefore be closer to the autograph than an old manuscript.

[5] "Food for mutual entertainment." For the term *Nishwār,* see L., pp. 1617c–1618a.

[6] "What is Deemed Excellent of the Deeds of the Generous," or "Memorable Deeds by the Generous." Note the play on the root *j-w-d* .

[7] Cf. below, Index, s.v. *shahāda.*

which leaves very little to be desired (it even offers a survey of all the stories, tables locating the stories in the two early editions, etc.), it is perhaps sufficient to mention here F. Gabrieli, "Il valore letterario e storico del Farağ ba'd al-Šidda di Tanūḫī," in *RSO* XIX, 1 (1940), 16–34 (text corrections in the appendix); A. Wiener, "Die Farağ ba'd aš-Šidda Literatur," in *Der Islam* IV (1913), 270–98, 387–413 (important also as a study of the manuscript problem); *EI2*, s.v.; and, recently, an important contribution by Antonella Ghersetti, "Il qāḍī al-Tanūkhī e il Kitāb al-farağ ba'd al-šidda," in *Annali dell'Istituto Universitario Orientale [di Napoli]*, Vol. 51, fasc. 1 (Napoli 1991), 33–51 (on the biography of al-Tanūkhī and the structure of his *al-Faraj ba'd 'l-šidda,* with extensive references to earlier studies).

A volume of translated selections exists entitled *Ende Gut, Alles Gut* by A. Hottinger, Zürich 1979, which unfortunately is not always reliable and omits some of the (in the opinion of the author of this reader) most interesting stories.

The Leiden University Library has a manuscript of al-Tanūkhī's book. Although of very poor quality—at times the scribe makes mistakes suggesting that he knew little Arabic—and makes changes at will, there are some places where he supports a reading or clarifies a sentence. Moreover, he may have used a good original, and for this reason I have quoted this manuscript in a few places.

From: Abū ʻAlī al-Muḥassin b. ʻAlī al-Tanūkhī, *al-Faraj baʻd al-shidda,* ed. al-Shāljī, Beirut 1398/1978, III, 389-92 (no. 364).[8]

من زرع الإثم حصد الدمار

وحدّثني عُبَيد الله بن محمد بن الحفا، قال: حدّثني رجل من أهل الجند، قال: خرجت من بعض بلدان الشام، وأنا على دابّة لي، ومعي خُرج لي، فيه ثياب ودراهم.

فلمّا سرت عدّة فراسخ، لحقني المساء، وإذا بدير عظيم، فيه راهب في صومعة.

فنزل واستقبلني، وسألني المبيت عنده، وأن يُضِيفني، ففعلتُ.

فلمّا دخلت الدير، لم أجد فيه غيره، فأخذ دابّتي، وطرح لها شعيراً، وعزل رحلي في بيت، وجاءني بماء حارّ، وكان الزمان شديد البرد، وأوقد بين يديّ ناراً، وجاءني بطعام طيّب من أطعمة الرهبان، فأكلتُ، وبنبيذ، فشربتُ.

ومضت قطعة من الليل، فأردت النوم، فقلت: أدخل المستراح قبل أن أنام، فسألت عنه، فدلّني على طريقه، وكنّا في غرفة.

فلمّا صرت على باب المستراح، إذا بارية مطروحة، فلمّا صارت رجلاي عليها نزلتُ، فإذا أنا في الصحراء، وإذا البارية قد كانت مطروحة على غير تسقيف.

وكان الثلج يسقط في تلك الليلة سقوطاً عظيماً، فصحت، وقدّرت أنّ الذي

---

8 Corresponding to II, 56-57, of the Cairo edition of 1903, and (II), 266-68, in the Cairo edition of 1375/1955. See Fakkar (above, Introduction), pp. 54, 123, for other editions.

استمرّ عليّ من غير علمه، فما كلّمني.

فقمت وقد تجرّح بدني، إلّا أنّي سالم، فجئت واستظللت بطاق باب الدير من الثلج.

فما وقفت حيناً حتى رأيت فيه برابخ من فوق رأسي، وقد جاءتني منها حجارة لو تمكّنت من دماغي لطحنته.

فخرجت أعدو، وصحت به، فشتمني، فعلمتُ أنّ ذلك من حيلته، طمعاً في رحلي.

فلمّا خرجت، وقع الثلج عليّ فعلمت أنّي تالف إن دام ذلك عليّ، فولّد لي الفكر أن طلبت حجراً فيه ثلاثون رطلاً وأكثر، فوضعته على عاتقي تارة، وعلى قفاي تارة، وأقبلت أعدو في الصحراء أشواطاً، حتى إذا تعبت، وحميت وجرى عرقي، طرحت الحجر، وجلست أستريح خلف الدير، من حيث تقع لي أنّ الراهب لا يراني.

فإذا أحسست بأنّ البرد قد بدأ يأخذني، تناولت الحجر وسعيت من الدير ولم أزل على هذا إلى الغداة.

فلمّا كان قبيل طلوع الشمس، وأنا خلف الدير إذ سمعت حركة بابه، فتخفّيت.

فإذا بالراهب قد خرج، وجاء إلى موضع سقوطي، فلمّا لم يرني دار حول الدير يطلبني، ويقول، وأنا أسمعه: ترى ما فعل الميشوم؟ أظنّ أنّه قدّر أنّ بالقرب منه قرية، فقام يمشي إليها، كيف أعمل، فاتني سلبي، وأقبل يمشي يطلب أثري.

قال: فخالفته إلى باب الدير، وحصلت داخله، وقد مشى هو من ذلك المكان يطلبني حول الدير، فحصلت أنا خلف باب الدير، وقد كان في وسطي سكّين، فوقفت خلف الباب، فطاف الراهب، ولم يبعد.

فلمّا لم يقف على خبر، عاد ودخل، فحين بدأ ليردّ الباب، وخفت أن يراني، ثرت عليه، ووجأته بالسكّين، فصرعته وذبحته.

وأغلقت باب الدير، وصعدت إلى الغرفة، فاصطليت بنار موقودة هناك، ودفئت، وخلعت عنّي تلك الثياب، وفتحت خرجي، فلبست منه ثياباً جافّة، وأخذت كساء الراهب، فنمت فيه، فما أفقت إلى قريب من العصر.

ثم انتبهت وأنا سالم، غير منكر شيئاً من نفسي، فطفت بالدير، حتى وقفت على طعام، فأكلت منه، وسكنت نفسي.

ووقعت مفاتيح بيوت الحصن في يدي، فأقبلت أفتح بيتاً بيتاً، فإذا بمال عظيم من عَيْنٍ، وورقٍ، وثياب، وآلات، ورحال قوم، وأخراجهم.

وإذا تلك عادة الراهب كانت مع كلّ من يجتاز به وحيداً، ويتمكّن منه، فلم أدر كيف أعمل في نقل المال وما وجدته.

فلبست ثياب الراهب، وأقمت في موضعه أيّاماً، أتراءى لمن يجتاز بالموضع من بعيد، فلا يشكّون أنّني هو، وإذا قربوا منّي لم أبرز لهم وجهي، إلى أن خفي خبري.

ثم نزعت تلك الثياب، ولبست من بعض ثيابي، وأخذت جواليق، فملأتها مالاً،

وحملتها على الدابّة، ومشيت، وسقتها إلى أقرب قرية، واكتريت فيها منزلاً، ولم أزل أنقل إليها كلّما وجدته، حتى لم أدع شيئاً له قدر إلّا حصّلته في القرية.

ثم أقمت بها إلى أن اتّفقت لي قافلة، فحملت على دوابّ اشتريتها، كلّ ما كنت قد حصّلت في المنزل.

وسرت في جملة الناس بقافلة عظيمة لنفسي، بغنيمة هائلة، حتى قدمت بلدي، وقد حصلت لي عشرات ألوف دراهم ودنانير، وسلمت من الموت.

Notes to Page 80

الحفا identified by the editor (see *Faraj*, vol. V, index, pp. 173-74; *Nishwār* [Beirut 1393/1973], vol. VII, 85, note 2) as Abū 'l-Qāsim 'Ubaydallāh b. Muḥammad b. al-Ḥasan al-'Abqasī al-ma'rūf bi 'l-Ṣarawī, a poet whom al-Tanūkhī quotes frequently. Apparently the editor did not succeed in identifying this authority in a biographical dictionary. In *Faraj*, V, 23, he offers a sample of his poetry; III, 314 confirms the reading الحفا.

أَهْل الجُنْد inhabitants of a garrison city, militiamen.

بُلْدان plur. of بَلَد, 'city,' 'region.'

الشام Syria; in the Middle Ages it included Palestine, see Yāqūt, III, 312b; G. Le Strange, *Palestine under the Muslims*, reprint Beirut 1965, p. 27.

دابّة لي a horse/mule of mine; for this frequently used construction, see *Ar. Syntax*, p. 250. The Leiden manuscript simplifies and reads دابّتي.

خُرْج double bag for the saddle.

لَحِقَ to overtake, to catch up with.

إذا بِدَيْرٍ at that moment I [noticed] a monastery; see W I, 283D-284B; II, 157D-158A; 345C-D; *Ar. Syntax*, pp. 308-9. The *bi-* in إذا بِدَيْرٍ, or إذا أنا بِدَيْرٍ is explained by medieval grammarians as short for إذا أنا (مُحِسٌّ) بِدَيْرٍ, but one can also have sentences such as فَنَظَرْتُ فإذا آمْرَأَةٌ, "then I looked and [lo and behold], there was a woman." The technical term used by the Arab grammarians is *idhā al-mufāja'ati* or *idhā al-fujā'iyya*, 'the *idhā* of sudden encounter,' though the idea of an unexpected occurrence is not always clearly present and one should rather think of *idhā* as indicating an incident ('*Inzidenzschema*,' see *Admin*., p. 89a). Note also بَيْنَما النَّبِيُّ يُصَلِّي إذْ أَقْبَلَ عُقْبَةُ, "while the Prophet was praying, at that moment (or, lo and behold at that moment) 'Uqba came forward," where it seems more likely that إذْ has to be taken as an adverb of time (cf. حِينَئِذٍ and إذْ ذاكَ).

دَيْر hermitage, often constructed with fortifications. These hermitages or convents were open to Muslim travelers. They were also visited by dignitaries during excursions, see *EI*2, s.v. DAYR.

صَوْمَعَة tower; here: 'monk's cell' (often located in a tower, see L and Dozy, s.v.) .[9]

مَبِيت root بيت, passing the night.

أَضافَهُ to take someone in as a guest (ضَيْف), offer him hospitality.

شَعِير barley.

---

9 Dozy refers to E. Quatremère, *Mémoires. . . sur l'Égypte*, Paris 1811, I, 35-36, where we find an interesting description of a monastery inaccessible by its position and also provided with a *donjon*. See also Y. Hirschfeld, *The Judean Desert Monasteries*, New Haven 1992, pp. 172-76 and index.

عَزَلَ رَحْلِي في بَيْتٍ he set apart my saddle [and its bag] in a room, he stored my saddle, etc.

ماء حارّ hot water (so that the traveler could wash and warm himself).

بَيْنَ يَدَيَّ in front of me (lit. 'between my two hands')—see W II, 181B.

مِنْ أَطْعِمَةِ الرُّهْبانِ "belonging to the [excellent] foods of monks," "some of the [tasty] dishes that monks are accustomed to eat."

وبِنَبِيذٍ connect with *bi-* in جاءني بِماءٍ. *Nabīdh* is an alcoholic beverage said by some to be allowed because the Koran prohibits only *khamr;* see *EI*2, s.v. For its being offered in monasteries, see *EI*2, s.v. DAYR.

أَدْخُلُ المُسْتَراحَ I will enter/let me go to the toilet.

سَأَلَ عَنْ to ask for the whereabouts of a person/a thing; for عَنْ with verbs denoting uncovering, etc., see W I, 140A-D.

وَكُنّا في غُرْفَةٍ the implication seems to be that the two of them are not on the ground floor, where there would be a dunghill or a toilet. Cf. also L, who has غُرْفَة 'chamber in uppermost storey.'

صارَ not only 'to become,' but also frequently 'to end up in/at a place.'

وَإِذا بارِيَةٌ مَطْرُوحَةٌ the two older Cairo editions available to me read: وإذا بادية مطروحة , and in the next line وإذا البادية كانت مطروحة على غير سقف . A note by the editor mentions that two of his manuscripts have بِنَخٍّ مطروح على حفيرة , which is perhaps a reading substituted for the difficult reading in the original (*lectio facilior* for *lectio difficilior*). In vol. II, 46, the editor identifies بارِيَة as a mat woven from cane or reed (قَصَب), which can only be derived from بري/و, and claims that the term is still used in Baghdad. This translation is supported by E. Fagnan, *Additions aux dictionnaires arabes*, reprint Beirut, n.d., p. 11b, and D. R. Woodhead and W. Beene, *A Dictionary of Iraqi Arabic*,

Washington 1967, p. 33 (*baarya* 'large woven bamboo mat').[10] In any case
what seems to be intended is an open-air toilet jutting out and not resting on
any [solid] woodwork that is part of the roof (تَسْقِيف).

كَانَ ...يَسْقُطُ the snow had been falling; كَانَ + imperfect is often used in the
sense of an occurrence repeating itself in the past. A brief but clear
exposition of the use of كَانَ can be found in Bro., pp. 120-23.

قَدَّرَ to estimate, to assume.

Notes to Page 81

اِسْتَمَرَّ عَلى from the context it appears that the verb means 'to happen to' (perhaps
from اِسْتَمَرَّ in the sense of 'to have its course').

مِنْ غَيْرِ عِلْمِهِ without his knowledge. For بِلا ، بِدُونِ in the sense of 'without,' see
W II, 163A.

تَجَرَّحَ to have wounds, to be wounded.

إِلَّا أَنِّي 'except that I,' 'however, I was.'

سالِم intact, here apparently in the sense of 'having no broken limbs.'

اِسْتَظَلَّ مِنْ to shadow oneself from. . . ; here: to seek protection from. . . .

طاق vault, archway (i.e., an arched structure or gate in front of the door). Towers
were often next to the gate; see Hirschfeld (above, note 9), p. 174.

---

10 Ms. Or. 61 of the Leiden University Library also reads بارية adding على غير
تسقيف One could also think of reading بَرَّانِيَّة وإذا from بَرَّانِيّ 'exterior.' See
Dozy, I, 61b, and cf. 62a: "*tour au dehors de la muraille d'une ville.*"

فَما وَقَفْتُ حِيناً حَتَّى. . . 'and I had not stood there for a while before. . .'; 'but soon I. . . .'

بَرابِخ plur. of بِرْبَخ, passage for sewage, conduit pipe for water.[11]

جاءَتْني مِنْها *-hā* refers to the بَرابِخ.

تَمَكَّنَ مِنْ to get hold of; here: to hit, reach their [intended] goal.

طَحَنَ to grind, to crush.

صِحْتُ بِهِ I called out to him; *bi-* is used with intransitive verbs—see W II, 159A-B.

مِنْ حِيلَتِهِ part of his stratagem, a stratagem which he used.

طَمَعاً في رَحْلِي 'because he wanted to get hold of my saddle/my baggage.' For في, see Index.

تالِفٌ 'likely to perish'; the active participle may have the sense of a future, or may indicate that something is likely to happen.

وَلَدَ (وَلَّدَ ؟) لي الفِكْرُ the same idiom occurs in *Faraj* II, 109: reflecting [on the situation] gave birth [to the idea] / brought up in my mind [the idea that. . .].[12]

رَطْل measure of weight and capacity.

وأكثر one would expect أَوْ أكثر

---

[11] The Italian *barbacane* is said to derive from this term. See G. B. Pellegrini, *Ricerche sugli arabismi italiani con particolare riguardo alla Sicilia,* Supplementi al Bollettino 10, Centro di studi filologici e linguistici siciliani, Palermo 1989, p. 187.

[12] One could suggest reading وُلِدَ لي الفِكْرُ, 'the thought was born/came up in my mind,' but this vowelling is not supported by the dictionaries. The Leiden manuscript has وَلَدَ.

تارَةً . . . تارَةً now... then, one time... another time....

قَفاً back of the neck.

أَقْبَلَ to begin. أَقْبَلَ belonging to the 'verbs of beginning' is followed by an imperfect; for verbs with similar meanings see W II, 108B-109B.

شَوْط heat, single run.

طَرَحْتُ depends on حَتَّى, 'until'; إِذا تَعِبْتُ وَحَمِيتُ وَجَرَى عَرَقِي is the first part of a conditional sentence in parenthesis, the condition being fulfilled by طَرَحْتُ. . . . وَجَلَسْتُ. . .—see W II, 12C-14B. In this type of sentence إِذا always has the sense of 'when'—see Bro., p. 198: أَتْبَعُهُ حَتَّى إِذا دَخَلَ البَيْتَ أَدْرَكْتُهُ, "I will follow him until, when he enters the house, I will catch up with him."

عَرَق sweat.

مِنْ حَيْثُ يَقَعُ لي 'where (or: 'since,' see Dozy I, 344a) the chance would be there for me...,' 'where I/since I would have a chance....' For وَقَعَ لَهُ see Dozy II, 830a. Towers as living quarters often stood at a distance from the main building(s); see Hirschfeld (above, p. 389, note), *passim.*

أَخَذَ here: to overwhelm.

تَناوَلَ to take in hand, to pick up.

مِنَ الدَّيْرِ the two older editions add here إلى الحِصْنِ from the monastery to the (its) fortification(s).

لَمْ أَزَلْ على هذا I continued to be in this situation/continued this practice.

كانَ it was, the time was. Cf. XII, 203, كانت الليلةُ القابِلةُ.

قُبَيْلَ a little before, see W II, 186C.

إذْ 'at that moment' (here introduced by لَمَّا instead of بَيْنَما), see Index.

دارَ حَوْلَ الدَّيْرِ he walked around the monastery.

تُرَى (often يا تُرَى) usually vocalized this way and explained as an imperfect of أُرِيَ, passive of أَرَى, 'to show,' 'to make understand' (cf. رَأْي , 'opinion'); translate: 'would you think,' or translate as an adverb, 'possibly'—see W II, 48D-49B.

For مَيْشوم read مَأْشوم ('miserable'), as in the older edition.

أَظُنُّ. . . سَلْبَهُ this sentence is still part of what the monk is saying audibly to himself.

بِالقُرْبِ مِنْهُ close to it (i.e., the monastery).

فَقامَ يَمْشِي إِلَيْها and that he stood up (began/undertook) to walk to that [village].

فاتَنِي سَلْبُهُ [the chance of] plundering him [after his expected death] has escaped me; cf. فاتَتْهُ الصَّلاةُ, 'he has missed [the correct time for performing] the صلاة.

Notes to Page 82

قالَ the subject is the narrator—in this case the hero of the story himself.

فَخالَفْتُهُ the verb خالَفَهُ usually means 'to disagree with somebody,' but here it means 'to go to a place during the absence of somebody.'

حَصَلَ the verb can have many meanings; here: 'to end up,' 'to manage to reach.'

داخِلَهُ inside (in the accus. as an indication of place).

وَقَدْ مَشَى هُوَ leave قَدْ untranslated, or translate 'naturally,' 'as one would expect'; هُوَ, 'he,' i.e., the monk.

حَوْلَ الدَّيْرِ 'around the monastery' (in the sense that he looks around in the vicinity).

وَسَط Dozy: belt.

أَبْعَدَ to go far. Form IV often indicates reaching a certain point, concrete (time, place, state) or abstract, e.g., أَقْفَرَ, 'to become desert,' أَبْلَغَ, 'to be eloquent'—see W I, 34D-36B.

وَقَفَ على frequently in the sense of 'to find.'

لَمْ يَقِفْ لي على خَبَرٍ the position of *li-* preceding the noun it qualifies is common; see *Ar. Syntax*, pp. 228-29.

بدأ ليردّ Read: بَدا لِيَرُدَّ as in Leiden ms Or. 616.[13]

ثُرْتُ عَلَيْهِ from ثارَ على to jump upon.

وَجَأَ to stab.

اِصْطَلَى to warm oneself (VIII from root صلي).

فَما أَفَقْتُ unless one reads إِلَّا قَرِيباً مِنَ العَصْرِ, these words have to be taken as a parenthesis: 'without waking up [a single time].' The old editions simplify this sentence and read فَنِمْتُ فيه إِلَى العَصْرِ.

غَيْرُ مُنْكِرٍ شَيْئاً مِنْ نَفْسِي asyndetic (cf. أَنْبَأَنا قال , and حَدَّثَنا قال): "without finding anything wrong with myself/my body."

طُفْتُ from the verb طاف.

---

13 The old editions have بَدَأَ يَرُدُّ.

سَكَنَتْ نَفْسِي "my mind was at rest," "I felt comfortable again."

وَقَعَتْ. . . فِي يَدِي "and the keys of the rooms of the fortification came into my hands" (بَيْت can even be used in the sense of 'drawer in a cabinet'; cf. also بَيْت الإِبْرَة 'compass').

عَيْن here: 'gold [*dīnārs*?]'; for other meanings of عَيْن, see the long article in L, and for different broken plurals, often depending on these various meanings, W I, 226B.

وَرَق silver [*dirhams*?]; cf. Dozy.

آلات pl. of آلة, utensils, implements.

وَإِذا تِلْكَ عادةُ الرَّاهِبِ كانَتْ مَعَ. . . "and apparently (lit.: lo and behold) this had been the custom which this monk followed in dealing with. . ."; see *Ar. Syntax*, pp. 101-2: كانَ as a parenthesis puts the statement in this nominal sentence in the past.

وَيَتَمَكَّنُ مِنْهُ cf. above, p. 390; "and [those lonely travelers] he would overpower/would get hold of."

فِي 'when it came to,' 'in dealing with'—see Index.

نَقْل The two earlier editions and the Leiden manuscript have ثِقْل, 'weight' for نَقْل.

فَلَبِسْتُ *fa-* has here the sense of "and therefore"—see W I, 291A.

فِي مَوْضِعِهِ in his (the monk's) abode.

تَراءَى to show oneself.

أَنَّنِي هُوَ that I was he (i.e., the monk).

أَبْرَزَ to bring into the open; here: to let see/show: see Bla., s.v.

إِلى أَنْ خَفِيَ خَبَرِي "till my story was hidden/could not be easily detected." The author probably means that the monk would appear from time to time in the village. They would now miss him but not harbor any suspicions, because seeing him regularly from a distance, they believed him to be alive and well. The Leiden manuscript adds عَنْهُمْ.

نَزَعَ to take off.

لَبِسْتُ مِنْ بَعْضِ ثِيابِي 'some of my own clothes.'[14]

جَوالِيقُ / جَوالِقُ plur. of جُوالِق or جُوالَق, see W I, 229A-C: the type فَعالِلُ instead of فَعالِيلُ is chiefly used as a poetic license.

Notes to Page 83

لَمْ أَدَعْ root ودع—see W I, 79C.

لَهُ قَدْرٌ having [any] value.

حَصَّلَ to make [something] end up [in a place]; to bring over.

اِتَّفَقَتْ لِي قافِلَةٌ I chanced to find a caravan [I could join].

قافِلة عظيمة لِنَفْسِي an enormous caravan of my own [within the larger caravan].

هائِل frightening, impressive.

حَصَلَ لِ to come into [somebody's] hands, to be acquired by [somebody]. Cf. above

---

14 مِن appears to be pleonastic, but the idiom is supported by the *Dictionnaire* of Blachère, I, 718a-b. The older edition omits this sentence.

p. 391 and Index.[15]

عَشَرَاتُ أُلوفٍ – عَشَرَات is plur. of عَشَرَة 'numbered by the tens of thousands.' For the pl. أُلوف see W I, 259C.

---

15 Cf. *EI*2, s.v. LUḲAṬA: according to Islamic Law, he should have advertised his find and should not have taken possession of it until a year had passed.

VIII. Muḥammad b. Hilāl al-Ṣābī
al-Hafawāt al-nādira

The author of *al-Hafawāt al-nādira*, from which the following selections were taken, Muḥammad b. Hilāl al-Ṣābī, was born in 410 and died in 480. His ancestors had been known as men of letters and historians. His great-grandfather, Ibrāhīm, distinguished himself as a letter writer and a poet. His father, Hilāl b. al-Muḥassin al-Ṣābī (359–448),[1] the most famous member of the family, was the author of a *Rusūm Dār al-khilāfa* (on court etiquette and the proper form of official correspondence)[2] and a *Ta'rīkh al-wuzarā'*,[3] both of which have been preserved.

Muḥammad's great-grandfather, Ibrāhīm b. Hilāl (313–384), though a Sabian, had observed the Fast, knew the Koran by heart, and used Koranic phrases in his letters. Perhaps for this reason he had won aceptance in Muslim society and had held official functions. His grandson converted to Islam after seeing the Prophet in a dream, but continued to be known as Hilāl al-Ṣābī.

Muḥammad b. Hilāl, the author of the *Hafawāt,* wrote a supplement (*Dhayl*) to the *Ta'rīkh* of his father; this *Ta'rīkh* was the continuation of a work by Thābit b. Sinān which was, in its turn, a continuation of the *Ta'rīkh Baghdād*. This sequence of supplements is one more interesting example of the inspiration which the *Ta'rīkh Baghdād* provided to various continuators[4] and of the widespread custom of composing a *Dhayl* or a *Ṣila* to an earlier collection of biographies.

The considerable fortune which the son inherited from his father enabled him to stay away from the turbulence of a public career and the atmosphere of mistrust, betrayal, and violence so often described in the works of Tanūkhī as well as in his own *Hafawāt*. The only function he held was that of an official in the *Dīwān al-Inshā'* during the reign of the Abbasid al-Qā'im (422–467). He was known for his honesty and his generosity which manifested itself, among other things, in the public library which he founded. The exact location of this library is mentioned by the biographers. They also mention the sad fact that very soon the librarian began to

---

1 See *EI* 2, s.v.

2 Ed. M. 'Awwād, Baghdad 1383/1964.

3 H. F. Amedroz, *The Historical Remains of Hilāl al-Ṣābī*, Leiden 1904.

4 See C. E. Farah, *The Dhayl in Medieval Arabic Historiography*, American Oriental Society, New Haven 1967, p. 8; F. Rosenthal, *A History of Muslim Historiography*, Leiden 1968, pp. 82–83; C. Cahen, "The Historiography of the Seljuqid Period," in B. Lewis and P. Holt, *Historians of the Middle East*, London 1964, p. 61. For details about further continuations, see Ibn al-Qifṭī, *Ta'rīkh al-ḥukamā'*, ed. J. Lippert, Leipzig 1903, pp. 110–11, and quoted by I. 'Abbās (see below), pp. 327–28.

sell off books from this library. Being reminded by several critics that the library was a *waqf*[5] and could not be sold, the librarian excused himself by stating that Muḥammad b. Hilāl's library was duplicating the library of the Madrasa Niẓāmiyya and that he had spent the revenues of the sales on alms.

Only the *Hafawāt al-nādira* is known to have survived, while the *Ta'rīkh* and a *Kitāb al-Rabī'* are known only by name. However there exist a considerable number of quotations from the *Kitāb al-Rabī'*, and these have been brought together by I. 'Abbās in a collection named *Shadharāt min kutub mafqūda fī 'l-ta'rīkh* (Beirut 1408/1988), pp. 327–50. The book seems to have been a continuation of Tanūkhī's *Nishwār al-muḥāḍara.*

The author is also known as Ghars al-Ni'ma al-Ṣābī, the first term being a nickname, 'the planting/planter of bounty,' 'the Beneficient', see L, p. 2247a; the second is a reference to his ancestors' having been Sabians. There was a Jewish-Christian sect of this name, but a hellenized pagan community of the same name which bore no resemblance to this Jewish-Christian sect also survived for a long time and won a certain degree of respect and interest from Muslim authors. It was centered in Ḥarrān. See *EI* 2, s.v. ṢĀBI'A (pp. 677a–678b).

A few references: the Introduction of the edition of the *Hafawāt* by Ṣ. al-Ashtar, pp. 7–53, and the literature quoted on p. 18; the above mentioned collection by I. 'Abbās, pp. 325–30; Ibn Khallikān, *Wafayāt al-a'yān,* ed. I. 'Abbās, Beirut 1971-76, VI, 101-5; *Wāfī,* V, 168–69; *GAL,* G I, 324; B. Lewis and P. M. Holt, *Historians of the Middle East,* Oxford 1964, p. 61; F. Rosenthal, *Muslim Historiography,* Leiden 1968, p. 82; *EI* 2, III, 752b, VI, 198b, 243a.

---

[5] See *EI* 1–2, s.v.: the *waqf* is a foundation or trust, often, but not necessarily a pious foundation; one can also make a *waqf* for one's children. Many manuscripts still carry *waqf* notes.

From: Ghars al-Ni'ma Abū 'l-Ḥasan Muḥ. b. Hilāl al-Ṣābī, *al-Hafawāt al--nādira*, ed. Ṣ. al-Ashtar, Damascus 1387/1967, pp. 100-101, no. 113.

وقيل لمَّا قَلَّد السفَّاحُ يحيى أخاه الموصل ونواحِيَها، وكان مقداماً ناقص العقل، متخلِّفاً في جميع أموره، وكان يفعل أشياء غير مُشاكِلَة لِشَرَفه وأبُوَّته، فوجَّه معه السفَّاح بجماعة من مشايخ الدَّعوة، يُقوِّمون أمرَه ويُسدِّدونه، ويكاتبون النَّاسَ عنه، وكان يحيى مشتهراً بالشَّراب وحُبِّ المُخَنَّثين، لا يختار عليهم غيرَهم، فتقدَّم إلى رجل بالموصل حاذقٍ بصنعة الطُّبُول باتِّخاذ عددٍ منها، واستعمله على تقديم عملها، فتهَيَّأَ أن فَرَغ من واحدٍ في يومِ جُمعة عند النِّداءِ بالأذان، فصار به إلى يحيى في دار الإمارة، وهي بقُرب الجامع، وبينها وبين الجامع باب في ممرٍّ طويلٍ قد فُرِش بالبلاط، فصادف يحيى وقد ركب بغلة مُحَرَّمَةً، وهو ماضٍ في المَمَرِّ إلى الجامع، وعليه سَوادُه وشَاشِيَّتُه، فقال له: أين تلك الحاجة؟ فقال: معي منها واحدٌ، فقال هاته، فلمَّا رآه استفزَّه السُّرورُ به إلى أن جعله في عنقه، ووقَّع عليه بيدِه لِيَذُوقَه بزعمه ويعرفَ صفاءَ صوته، فساعةَ سمعت البغلةُ صوته حملت به نحو الجامع، وسمع المكبِّرون وقْع حافر البغلة على ذلك البلاط فرفعوا الستر، واقتحمت به البغلة إلى وسط النَّاس على حاله القبيحة، فنظر الناسُ منه إلى منظرٍ لم يكُ في الإسلام مثلُه، فمن مُتعجِّبٍ وضاحكٍ وقاذِفٍ، وأخذه الحصى من جميع المسجد، فما أفلتَ إلَّا بحُشاشةِ نفسه! وشُغِلَ النَّاس به عن صلاتهم، وكُتب إلى السفَّاح بذلك فاسْتَعْظَمَهُ وصرفَه ولم يَسْتَعِنْ به مُدَّةَ أيَّامه.

Notes to Page 96

قَلَّدَ (with double object) to appoint to, to invest [with a dignity], (originally: to hang the suspensory of a sword around somebody's neck).

السَّفَّاحُ the first Abbasid caliph (132-136).

يَحْيَى appointed and deposed in 133 A.H., or appointed in 132 and deposed the next year. He died in 136 A.H.[6]

المَوْصِل Mosul.

نَوَاحٍ pl. of نَاحِيَة district.

مِقْدَام impetuous; the pattern *mif'āl,* common as a noun of instrument, is also used as an intensive adjective; note that when used as an adjective, it does not take the feminine ending, e.g. جَارِيَة مِعْطَار, a girl who uses much perfume—see W I, 138B, 186C.

نَاقِصَ العَقْلِ here probably: falling short in common sense.

مُتَخَلِّف incompetent.

أَشْيَاءُ plur. of شَيْءٌ; although of the pattern *af'āl,* this plural is irregularly treated as a diptote—see W I, 240B.

غَيْرُ مُشَاكِلَةٍ not in keeping with.

---

6 Ibn Qutayba, *K. al-Ma'ārif,* ed. Th. 'Ukāsha (Cairo 1960), p. 377, mentions that this Yaḥyā [b. Muḥ. b. 'Alī] was appointed in Mosul by al-Manṣūr, the successor of al-Saffāḥ, but this is not confirmed by other texts, such as al-Ṭabarī, *Annales* (ed. M. J. de Goeje, et. al., Leiden 1897-1901), III, 72, 74. Judgments on his character are unfavorable, and he was notorious for his cruelty; see, for example, al-Balādhurī, *Ansāb al-ashrāf* III (ed. 'A. al-Dūrī, Wiesbaden, 1978), 281; and Ibn Ḥazm, *Jamharat ansāb al-'Arab,* Beirut 1982, pp. 20-21.

أُبُوَّة paternity; here: [noble] ancestry.

فَ in later prose فَ often introduces the main clause after لَمَّا—see W II, 347B.

وَجَّهَ بِ *bi-* is often used with transitive verbs of motion, but the difference between وَجَّهَ and وَجَّهَ بِ is not always clear—see W II, 159D-160C; Bro., pp. 154-55.

مَشايِخ الدَّعْوَة the veterans of the [Abbasid] revolution. مَشايِخ is used as an irregular plur. of شَيْخ and a plural of plural of مَشْيَخة (see L and W I, 227B-D). We find مَشْيَخة in the sense of 'old [revered] men' and 'list of teachers' which a scholar draws up to show that he is entitled to transmit, teach, and explain certain texts. To justify his claims, he may quote *isnāds* for these texts sometimes reaching as far as the author; see *EI*2, s.v. FAHRASA. For *da'wa,* see *EI*2, s.v., p. 168b.

سَدَّدَ to direct, to keep on the right track.

كاتَبَ 'conduct [official] correspondence.'

عَنْهُ in his stead; cf. يُقاتِلُ عَنْهُ, he fights to protect him—see W II, 139D-140B, and cf. below, p. 102 (note on عَنْ), and index.

اِشْتَهَرَ بِ to be known for [a practice, a habit], cf. مَشْهور, 'famous.'

شَراب euphemism for 'wine.'

مُخَنَّث literally 'effeminate,' often used in speaking of artists; see E. K. Rowson, "The Effeminates of Early Medina," in *JAOS* III, 4 (1991), esp. 692b-693a (on the period of the early Abbasids).

عَلَيْهِم over them, in preference to them—see W II, 169B-C.

تَقَدَّمَ إلى . . . بِ to order somebody [to do] something.

حَذِقَ بِ to be skillful in.

طَبْل drum; essential in Arabian music and also, at least in modern times, used as a solo intrument. *Ṭabl* seems to have been a general term for various types of drums.

اتَّخَذَ here: to build, to make; cf. also below, index.

اِسْتَعْمَلَهُ على he employed him on condition that. . . .[7]

قَدَّمَ 'to expedite.'

تَهَيَّأَ أَنْ here: "it so happened that" (synonym of اِتَّفَقَ أَنْ).

النِّداء بِالأَذانِ the proclamation of Prayer Time, Call to Prayer; cf. W II, p. xix of the Addenda.

بِقُرْبِ الجامعِ frequently the governor's mansion in Islamic cities was close to the Friday Mosque (جامع).

وبينَها وبينَ cf. W II, 180C: بيني وبينَهُ, 'between me and him.'

في giving access to.

مَمَرّ street, passageway, corridor.

فُرِشَ بِالبَلاط paved with stone/with slabs of stone; see the interesting article BALĀṬ in *EI*2.

---

7 Following the editor, one could read اِسْتَعْجَلَهُ على تَقْدِيمِ عَمَلِها "he ordered him to make haste in delivering [his] work on these [drums]"—see Dozy under استعجل and تقديم.

فصادَفَ the subject is the maker of the طُبول.

مُحَرَّمَة intractable.

مَضَى في... to progress/advance on. . .

سَوادُهُ his [official] black [attire]. Black was the color of the Abbasids.

شاشِيَّة kind of headgear (شاش muslin).

هاتِهِ give it here!

اِسْتَفَزَّ to excite.

إلى أَنْ جَعَلَهُ في عُنُقِهِ to such an extent that/so that he could not keep himself from putting/from hanging it on his neck.

وَقَّعَ here: 'to play a musical instrument.'

ذاقَ to taste; here: to try out.

بِزَعْمِهِ as he was claiming, 'ostensibly,' 'pretending that he was. . . .'

وِيَعْرِفَ صَفاءَ صَوْتِهِ ". . . and to come to know/and to try whether its sound was clear."

ساعة the sentence سَمِعَتِ الْبَغْلَةُ is in the construct state to ساعة; see W II, 200B-D, which gives the example زَمَنَ الْحَجّاجُ أَميرٌ.

حَمَلَتْ بِهِ *bi-* clearly means here that Yaḥyā is being carried along [against his will]. Cf. the interesting paragraph in *Ar. Syntax*, pp. 237-39 (b α-β).

الْمُكَبِّرون Form II may be used in the sense of pronouncing a formula—seeW I, 32B. The تَكْبير (the formula الله أَكْبَرُ) opens the صَلاة proper and follows immediately upon the "statement of intention" (نِيَّة). This means that Yaḥyā is late!

حافِر hoof.

فرَفَعوا السِّتْرَ and they lifted the curtain (i.e., the curtain on the door of the mosque) as a polite gesture to Yaḥyā, whom they expected to dismount.

اِقْتَحَمَ . . . إلى to rush into, to throw oneself headlong (precipitately) into.

على حالِهِ القَبيحةِ while he (i.e., Yaḥyā) was in his (i.e., this) unseemly situation. The question of the legality of music has been debated till the present day.[8] However, it certainly is not appropriate to enter a mosque having the appearance of somebody engaged in some trivial pastime.

مِنهُ 'of him,' 'in him': مِنْ indicates the person or thing in which the quality mentioned in the context is prominent—e.g., لَقيتُ منهُ الأَسَدَ, "I encountered in him a lion," a classical example mentioned in works on rhetoric as a form of simile—see W II, 138D.

مَنْظَر spectacle.

فمِنْ بَيْنَ . . . و . . . و and there were. . . , and. . . , and. . . . Cf. W II, 135C: فمِن قائلٍ بِالرُّوحانيّات ومن قائلٍ بِ 'there are some who believe in the spiritual beings. . . and others who believe in. . . ; and II, 180C-181A: بَيْنَ . . . بَيْنَ, and ما بَيْنَ . . . و, 'both. . . and. . . .'

قَذَفَ to throw [stones], to reproach, to accuse; in view of the context, the first translation is more likely.

أَخَذَهُ الحَصَى the pebbles hit him; cf. أَخَذَني بَطْني, above, IV, 41 (text), 42 (note).

---

8 See, among the many relevant texts and articles, J. Robson, *Tracts on Listening to Music*, London 1938. There is an extensive bibliography in W. J. Krüger-Wust, *Arabische Musik in europäischen Sprachen: Eine Bibliographie*, Wiesbaden 1983.

حُشاشة النَفْسِ 'last breath of life'— i.e., he barely escaped.

عَنْ عَنْ is used with verbs which mean or imply 'abandonment,' 'neglect,' 'being able to do without,' etc.—see W II, 140D-141C. Here: "people were occupied by him [and turned] away from their صلاة." (Understandably, one may not disturb somebody's صلاة.)

كُتِبَ the passive indicates that the author does not know or does not want to specify the agent (cf. W I, 50A): 'people wrote,' 'a letter went out.'

بِذلِكَ "describing the event," "dealing with these complaints"; بِ very often indicates the contents of a communication, oral or written.

اسْتَعْظَمَ to deem something serious.

صَرَفَ to remove.

اسْتَعانَ بِ to seek help from somebody, here appparently: to employ somebody in a government position.

أيّامِهِ the pronoun refers to Yaḥyā.

The following anecdote contains a rather confusing sequence of names. This shows that *al-Hafawāt al-nādira* was written for an educated audience that must have been thoroughly acquainted with the history of Muslim officialdom. One finds the same characteristic in many collections of stories in medieval Arabic literature. Is the well-known thesis that medieval Arabic literature was intended for an elite sufficient to explain this phenomenon? One has to keep in mind that we are dealing with a manuscript culture: handbooks were not easily accessible, and it must have been a time-consuming undertaking to acquire the background necessary to identify the individuals mentioned so as to be able to grasp all the detail found in some anecdotes.

Fortunately, one can enjoy the story even when one finds it difficult to keep track of all the personalities and the family relations involved!

Hafawāt, pp. 202–4, no. 194; cf. Hilāl al-Ṣābī, *Tuḥfat al-umarā' fī ta'rīkh al-wuzarā'* (abbreviated: *Wuzarā'*), ed. H. F. Amedroz, Beirut 1904, pp. 159–60, for a somewhat different version of the same story.

Dramatis Personae

Ibn al-Qunnā'ī, Abū 'Alī [Isḥāq b. 'Alī] al-Naṣrānī: later appointed in the *dīwān* of al-Khāqānī. Relates a harrowing story in which he himself (therefore no *isnād*), his father, and his brother were involved. According to L. Massignon, *La passion de Hallâj* (abbr. *Passion*), nouvelle ed., Paris 1975, I, 490–91, his father, his brother, and a brother-in-law were living in the same house, which would agree with the version in *Wuzarā'*, but not with this version. See also D. Sourdel, *Le Vizirat 'abbāside de 749 à 963* (abbr. *Vizirat*), Damascus 1959–60, (II) pp. 437, note 4, 478, 741.

Bishr b. 'Alī [Abū Naṣr al-Naṣrānī]: secretary of Ḥāmid and a friend of al-Qunnā'ī. See *Passion,* I, 491; Ibn Miskawayh, *Tajārib al-umam,* ed. H. F. Amedroz and D. S. Margoliouth, London 1920–21, I, 57, line 9; Hilāl al-Ṣābī, *Wuzarā',* pp. 33, 159, 243.

Ḥāmid: vizier of al-Mu'tamid, imprisoned by Ibn al-Furāt, murdered by Muḥassin. See *Passion,* I, 467–68; *Vizirat* (II), 413–26, and Index; al-Dhahabī, Shamsaddīn Muḥ. b. Aḥmad, *Siyar a'lām al-nubalā',* ed. Sh. al-Arna'ūt and Ḥ. al-Asad, Beirut 1401–/1981–, XIV, 478–79, 356–59.

Abū Ya'qūb: brother of al-Qunnā'ī and also a friend of Bishr. According to *Passion,* I, 490, the *kunyas* of the brothers of al-Qunnā'ī were Abū Ya'qūb and Abū 'Alī, and that of his father was Abū 'l-Ḥasan.

Abū 'l-Ḥasan ibn al-Furāt: vizier; in this story he holds his third—disastrous and final—vizirate. See *Passion* I, 463–66, and index; *Vizirat* (II), pp. 424–34, and Index.

Muḥassin, son of Ibn al-Furāt: persecutes on behalf of his father, but also by his own initiative. See *Passion,* Index; *Vizirat,* pp. 423–34, and Index.

Abū Muḥ. b. 'Aynūna (or 'Aynawayh, *Passion* I, 491): governor persecuted by Muḥassin.

Abū 'l-Qāsim ['Abdallāh] al-Khāqānī: vizier. See *Vizirat* (II), pp. 433–38, 746, and index.

Abū Aḥmad 'Ubaydallāh: governor of Naṣībīn (not identified with certainty).

Abū Ibrāhīm: his brother (not identified with certainty).

'Abdarraḥmān b. 'Īsā b. Dāwūd: brother of 'Alī b. 'Īsā, "the Good Vizier." See *Passion* I, 457; *Vizirat* (II), pp. 482–83, and index; *EI* 2, s.v.

Abū Manṣūr b. Farrukhānshāh: son-in-law or perhaps brother-in-law of al-Qunnā'ī. See *Passion,* I, 490.

Murīb: servant of Muḥassin (not identified).

Ibn Hindī: tells the second part of the story; perhaps identical with the Zahmān b. Hindī mentioned on p. 370 of *Wuzarā'*. Or perhaps one should read Ibn Hibintā. See *Passion,* I, 490, note 3: Ibn al-Qunnā'ī was sometimes called Ibn Hibintā, referring to his ancestor.

For a not always reliable translation of (Ibn) Miskawayh see: H. F. Amedroz and D. S. Margoliouth, *The Eclipse of the Abbasid Caliphate*, 6 vols. and index, London 1920–21. See also the extensive bibliography in D. Sourdel, *Le vizirat 'Abbāside* (see above), pp. xxiii–lxv.

From: Ghars al-Niʿma Abū 'l-Ḥasan Muḥ. b. Hilāl al-Ṣābī, *al-Hafawāt al-nādira*, ed. Ṣ. al-Ashtar, Damascus 1387/1967, pp. 202-4, no. 194.

وحدَّث أبو علي بن القُنَّائي النصراني قال: كان بشر بن علي كاتبُ حامدٍ صديقاً

لي ولأبي يعقوبَ أبي، فلما تقلَّد أبو الحسن بن الفرات الوزارة الثالثة، واسْتَعَرَتِ

الدنيا ناراً بالمحسِّن ابنه وشرُّه وتسلّطه وتبسّطه، طلب بشراً. وأبا محمد بن عَيْنُونَهْ في

جملة من طلبه، وتتبَّعه وكبس عليه واستقصى في أمره، فأما بشرٌ فإنَّه أخذ لنفسه عند

القبض على حامد صاحبه، واستتر عندي، ولم أعلم أبي وأخي به خوفاً أن يُحلَّفا فيدلّا

عليه، واتَّفق أن كتب أخي إلى بشرٍ رُقعةً ضمَّنها كلَّ إرجافٍ وفضولٍ، وما اطَّلع عليه

من تَقَرُّر الأمر لأبي القاسم الخاقاني وقُرب تقلّده الوزارة، وبأنَّه قد أحكم له ما يُريده

منه، وأجابه بِشْرُ في تضاعيفها بما شاكل الابتداء، من غير تحفُّظ ولا تحرُّزٍ، واختلطت

الرقعة بين يدي أخي بمكاتبات وكلائه وحسابات صنيعته، وغير ذلك ممّا لا فِكْرَ فيه؛

وكتب أبو أحمد عبيد الله بن محمد أخو أبي إبراهيم موسى بن محمد، وكان يتولَّى

نصيبين، إلى المحسِّن بما قال فيه: «إن أردت ابن عينونه وعبدَ الرحمن بن عيسى بن

داوُدَ فهما عند ابن القُنَّائي»، فما شعر أبي وأخي في يوم واحدٍ إلّا بمُريبٍ خادم

المحسِّن وقد كبسهما في جماعة من الرَّجَّالة، وفتَّش جميع الحُجَر والبيوت، ولم تُبْقِ

غايةً إلّا بلغها في الاستقصاء والاحتياط في التفتيش والطلب، فلما لم ير أحداً عدل

إلى ما كان بين أيديهما من رِقاع حساب، فجمعه وحمله إلى المحسِّن، وفي جملته

الرقعةُ إلى بشر وجوابه فيها، المشتملة على العجائب! ورأى أخي ذاك فمات في جلده؛

ولم يَقْصِدْ أحدٌ داري اكتفاءً بما جرى على دار أبي وأخي، وسلم ابن عينونه، وكان في الوقت سكرانَ لا فضلَ فيه لحركة!

وقال ابن الهندي: فحدثني أبو منصور بن فرخانشاه صِهْرُنا قال: كان خبرُ الرقعة عندي، وأنها فيما أخذه مُرِيبٌ من الرقاع، فلم أزل أمشي خلفه، وهو متأَبِّطٌ بما أخذه، إذ انسلَّتِ الرقعةُ بعينها بتفضُّل الله تعالى من بين سائر تلك الكتب والرقاع وسقطت على الأرض، فأخذتُها وبادرت إلى مُسْتَراح رأيته في الطريق مفتوحاً، فطرحتُها فيه، وهدأَت نفسي عند ذلك.

قال: ومضى أبي وأخي مع مُرِيبٍ إلى المُحَسِّن، ووَقَفَ على الرقاع والكتب، فلم يجد فيها ما أنكره، فخاطبَهما بالجميل، واعتذرَ إليهما، وعرَّفهما السبب الذي من أجله فعل ما فعل! وجاءته رسالة أبي الحسن والده يُنكرُ عليه فعلَه، وانصرفا مكرَّمَيْنِ، وزالت المحنةُ والبليَّةُ عنهما بانسلال تلك الرقعة من بين تلك الرقاع المأخوذة، ولله الحمدُ والفضلُ والمِنَّةُ والطَّوْلُ.

Notes to Page 105

النَّصْرانِيّ the Christian (see below, Index).

أبي read أخي with *Wuzarā'*, p. 159.

فلـمَّا the main sentence begins with طَلَبَ.

تَقَلَّدَ to take upon oneself/accept an appointment; cf. note on قَلَّدَ above, p. 97.

اِسْتَعَرَتِ الدُّنْيا ناراً the world was on fire, the realm was ablaze with fire; ناراً in the accus. specifies اِسْتَعَرَتْ ; cf. اِشْتَعَلَ الرَّأْسُ شَيْباً "the head is aflame with hoariness"—see W II, 122A-123B.

بِالمُحَسِّن through [the doings of] al-Muḥassin.[9]

تَبَسُّط Dozy: despotic, dictatorial behavior.

طَلَبَ (subject al-Muḥassin) 'to look for,' 'try to get hold of.'

فِي جُمْلَةِ مَنْ طَلَبَهُ "among the total of those he sought," "among others."

تَتَبَّعَ see W I, 37C: "The idea of reflexiveness is often not very prominent, especially in such verbs as govern the accusative, e.g. تَتَبَّعَ, 'to pursue step by step' (literally, 'to make oneself... into a pursuer' of something)."

كَبَسَ على to take/to catch by surprise; see *WKAS*, s.v.

اِسْتَقْصَى فِي أَمْرِهِ 'to go to great length in dealing with him/mistreating him'; cf. Dozy, s.v. استقصى على 'traiter quelqu'un avec la plus grande sévérité.' The object هُ refers in each case to مَنْ, so that one should translate "[among those whom] he... and treated harshly (when he found them)."

فَ often follows أَمَّا —see W I, 291A.

أَخَذَ لِنَفْسِهِ he managed to save his life; cf. al-Ṭabarī, *Glossarium*, p. cviii: 'sibi cavit, rem suam curavit'; Dozy: 'prendre ses précautions.'

عِنْدَ القَبْضِ على حامِدٍ at the moment/at the time Ḥāmid was seized.

صاحِبِهِ his overseer, his employer.

---

9 Al-Muḥassin b. al-Furāt is mentioned in *EI2*, I, 387a; III, 702b and 767b; VII, 397a and 653a.

اِسْتَتَرَ عِنْدِي he went into hiding with me/in my house.

أَعْلَمَ بِ to inform.

حَلَّفَ to impose an oath—i.e., for fear that they would be made to swear an oath stating that they did not know where Bishr was hiding; being good Muslims they would be unwilling to commit perjury (which, however, was allowed by some authorities if the person imposing the oath was an unjust ruler).

دَلَّ على to show the way to, to direct to.

كَتَبَ أَخِي إلى بِشْرٍ This would imply that, after all, he knew that Bishr was hiding in the house of Abū ʻAlī al-Qunnāʼī, or that a trusted go-between delivered messages to Bishr.[10]

رُقْعَة here: 'letter'; elsewhere often 'short note on a small piece of paper,' 'petition handed to a dignitary' (see below, p. 114 [text]).

ضَمَّنَها in which he included, to which he entrusted.

كُلَّ إِرْجافٍ all [possible] rumors; كُلّ followed by indefinite genit. can mean 'all of them [being. . .],' 'all of it,' 'purely,' 'all one could imagine,' etc.—e.g. مَعِي كُلُّ فَضْفاضِ القَمِيصِ, "with me were [comrades] all of them clad in loose-fitting tunics"—see W II, 205D; *Ar. Syntax*, p. 154; *WKAS*, s.v. (p. 294a).

فُضول sometimes considered as the plur. of فَضْل, 'excellence,' 'bounty'; often used in the sense of 'gossip,' 'indiscretions'; hence the wordplay فُضولٌ بِلا فَضْلٍ.[11]

---

[10] The version in the *Wuzarāʼ* suggests that only Ibn ʻAynūna was hiding with al-Qunnāʼī, which would mean that Bishr was somewhere else in a place known to al-Qunnāʼī's brother, or that the second brother of Abū ʻAlī al-Qunnāʼī is intended.

[11] A فُضُولِيّ is a person who busies himself with things that do not concern him.

ما اطَّلَعَ عَلَيْهِ مِنْ . . . what he had come to know of. . . .

تَقَرَّرَ . . . لِ here probably: 'to be assigned to.'

الأمر i.e., the vizirate.

أَحْكَمَ له ما يُرِيدُهُ مِنْهُ probably: he (al-Khāqānī) had set up/had decided for him (the brother of Isḥāq b. 'Alī?) what he wanted from him [in the way of administrative service], cf. *Passion*, I, 490: Subsequently Isḥāq b. 'Alī and his brother, Muḥ. b. 'Alī, were put in charge of administration of finances; see Arīb, *Ṭabarī continuatus*, ed. M. J. de Goeje, Leiden 1897, p. 125, line 14.

في تَضاعيفها (pl. of تَضْعيف) the interlinear spaces [of a letter]—see L., s.v. (p. 1792a). The pronoun ها refers to the *ruq'a* sent by the brother of al-Qunnā'ī.

شاكَلَ to be of the same form, shape, character; "in the same vein."

الابْتِداء the beginning [of the correpondence]—i.e., the initial letter (which came from the brother of al-Qunnā'ī); cf. Dozy: ابْتَدَأَهُ بِالكَلام, 'il lui parla le premier.'

اخْتَلَطَ بِ to become mixed up with, to end up among.

بَيْنَ يَدَيْ أخي see below, Index: 'in front of my brother'—i.e., on the desk of my brother.

مُكاتَبات here: letters, correspondence (elsewhere often 'contract with a slave buying himself free'); cf. p. 30 (تَحْرير الكُتُب) and below, Index, fem. plurals.

وَكيل agent, i.e., supervisor of an estate who collects the revenues for the owner of the estate.

حُسْبانات accounts; the fem. plural is used with many substantives that have no broken plural, e.g., حَيَوان plur. حَيَوانات—see W I, 198B-D.

صنيعة is probably a misprint for ضَيْعَة 'estate.'

مِمَّا لا فِكْرَ فيه to which one gives no [special] thought, which do not deserve special attention.

نَصِيبِين or نصيبِين. See G. Le Strange, *The Lands of the Eastern Caliphate,* Cambridge 1930, pp. 94-95; *EI*2, s.v. NAṢĪBĪN; a city about 100 miles northwest of Mosul. According to Yāqūt, *Mu'jam al-buldān,* Beirut 1374-76/1955-57, s.v.: "some Arabs" used to read the name of this town with three case endings, but Yāqūt prefers two.

بِ See Index; بِما قالَ فيه '[he wrote] something (a paragraph in a letter, a report) in which he said. . .'

ابن القُنَّائي apparently the father is meant.

ما شَعَرَ . . . إلّا see above, p. 47 (text), 59 (note).

رَجَّالة foot soldiers; here apparently used as a quasi-plural. The "feminine ending" (which originally may not have been an indication of gender) has various functions. It can indicate a:

- Single individual of a species: حَمامة quasi-singular of حَمام, 'pigeon' (W I, 147B-148A);
- Single occurrence of an action: نَصْرَة, singular of نَصْر, verbal noun of نَصَرَ, 'a single instance of helping' (W I, 122D-123D);
- Collective: مارّة, 'passers by,' quasi-plural of مارّ, 'passing by' (W I, 232D-233A);
- Intensive: راوِيَة, intensive of راوٍ, 'transmitter of much [poetry]' (W I, 139A-140A);
- Intensive and extensive: عَلّامَة, 'most learned,' intensive of the already intensive pattern فَعّال (W I, 139C)—cf. above, p. 30 (text), 32 (note);

- ة is also used to form substantives from verbal adjectives: مُصِيبَة , 'disaster,' from مُصِيب , 'hitting, afflicting'—see *Ar. Syntax*, p. 62.[12]
- It also forms abstracts (W I, 165C-166A): اليَهُودِيَّة , 'the Jewish religion,' الحَنَفِيَّة , 'the Ḥanafi *madhab*,' and occasionally those representing the Jewish religion or the Ḥanafi *madhab* as a group. Cf. also المُعْتَزِلَة , 'the Mu'tazilites,' which may be more easily explained as a collective.

بَيْت possibly: closet.

لَمْ يُبْقِ غايةً إلّا بَلَغَها (lit., he did not leave any extreme except that he reached it), 'he went as far as he could.'

اِحْتاطَ to be circumspect; here: to be careful, thorough.

عَدَلَ إلى to turn towards.

أَيْدٍ plur. of يَد on the pattern *af'ulun* (with contraction), derived from a fictive root يدي —see W I, 209D; Bro., p. 24 (ch. 13), line 20-22.

فَجَمَعَهُ the pronoun refers to ما in ما كان .

فيها on it, in it; cf. above في تَضاعِيفِها .

اِشْتَمَلَ على to contain.

عَجائِب plur. of عَجِيبة , here to be taken in the ironical sense of marvellous information (i.e., material to support an accusation, or marvels to be expected after the removal of Ibn al-Furāt).

---

12 The technical term is النقل من الوصفيّة الى الاسميّة (the last two terms in W I, 165D). The above reproduces W and *Ar. Syntax* in a simplified form. See also Bro., pp. 81-83; and the interesting observations by H. Fleisch, *Traité de philologie arabe*, I, 311-38 (esp. I, 324-38), and the shorter exposition by the same author in *L'Arabe classique*, nouvelle éd., Beirut 1968, pp. 46-48.

ماتَ في جِلْدِهِ he died when [his soul] was still in its skin, "he died a thousand deaths."

Notes to Page 196

اِكْتِفاءٌ بِ deeming sufficient.

ما جَرَى على what happened to, what had been done in [the house of my father and my brother].

وسَلِمَ ابْنُ عَيْنونة I. 'A., too, was safe (escaped). See above, p. 105 (l. 3 of text).

لا فَضْلَ فيهِ لِحَرَكةٍ he had no energy left to move; apparently to be taken in the sense that he could not even have tried to escape.

Ibn Hindī perhaps = Ibn Hibintā (see above, Dramatis Personae).

عِنْدِي with me, known to me.

خَلْفَهُ the pronoun refers to Murīb.

تَأَبَّطَ بِ to carry something under one's armpit (إِبْط).

إِذْ see below, Index, *idhā, idh*; here 'then (i.e., when I continued to walk behind him, at that moment, then/then suddenly).'

اِنْسَلَّ to slip.

بِعَيْنِها precisely the one [that was dangerous]; بِعَيْنِهِ often means 'the very same,' 'the very same thing [under discussion, mentioned earlier]'—seeW II, 281B-C. Cf. Index, s.v. *'ayn*.

كِتاب here and often elsewhere used in the sense of 'letter.'

مُسْتَراح [public] toilet.

عِنْدَ ذٰلِكَ at that moment, when that had been done.

وَقَفَ على to inspect (literally: to stop [and look] at).

أَنْكَرَ (على) to disapprove; أنكر has several other meanings which all appear frequently, e.g., 'to disown,' 'to find unpleasant,' 'to be ignorant of.' One of the duties of a good Muslim is الأَمْرُ بالمعروف والنَّهْيُ عن المُنْكَر , 'to order/encourage what is good and to forbid/discourage what is bad/disapproved.' *Munkar* is also a category in Islamic law.

خاطَبَهُما بِالجَمِيل he addressed/spoke to the two of them in a friendly manner.

مِنْ أَجْلِه (the pronoun refers to سَبَب).

جاءَتْهُ the object pronoun refers to al-Muhassin.

Abū 'l-Ḥasan = Ibn al-Furāt.

مِحْنَة here: 'ordeal'; also: 'trial,' 'torture'; see *EI*2, s.v.

مِنْ بَيْنِ *bayna,* which is really a noun of place in the adverbial accus. (W II, 111B-C), is put in the genit. when dependent on مِنْ; see W II, 188C-D.

طَوْل reference to ذو الطَّوْل in Koran xl, 3, interpreted as 'The Possessor of Power,' or 'The Possessor of Bounty'; see L, p. 1806c.

* * *

The following is the last of a series of anecdotes about the vizier Abū ʿAlī Muḥ. b. ʿUbaydallāh b. Yaḥyā al-Khāqānī (299-301).[13]

From: Ghars al-Niʿma Abū ʾl-Ḥasan Muḥ. b. Hilāl al-Ṣābī, *al-Hafawāt al-nādira*, ed. Ṣ. al-Ashtar, Damascus 1387/1967, p. 209.

وعُرِضَتْ عليه رُقعتان: إحداهما عن بعض الجند في استطلاق ما تأخّر من رزقه، والأخرى من بعضِ حُرمه، تستأذنه في دخول الحَمَّام، فوقَّعَ تحت رقعة حُرمته – وعنده أنها رقعة الجندي – «قد حَظَرَ أميرُ المؤمنين ذلك، فلا سبيلَ إليه!» وتحت رقعة الجندي: «إذا خَلَوْنا كان الخطابُ شِفاهاً إن شاء الله!» فعجب الجندي والكُتَّابُ من هذا التوقيع، ووقعت المرأةُ على ذكر الخليفة وأنه حَظَرَ عليها دخول الحمام فلَطَمَتْ واغتمَّتْ كيف عرَف الخليفة ذلك ومَنَعَ منه!

Notes

رُقْعة see note, p. 108.

عَنْ '[coming] from,' or 'on behalf of'; مِنْ and عَنْ appear occasionally as synonyms; moreover there is graphic similarity. This means that copyists of manuscripts could confuse the two particles or arbitrarily adopt one particle instead of the other—see W II, 143C-D. عَنْ has to be understood here as meaning 'originating from,' 'coming from'—see W II, 142B-D.

بَعْض الجُنْد here probably: a member of the armed forces, possibly under the direct command of the caliph. See *EI*2, I, 729b; II, 601b.

---

[13] See *Vizirat*, pp. 394-99 (p. 397 for references to texts dealing with his stupidity), and index, p. 774a, bottom; *Passion*, I, 466-67; *Tajārib*, index, p. 73.

فِي often used to indicate the contents of a book, less frequently of a letter—see W II, 155B.

اِسْتِطْلاق desiring that something be set free, released; remission.

تَأَخَّرَ to be delayed/due/outstanding.

رِزْق sustenance, soldier's allowance.

حُرَم plur. of حُرْمَة, wife.

وعِنْدَهُ in his opinion; here: "he thought that. . ." Cf. the variant in one of the manuscripts: ويُقَدِّر. See W II, 179C-D, for the frequent use of عِنْدَ in the sense of 'holding an opinion,' e.g., كان عِنْدَهُ أَنَّ القرآنَ مَخْلوق, "he held that the Qur'ān was created (i.e., not coeternal with God)"; and الصَّوابُ عِنْدي ما فَعَلَهُ, "the right thing in my opinion is what he did."

اِسْتَأْذَنَ to ask for permission (إِذْن), often in the sense of 'to ask for an audience,' but here for permission to go to the bathhouse

وَقَّعَ frequently used in contexts of answering a petition (قِصَّة, plur. قِصَص) written on a small piece of paper (رُقْعَة). The dignitary writes his reply at the bottom or on the reverse side of the slip of paper.[14] The term التَّوْقيع على القِصَص became a technical term in Muslim administration; see the article DIPLOMATIC in *EI*2, p. 306a. قِصَّة also means 'story.' For other important terms derived from the root ق ص ص, see L, and *EI*2, s.v. ḲIṢṢA.

وعِنْدَهُ أَنَّهُ رُقْعَةُ الجُنْدِيّ cf. above: "thinking that it was the petition of the man from the army."

---

14 See Ibn al-Ṣayrafī (Çaïrafî), "Code de la chancellerie d'état," trad. par H. Massé, *Bull. de l'Institut des Études Orientales,* Damascus 1913, pp. 112-13. This reply may then be copied and frequently elaborated by a secretary (*kātib*).

حَظَرَ to prohibit, to disallow.

لا سَبِيلَ إلَيْهِ there is no way to [do] it, it cannot possibly be done. لا when it categorically denies the existence of the following substantive puts that substantive in the accusative; see below, p. 124 (note on لا بَقاءَ).

إذا خَلَوْنا كان الخطابُ شِفاهاً literally: "when we are alone, the discussion will be oral"—i.e., it is better to discuss this between the two of us when we are alone.[15]

عَجِبَ الجُنْدِيُّ والكُتّابُ See above. This probably means that the scribes either saw the reply or had to copy it, one copy staying in the files of the office.

وَقَعَ على take note of, take notice of.

لَطَمَ to slap [one's face as a sign of sorrow].

اغْتَمَّتْ كَيْفَ she grieved, [saying]: 'How... ?' Her saying something is implied in اغْتَمَّتْ; see *Ar. Syntax*, p. 380, e.g., أَوْمَأَ إلَيَّ قِفْ, 'he gave me a sign [meaning]: Stand still!'.

---

15 Some men, especially those in the public eye, may not have been eager to allow their wives to visit a public bath; see H. Grotzfeld, *Das Bad im arabisch-islamischen Mittelalter*, Wiesbaden 1970, pp. 100-101.

XI. Abū 'Ubayd al-Bakrī, *Kitāb al-Masālik wa-'l-mamālik*

Abū 'Ubayd al-Bakrī, 'Abdallāh b. 'Abdal'azīz was one of the most interesting among the many outstanding scholars who were active in Islamic Spain. The exact date of his birth is unknown, but it must have been around 410. His father was the ruler of a small principality in Huelva and Saltes, but he lost this principality to the king of Seville. Abū 'Ubayd followed his father to Cordoba or, according to a different account, to Seville itself. However that may be, Abū 'Ubayd ultimately settled in Cordova sometime after the conquest of Spain by the Almoravids.

Abū 'Ubayd's scholarly activity covered many branches of learning: geography, philology, botany, and theology. His career was different from that of most scholars in that he does not seem to have undertaken any journeys. His biographers depict him as an unrepentant alcoholic and quote some of his bacchic verses; but his addiction did not keep him from writing handbooks that even today enjoy a considerable reputation. Those that have survived are: *Faṣl al-maqāl fī sharḥ Kitāb al-Amthāl*, a most valuable supplement to an earlier collection of proverbs (the index of the edition by I. 'Abbās and 'A. 'Ābdīn lists useful references to a variety of other collections of proverbs); *al-Tanbīh 'alā awhām Abī 'Alī fī Kitāb al-nawādir* and *Simṭ al-la'ālī fī sharḥ al-Amālī*, both dealing with a famous earlier collection of *amālī* (lectures) by al-Qālī (d. 356, known by this *nisba*, al-Qālī, in the East, but in the Maghrib as Abū 'Alī); *Mu'jam mā 'sta'jama*, a geographical dictionary dealing mainly with the Arabian peninsula; and *al-Masālik wa-'l-mamālik* which, as far as we know, has not survived in its entirety. The present selection was taken from the recent edition of a fragment from this last work dealing with western Europe.

For further details, see the introduction to this edition; *EI* 2, s.v. ABŪ 'UBAYD AL-BAKRĪ, and the Index of *EI* 2 to vols 1–7, passim; *GAL*, G I, 106, S I, 166; *GAS* I, VII, VIII, s.v.; and *Wāfī*, XVII, 290–92 (the last has, in the footnotes by the editor, some references not yet listed in the *EI*). For some very interesting observations, see J. Vallvé, "Nuevas ideas sobre la conquista árabe de España toponimia y onomástica," in *al-Qanṭara* X, 1 (1989), 51–150 (particularly pp. 53–54).

The following story appears in E. Lévi-Provençal, who edited and translated the sections by a certain al-Ḥimyarī dealing with Spain in *La Péninsule ibérique au moyen âge* (Leiden 1938), pp. 42–43 (text), pp. 54–55 (translation). The translation at times does not stay very close to the original. This al-Ḥimyarī (8th/14th century)[1] borrowed from al-Bakrī in his geographical dictionary *K. al-Rawḍ al-mi'ṭār fī khabar al-aqṭār*. In the meantime, a complete edition of his dictionary has been prepared by I. 'Abbās (Beirut 1975). The entry on Barcelona appears on pp. 86–87, but reaches only as far as the third line (*khārijun 'anhā* for *khārijun minhā*). The story of Ramon was therefore taken by Lévi-Provençal directly from a manuscript of al-Bakrī.

This selection is a true exercise in determining subjects of sentences and the reference of some prononominal suffixes!

[1]The identity of the author has been discussed by several scholars, but seems now to be well-established. See Adelgisa De Simone, "Trapani, Marsala e Mazara in una compilazione araba del secolo XIV," in *Studi arabo-islamici in memoria di U. Rizzitano*, Ist. del Liceo Ginnasio Gian Giacomo Adria di Mazara del Vallo (Trapani 1980), pp. 454–56.

From: Abū 'Ubayd al-Bakrī, *The Geography of al-Andalus and Europe from the Book al-Masālik wa-'l-Mamālik*, ed. Abdurrahman Ali El-Hajji, Beirut 1387/1968, pp. 96-99.

وأمّا مدينةُ بَرْشِلُونَة فهي من القسم الثالث من الأنْدَلُس، مُسَوَّرَةٌ على ساحل البحر. واليهود بها يَعْدِلون النصارى كَثْرَةً. ولها رَبَضٌ خارجٌ منها.

وصاحبُ بَرْشِلُونَة اليومَ رايْ مُنْدُ بن بَلَنْقِير بن بُرَّيل، وكان خرج يُريد بَيْتَ المَقْدِس سنةَ ستٍ وأربعين وأربعمائة، فنزل في مدينة نَرْبونَة على رَجُل من كُبَراء أهلها، فتَعَشَّقَ امرأتَه وتَعَشَّقَتْه؛ ثم تَمادَى في سَفَره حتى وصل بيتَ المَقْدِس، ثم كَرَّ راجعاً حتى أتى نَرْبُونَة فنزل على ضَيْفه بها وليس له هَمٌّ إلّا امرأتَه؛ فحَكَمَ ذلك التعاشُقُ بينهما واتَّفَق معها على أنْ تَعْمَلَ الحيلةَ في الهروب إليه من بلدها فيُزَوَّجها من نفسه؛ فلما وصل إلى برشلونة أرسل إليها قوماً من اليهود في ذلك. ودخل صاحبُ طُرْطُوشَة في الأمر فأَوْصَلَهم في الشَوَاني إلى نَرْبونة، فلم تَتَوَجَّه لليهود الحيلةُ في أمرها وحَسَّ زَوْجُها ببعض شأنِها، وكان بها كَلِفاً، فثَقَّفَها فكان تَثْقِيفُه لها سبباً لمعونة أهلها على مُرادها؛ فوَصَلَتْ مع قومٍ منهم إلى بَرْشِلونة، فنزل رايْ مُنْدُ عن امرأته وتزوّج النَرْبونيَّة. فلَبِسَتِ الأولى المُسُوح وخرجت مع جماعة من أهل بَيْتِها إلى رُومَة حتى أَتَتْ عظيمَها وصاحبَ الدِّين بها، وهو الذي يُسَمُّونَه البابَه، فشَكَتْ إليه ما صنع زوجُها وأَنَّهُ تركها بغير سبب، وهو أَمْرٌ لا يَحِلُّ في دينهم وأنّه لا يجوز لهم فِعْلُه، وإنّما حَمَلَه على ذلك عِشْقُه للنَرْبُونِيَّة، وشَهِدَ لها شُهُودٌ قِبَلَهم، فحَرَّمَ البابَه

على صاحب بَرْشِلونة دخولَ الكنائس وأَمَرَ ألّا يُدْفَنَ له ميت وأَنْ يَتَبَرَّأَ منه جميعُ مَن يَعْتَقِدُ النصرانيةَ. فلمّا عَلِمَ أَنَّهُ لا حيلةَ له معه ولا بَقاءَ في أُفُقٍ يكون فيه لنصرانيٍّ حُكْمٌ، فبَذَلَ الأموال ودَسَّ مشاهيرَ الأساقِفةِ والقِسِّيسِينَ، وأَوْطَأَهم على الشُّخُوص إلى البابَه وأَنْ يَشْهَدوا له أَنَّه تَقَصَّى عن نَسَب المرأة التي تَرَكَ فوَجَدَها منه بقُرْبَى يُحَرِّمُها عليه وأنّ النَرْبونيَّة فَرَّتْ من زوجها لذلك، لأنّه كانت منه بنَسَبٍ وكان يُكْرِمُها على المُقام معه. فنَفَذَ القومُ إلى البابَه وشَهِدوا للقُومِس ما أَوْطَأَهم عليه، فقَبِلَهم وأباح له دُخُولَ الكنائس ودَفْنَ مَن مات له وسائرَ ما حَجَرَ عليه.

Notes to Page 119

القِسْم الثالث See pp. 59 and 63 of this text: al-Bakrī attributes this division to 'the Ancients,' notably Constantine (the Great?), but fails to explain clearly what type of division is meant. See, however, al-'Udhrī, Aḥmad b. 'Umar, *Fragmentos Geográfico-Históricos*, ed. A. al-Ahwānī, Madrid 1965, p. 147 (note to p. 20, line 12). Al-Ahwānī attributes this division to [Pomponius] Mela (about 50 A.D.) and Pliny the Elder (died 79 A.D.).

مُسَوَّرَةٌ nominal sentence without subject: "[it is] walled."

نَصارَى (plur. of نَصْرانِيٌّ) and نَصْرانِيَّة, see below, Index.

ولَها *Ar. Syntax*, p. 26; Vagl. I, 64: names of peoples and tribes are sometimes feminine, and the pronoun could refer to the Jews; the text as it appears in Muḥ. b. 'Abdalmun'im al-Ḥimyarī, *Kitāb al-Rawḍ al-mi'ṭār*, ed. I. 'Abbās (Beirut 1975), p. 86b, which often borrows from al-Bakrī, suggests that it refers to مدينة ; in cases such as this, using لهم to refer to the Jewish colony would be far more likely.

رَبَض suburb.

رايْ مُنْد Raymond. For Ramón Berenguer I, see J. F. O'Callaghan, *A History of Medieval Spain* (Cornell 1975), index. Lévi-Provençal identifies *Burrīl* as Borell.

بَيْت المَقْدِس Jerusalem.

نزل . . . على he took up lodgings [as a guest]. . . with. . . .

نَرْبُونة Narbonne.

تَعَشَّقَ اَمْرَأَتَهُ he fell in love with his wife (i.e., the wife of his host).

تَمادَى في here: 'to continue.' Cf. Dozy: تَمادى على 'continuer.'

كَرَّ to return; also 'to return to the fight after fleeing'; here perhaps 'to return immediately.'

ضَيْف here 'host' (i.e., his former host).

وليس له هَمٌّ إلّا اَمْرَأَتُهُ (اَمْرَأَتَهُ) "he could think of nothing but his (the host's) wife," "his only intention was to meet. . . ." When a sentence preceding إلّا is negative, the exception is usually put in the same case as the general term, but may also be put in the accusative. This last alternative is obligatory when the exception is wholly different in character from the general term. See Vagl. II, 157; W II, 336B-C and. 337B-D; and cf. *Ar. Syntax*, pp. 503 and 504-5; *Admin.* p. 55.

حَكَمَ or حَكُمَ here: 'to become firmly established.'

فاتَّفَقَ معها على أنْ تَعْمَلَ . . . "and he arranged with her that she would carry out. . ."

فِي الهُرُوبِ . . . في ذلك *fī* is used in the sense of 'in order to, for the purpose of, having in mind to': see W II, 155C-D, and Index.

إليه to her beloved

مِنْ نَفْسِهِ *min* may indicate the side who makes a payment in a transaction; hence its use with زَوَّجَ since this involves payment of a dowry. See W II, 131C-D.

إليها i.e., to his beloved.

دخل . . . في الأمر he took part in the undertaking.

صاحبُ طُرْطوشة the ruler of Tortosa.

شَوانٍ pl. of شينية, galley, see Dozy I, p. 812b, and W I, 220D-221B..

تَوَجَّهَ here: to take its course, to be realized, to succeed.

حَسَّ . . . بِبَعْضِ شَأْنِها he had an inkling of what she was about to do / of her plans.

شَأْن often a synonym of أَمْر.

كَلِف deeply in love.

ثَقَّفَها he restricted her movements, he held her in custody; see Dozy I, p. 160.

مَعُونة أَهْلِها على مُرادِها help provided [to her] by her family to achieve her goal. على like في may indicate the goal of some activity. See W II, 168C-D.

منهم i.e., her family.

نزل . . . عن here: to give up, divorce.

الأُولى the first, i.e., the woman he divorced.

مُسُوح, plur. of مِسْح course garments; see Dozy II, 589b; also penitential garments.

جَماعة من أهْل بَيْتِها a group of people from her family.

حَتّى أتَتْ *ḥattā* should here be translated 'thereupon,' 'and so'; see *Ar. Syntax*, p. 479: بُعِثْتُ طَلِيعَةً حتى دَخَلْتُ الغُوطة *I was sent as a scout, whereupon*, or, *and so, I entered al-Ghūṭa*. I.e., his work as a scout began at al-Ghūṭa; it did not last 'until' he reached al-Ghūṭa.

عَظِيمَها its upper [religious authority].

وهو this being. . . .

شَكَتْ the object is the clause beginning with ما.

وأنّه لا يُجَوِّزُ لهم فِعْلَهُ (alternative reading) unless there is a lacuna, the clause introduced by the second أنه depends on the notion(s) implied in شكت. Translate: "and [she argued] that he [the Pope] should/would not allow them (the Christians) [to commit] such a deed." One of the manuscripts of al-Bakrī reads وأنهم لا يَجُوزُ لهم فعلُه "and that they (the Christians) were not allowed to do such a thing." This is also the reading preferred by Lévi-Provençal. It is not necessarily a better reading.

حَمَلَهُ على . . . [there] prompted him (i.e., the husband who had divorced her) to [do so]. . . .

قَبَلَهُم 'which were with them' (i.e., the party accompanying her on her journey to Rome?); see W II, 180A: قَبَلَ is the acc. of قَبَلٌ, 'front,' used in the sense of 'with,' 'towards,' 'in front of.' Perhaps one should read مِن قِبَلِهِم, 'on their behalf' (W II, 189D).

Notes to Page 120

أَلَّا يُدْفَنَ له مَيِّتٌ that no dead [member] of his [family] could be buried (i.e., given Christian burial).

تَبَرَّأَ to be innocent, not subject to punishment [in case he killed this ruler].

اِعْتَقَدَ to adopt as a doctrine / religion.

النَّصْرانيّة the Christian religion, Christendom: the *nisba* ending *-iyyun* combined with the fem. ending can be used to form both abstracts and, occasionally, collectives, e.g., al-Ḥanafiyya, 'the school of law of Abū Ḥanīfa'; see W I, 165C-166A, and IX, 203.

عَلَم i.e. Raymond.

معهُ i.e., with the Pope.

لا بَقاءَ (lit.: [that] there was no survival)—i.e., that he was not safe anywhere. *Lā* when it categorically denies the existence of the following substantive puts that substantive in the accusative—see W II, 94C-95B, and cf. above, p. 116 (note on لا سبيلَ إليه).

أُفُق horizon; here: 'region,' 'country.'

يكون فيه لِنَصْرانِيٍّ حُكْمٌ . . . where a Christian would have authority over him.

فَ introduces the main clause, see W II, 347B: it does so frequently after لَمَّا.

دَسَّ to send secretly; see Dozy I, 439b-440a.

مَشاهير plur. of مَشْهور 'well-known,' 'famous'; here: 'who had a [good] reputation, had much authority.'

أَساقِفة plur. of أُسْقُف, bishop.

قَساوِسة 'priests,' may be plur. of قِسِّيس.

أَوْطَأَهم على . . . he made them ready to, he put them in the right frame of mind to, persuaded them to. . . .

شَخَصَ to go out.

تَقَصَّى عن . . . to go far in investigating, to investigate thoroughly; see Dozy II, 260a-b.

نَسَب genealogy, ancestry.

تَرَكَ one would expect تَرَكَها, but the pronoun may be omitted if the sentence is sufficiently clear without it; see W II, 320A-B.

مِنْهُ in relation to him.

قُرْبَى This type of verbal noun is listed in W I, 111B; the context indicates that the term means 'proximity in family relationship such as would make marriage unlawful'; see *EI*2, s.v. NIKĀḤ for a discussion of the degrees of blood relationship to be considered.

لِأَنّهُ كانت مِنْهُ بِنَسَبٍ because she (the woman from Narbonne) stood in relation to him (i.e., her former husband) [also] in an unlawful degree of relationship. The sentence can be seen as a *jumla dhāt wajhayn*, a 'two-faced sentence,' a sentence within a sentence: i.e., 'because he (his situation was that) she was in relation to him having the same ancestor(s)'; see W II, 256A-B; but *hū* can also be interpreted as a *ḍamīr al-sha'n* (pronoun anticipating the following statement), i.e., "because it was the case that. . . " or "because it was so that. . ."; see W II, 81C-D, 299B; see also *Synt. Verh.*, p. 806.

كان يُكْرِهُها على . . . he (i.e., her former husband in Narbonne) had been compelling her to. . . .

مُقام can be used in the sense of إقامة ; see W I, 129D-130A.

قُومِس count.

وشَهِدوا لِلقُومِسِ ما أَوْطَأَهُم عليه and they testified on behalf of the count by [mentioning] what he had persuaded them [to say].

XII. Abū 'l-Faraj al-Iṣfahānī
Kitāb al-Aghānī

Although many biographies of Abū 'l-Faraj al-Iṣfahānī have survived, their contents are often rather meager and, as happens often, repetitive in the sense that later authors copy verbatim what they found in earlier collections of biographies.[1] They agree that al-Iṣfahānī was born in 284 but disagree on the date of his death, 356 or 357, the *Ta'rīkh Baghdād* asserting that only the first date is accurate, but others quoting strong evidence that only the second can be accepted. His incredibly dirty habits are described in sickening detail. Long tolerated by one of his patrons, the vizier al-Muhallabī, famous as a patron of the arts, the latter ended up arranging a special table for guests, so that he no longer had to witness al-Iṣfahānī's table manners from close by.

A curious fact of al-Iṣfahānī's biography is his adherence to the Shī'a, as illustrated by a monograph about the sufferings of the Alids, *Maqātil al-Ṭālibiyyīn,* which has survived; this in spite of his being direct descendant from the Umayyad caliph, Marwān b. al-Ḥakam (or according to one report, from the last of the Umayyads, Marwān II, al-Ḥimār). All biographers praise his vast memory and wide sphere of interest, which included even medicine. An exception is a tradition reported in the *Ta'r. Bagh.,* XI, 399, quoting a certain Abū Muḥammad al-Ḥasan b. al-Ḥusayn al-Nawbakhtī (d. 402, *Ta'r. Bagh.* VII, 299), apparently a Mu'tazilite, who asserted that Abū 'l-Faraj al-Iṣfahānī gained his wealth of data from books he would buy in the market; for that reason he called him the greatest liar in existence (*akdhab al-nās*).[2] Ibn al-Nadīm (d. 385) makes the same observation in his *Fihrist,* p. 115, but only in order to emphasize that Abū 'l-Faraj was extremely careful in the choice of written documents he used for his books. This curious observation can therefore be taken as a reminder of the importance attached to *samā'* (oral transmission with or without the use of written material), as well as an indication that the use of written documents had become, at least among philologists, an accepted practice. A frequently quoted anecdote emphasizes Abū 'l-Faraj's intellectual honesty.

---

[1] In some cases this is to our advantage when the older biographies are no longer extent.

[2] See also Ibn Wāṣil (under the title Abū 'l-Faraj al-Iṣfahānī, *al-Aghānī,* hadhdhabahū Ibn Wāṣil al-Ḥamawī, Cairo 1382/1962, I, 6, last line, p. 7, line 2).

Another interesting note tells us that the *Aghānī* was presented to Sayfaddawla, and that Abū 'l-Faraj himself never prepared more than this one copy of his sizable work which took him fifty years to complete.

The biographers are also helpful in the sense that they list in great detail the works of Abū 'l-Faraj that were known to exist, thereby confirming the authenticity of some short monographs that have appeared in print in recent years. Some of his books were written for Umayyad rulers in Spain, and payment was conveyed secretly. According to one biographer, not much of this payment ultimately reached him.

Abū 'l-Faraj himself wrote a *Mujarrad al-Aghānī,* anticipating the abridgment by Ibn Wāṣil (d. 697). His poetry, of which a good deal is cited by biographers, is qualified as showing the technical skill *(itqān)* of a scholar and the charm (*ẓarf*) of a poet. *Hijā',* 'lampoon,' seems to have been the genre in which he did best, thereby raising fears among his enemies!

For further information, see, apart from the excellent but now outdated article ABŪ 'L-FARAḎJ AL-IṢFAHĀNĪ in *EI* 2, the introduction to *Agh.* 2 (Cairo 1927/1371) I, 15–38; *Irshād,* V, 149–68, and for detailed references *Wāfī*, XXI, 20; *Inbāh,* II, 251; and Muḥ. b. Aḥmad al-Dhahabī, *Siyar a'lām al-nubalā',* ed Sh. al-Arna'ūṭ and A. al-Bustānī, Beirut 1401/1981, XVI, 201–3. M. Fleischhammer, *Altarabische Prosa,* Reclam Verlag, Leipzig 1990, pp. 265–70, has translated the author's introduction to the *Kitāb al-Aghānī;* for further selections in translation, see G. Rotter, *Abu l-Faradsch: Und der Kalif beschenkte ihn reichlich,* H. Erdmann Verlag, Tübingen/Basel 1977.

A free translation of the following story appears in C. Bernheimer, *L'Arabia antica e la sua poesia,* Napoli 1960, pp. 274–76.

The *Kitāb al-Aghānī* of Abū 'l-Faraj al-Iṣfahānī: Publication History

The oldest edition, Būlāq 1285, is in twenty volumes. It is poorly printed and difficult to use. A twenty-first volume was published by Brünnow, Leiden 1888. This volume is not authentic.

There is an edition by the Maṭba'at al-Taqaddum, Cairo 1323/1905, in twenty-one volumes. Is this a reprint of the Būlāq edition of 1285? *EI* 2 and *GAL* G I, 147 (p. 156), and S I, 226, also mention a reprint of the Būlāq edition dated Cairo 1323/1905 ("with Fihrist"). This edition is marked in *EI* 2 as *Agh.* 2.

Ignazio Guidi, *Tables alphabétiques du Kitâb Al-Aġânî,* Leiden 1895–1900, made an index to the twenty volumes of the Būlāq edition and the twenty-first volume edited by Brünnow (index of poets, general index of names, index of rhymes). Given the quality of the Būlāq edition, this is a monumental work with much "hidden scholarship."

Agh. 1 is the usual abbreviation for this 20+1 volume edition.

From here on the publication history of the *Aghānī* becomes extremely complicated. As far as I know, no up-to-date bibliography exists.

An edition by I. al-Abyārī, Cairo 1389/1969 in thirty-one volumes, has comprehensive indexes, but no rhyme index.

The edition marked in *EI* 2 as *Agh.* 3 is often marked by others as *Agh.* 2. This is the standard edition prepared by the Dār al-Kutub al-Miṣriyya. *I have simply marked it as* Aghānī *since the Būlāq edition, as well as other editions, are not often used.* The first volume appeared in 1345/1927 (according to Brockelmann S I, 226, in 1923). It was beautifully printed by the Maṭba'at Dār al-Kutub al-Miṣriyya, and the series was continued until 1381/1961. At that time the sixteenth volume was completed. It marks the volume and page numbers of the old Būlāq edition in the margin, so that Guidi's index can be used with it. There are, however, also separate indexes to each volume. These are much more detailed than those by Guidi and include, among other items, scholars mentioned in *isnāds*, book titles in text and notes, musicians and composers, proverbs, etc.

While this edition was still in progress, a reprint was begun, Cairo 1371/1952, by the same publisher.

The publication was resumed in 1970/1389 with volume 17, now published by al-Hay'ah al-Miṣriyyah al-'Āmmah li-'l-Ta'līf wa-l-Nashr. Volume 24 carries the date 1974/1394 and completes the work.

A recent bookseller's catalogue (Harrassowitz, no. 341) mentions on p. 60 a "reissue" by 'A. M. Farrāj in twenty-five volumes, volumes 24–25 containing the indexes. The author of this reader had occasion to glance briefly at the last volume, but found no more than an index of proper names. The relation of this edition to the Dār al-Kutub edition is not clear. This edition is dated 1401/1981. This author found what appears to be an earlier edition dated 1955.

Although the Dār al-Kutub al-Miṣriyya edition is the standard edition of the *Aghānī*, it is not yet a critical edition. It is based on no less than nine manuscripts, but still may not have taken into account all available manuscripts, some of them in Europe. Nor does the apparatus suggest that we have a complete list of all important variants, marginal notes, etc. Moreover, the order of the biographies in the later volumes is not the same as in the Būlāq edition, so that in these volumes it is not always easy to use Guidi's index with it. A comprehensive index to all volumes was apparently never planned.

In the meantime, a facsimile reprint of volumes 1–16 (Wizārat al-Thaqāfa, undated) appeared, selling in the sixties for as little as $30. Unfortunately, this reprint does not include the indexes, so that Guidi is needed to find one's way (unless one is prepared to copy the indexes from *Aghānī,* as this author did).

It is perhaps worthwhile to keep in mind that Ibn Wāṣil (604–97/1208–98), the author of a well-known history entitled *Mufarrij al-Kurūb fī akhbār Banī Ayyūb,* also put together a *Mukhtaṣar al-Aghānī,* published in Cairo in 1382/1963, which, as far as I can determine, has not been checked against the standard text of the *Aghānī.*

Several other editions may have appeared, both in the period between the first Cairo edition and the publication of the standard edition and in the period before the appearance of the facsimile reprint.

The *K. al-Aghānī* goes back to a collection of songs made by order of Hārūn al-Rashīd by Ibrāhīm al-Mawṣilī (d. 188/804) and others; this collection was revised by his son Isḥāq b. Ibrāhīm (d. 235/850).

Abū 'l-Faraj adds songs by other singers, and for each song he indicates the melody. But the songs serve only as an excuse for offering a wealth of information about the composers and their works and even more on the poets whose poems were set to music.

The *K. al-Aghānī* is therefore not so much a book on songs, as a collection of biographical data, some legendary, in which quotations from poems dominate. It has some of the characteristics of Ṭabarī (see above, Abbreviations, s.v. *Glossarium*) in the sense that it brings fragments of historical information—including much about social life and religion—introduced by an *isnād.* These bits of information are arranged without much system or order; yet precisely because Abū 'l-Faraj did not arrange this information in the form of a continuous story, they are often of great importance, because they reproduce (or claim to reproduce), the *ipsissima verba* of many of the earliest scholars of Arabic philology. Some of these scholars were still in touch with poets from the Umayyad era. In addition, it offers data that are of importance to geographers and anthropologists. It is not surprising therefore that I. Goldziher, who held that students of Islam should not study literature or religious law in isolation, derived much information from the *K. al-Aghānī.*

From: Abū 'l-Faraj al-Iṣfahānī, *Kitāb al-Aghānī*, VIII, 202-4.

وقالت جميلة: حدّثتني بُثَينة – وكانت صَدُوقةَ اللسان جميلةَ الوجه حسنةَ البيان عفيفةَ البطن والفرج – قالت: والله ما أرادني جَميلُ رحمةُ الله عليه بريبةٍ قطّ ولا حَدّثت أنا نفسي بذلك منه. وإنّ الحيّ آنتجعوا موضعاً، وإني لفي هَوْدج لي أَسيرُ إذا أنا بهاتفٍ يُنْشِد أبياتاً، فلم أتمالكْ أن رميتُ بنفسي وأهلُ الحيّ ينظرون، فبقيت أطلب المُنْشِدَ فلم أقف عليه، فناديتُ: أيها الهاتف بشعر جميل ما وراءَك منه؟ وأنا أحسَبه قد قضَى نَحْبَه ومضَى لسبيله، فلم يُجِبْني مُجِيب؛ فناديت ثلاثاً، وفي كل ذلك لا يردُّ عليّ أحدٌ شيئاً. فقال صَوَاحِبَاتِي: أصابَكِ يا بُثَينة طائفٌ من الشيطان. فقلت: كَلَّا! لقد سمعت قائلا يقول! قُلْنَ: نحن معكِ ولم نسمعْ! فرجعتُ فركبت مطيّتي وأنا حَيْرَى والهةُ العقل كاسفةُ البال، ثم سرْنا. فلما كان في الليل إذا ذلك الهاتفُ يَهْتِف بذلك الشعر بعينه، فرميتُ بنفسي وسعيتُ إلى الصوت، فلما قَرُبْتُ منه آنقطع؛ فقلت: أيها الهاتف، ارحمْ حَيْرتي وسكّن عَبْرتي بخبر هذه الأبيات، فإن لها شأناً! فلم يردّ عليّ شيئاً. فرجعتُ إلى رَحْلي فركبت وسِرْتُ وأنا ذاهبة العقل؛ وفي كل ذلك لا يُخْبرني صَوَاحِبَاتِي أنهنّ سمِعْنَ شيئاً. فلما كانت الليلةُ القابلةُ نزلنا وأخذ الحيُّ مضاجعَهم ونامت كلُّ عين، فإذا الهاتف يهتِف بي ويقول: يا بُثَينة، أَقْبِلي إليّ أُنبِئْك عمّا تريدين. فأقبلت نحوَ الصوت، فإذا شيخٌ كأنه من رجال الحيّ، فسألتُه عن آسمه وبَيْته. فقال: دَعِي هذا وخُذِي فيما هو أهمُّ عليكِ. فقلت له: وإن هذا لَمِمَّا يَهُمُّنِي. قال: اقنَعي بما

قلتُ لكِ. قلت له: أنت المنشدُ الأبيات؟ قال نعم. قلتُ: فما خبرُ جميل؟ قال: نعمْ فارقتُه وقد قَضَى نَحْبَه وصار إلى حُفْرته رحمة الله عليه. فصرَختُ صَرْخةً آذنتُ منها الحيَّ، وسقطتُ لوجهي فأُغْمِي عليَّ، فكأنّ صوتي لم يسمَعْه أحد، وبقيتُ سائرَ ليلتي، ثم أَفَقْتُ عند طلوع الفجر وأهلي يطلبونني فلا يقفون على موضعي، ورفعتُ صوتي بالعَويل والبكاء ورجعتُ إلى مكاني. فقال لي أهلي: ما خبرُكِ وما شأنُكِ؟ فقصصت عليهم القصّة. فقالوا: يَرْحَم الله جميلا. وٱجتمع نساء الحيّ وأنشدتُهنّ الأبياتَ فأسعدْنَني بالبكاء، فأَقَمْنَ كذلك لا يفارقْنَني ثلاثاً، وتحزَّن الرجالُ أيضا وبَكَوْا ورَثَوْه وقالوا كلُّهم: يَرْحمُه الله، فإنه كان عفيفاً صَدُوقاً! فلم أكتحلْ بعده بإثمِد ولا فرقتُ رأسي بمخيط ولا مُشط ولا دهَنْتُه إلّا من صُدَاع خِفْتُ على بصَرِي منه ولا لبِستُ خِماراً مصبوغاً ولا إزاراً ولا أزال أَبْكِيه إلى الممات. قالت جميلة: فأنشدتْني الشعرَ كلَّه وهذا الغناء بعضُه، وهو:

ألا مَن لقلبٍ لا يَمَلُّ فَيَذْهَلُ * أَفِقْ فالتعزِّي عن بُثَينةَ أجملُ

Notes to Page 131

جَميلة Jamīla, famous singer from the Umayyad period; founded her own school of music; see *EI*2, s.v. DJAMĪLA.

بُثَيْنة Buthayna, beloved of Jamīl al-ʿUdhrī. Jamīl and Buthayna were among the semi-legendary pairs of lovers whose tragic life stories, mostly in a bedouin setting, may date from the Umayyad period. These stories were probably enlarged in the early Abbasid period; see *EI*2, s.v. DJAMĪL, and *GAS* II, 406-8.

صَدُوقَة truthful: the pattern *fa'ūl* in the active sense does not need a fem. ending when used as an attribute to an expressed fem. noun or as a predicate to a fem., e.g. رَأَيْتُهَا صَبُوراً *I saw that she was/thought her patient*—see W I, 185C-D. The fem. ending here should therefore perhaps be taken as an intensive form, 'most truthful'—see W I, 139A-B.

حَسَنَةَ البَيان expressing herself clearly and eloquently. In later times the term *bayān* acquired a technical sense which became the subject of an extensive literature. See *EI*2, s.vv. BAYĀN and al-MA'ĀNĪ wa-'l-BAYĀN.

عَفيفَةَ البَطْنِ والفَرْجِ lit., chaste in belly and sexual organs. This frequently used phrase may be translated as 'modest in eating and chaste.'

ما أرادَني. . . بِرِيبَةٍ he never sought me/wished me to do a shameful thing.

حَدَّثَ نَفْسَهُ بِشَيْءٍ to expect/imagine that something can happen; cf. Bla., s.v., p. 2211a.

مِنْهُ coming from him, on his part.

لَ affirmative particle that may introduce the predicate after إِنَّ. See W II, 79A-D.

هَوْدَج camel litter/vehicle for women mounted on a camel.

لي cf. above, دابَّةٌ لي (text p. 80, notes p. 83), and Index.

إذا انا ب see below, Index, s. vv. *idh, idhā.*

هاتِف Interpreted by a medieval scholar as "a voice without a body"; often, but not invariably, associated with the jinn in the desert, and best translated by 'mysterious voice.' See *EI*2, s.v., and cf. *hātif*, 'telephone,' in contemporary Arabic.

أَنْشَدَ to recite. For further interesting details about the root نشد and the *hātif*, see I. Goldziher, *Abhandlungen zur arabischen Philologie*, I (Leiden 1896), pp. 6,

25, 37, 212; and W II, 339D. نَشَدَ (form I) has the sense of 'to beseech.'

أَبْيات plur. of بَيْت in the sense of 'line of poetry.'

تَمالَكَ عَنْ to restrain oneself from. Before أَنْ prepositions (in this case عَنْ) are often omitted—see W II, 193B.

رَمَى بِنَفْسِهِ he threw himself [down]. For بِ after transitive verbs see W II, 159D-160B.

بَقِيَ 'to remain,' 'to continue' is one of the 'sisters of *kāna*'—see below, Index, s.v. *zāla*.

أَقِفْ root وقف.

الهاتِفُ بِ *bi-* is used after verbs signifying communication, spoken or written, to indicate what is being communicated; see Index.

ما وَرَاءَكَ مِنْهُ ؟ lit., 'what is behind you of him?'; here: 'what news do you bring about him?' For وَرَاءَ, 'behind,' 'on the other side of,' etc., see W II, 187C-D.

قَضَى نَحْبَهُ he died; lit., he ended his vow, or term of life.

أَحْسَبُهُ قَدْ قَضَى نَحْبَهُ I reckon/have reason to believe that he has died. أَحْسَبُ governs here a double accusative consisting of a pronoun with following sentence.

مَضَى لِسَبِيلِهِ he went his way, i.e., 'he passed away.' لِ may indicate direction or goal—see W II, 147D-148A, and *WKAS*, s.v. (II, 1, 11b).

ثَلاثاً for ثَلاثَ مَرّاتٍ, with the number taking its gender from the understood noun—see W II, 240A-B. Cf. سِرْتُ خَمْساً for خَمْسَ لَيالٍ (the sing. لَيْلَة is fem.) and صُمْتُ خَمْسَةً for خَمْسَةَ أَيّامٍ (the sing. يَوْم is masc.).

في كلٍّ ذلك in [doing] all this, while doing all this.

صَواحِباتي some plurals of plurals use the fem. plural ending. The difference from the normal plural is often unclear, but in بُيُوتات العَرَب, the 'double plural' بُيُوتات means 'prominent families'—see W I, 132C.

طائِفٌ مِنَ الشَّيْطانِ a visitation from the Devil. The term شيطان is confusing, since it can also be used in the sense of جِنّي. In pre-Islamic times many poets had a *jinnī* inspiring them, and these *jinn* are often mentioned by name; see the above-mentioned *Abhandlungen*, I, (index) 221 and 227, under 'Ǧinnen' and 'Šejtân'; *EI*2, s.v. IBLĪS.

كَلّا by no means, certainly not—examples in W I, 287A..

قائِلاً يَقُولُ a speaker speaking. قال also means 'to recite,' and translating 'a reciter reciting' is probably more correct.

مَطِيَّة root مطو.

حَيْرَى for فَعْلَى as fem. of فَعْلانُ (to be distinguished from فَعْلانٌ) see W I, 184B and 185B.

وَلَهَ (or وَلِهَ) to be grief-stricken; hence والِهَةُ العَقْلِ, mentally unbalanced as a result of grief.

كاسِفُ البالِ dejected, gloomy—see *WKAS*, s.v. (p. 192b-193a).

كانَ في اللَّيْلِ night had fallen.

بِعَيْنِه precisely the same; see W II, 281D. For the various and often confusing meanings of عَيْن, see W II, 280D-282A, and Index.

انْقَطَعَ to be cut off, discontinued.

ارْحَمْ حَيْرَتي take pity on/show consideration for my state of confusion/my perplexity.

عَبْرَة tear(s).

. . . بِخَبَرٍ with the story of/by telling [me why you are reciting].

فإنَّ لها شَأنًا for they must have [been occasioned by] a momentous affair; for شأن, see below, XIII, 324.

ذاهِبَةَ العَقْلِ losing my mind; the corresponding verb is ذَهَبَ بِعَقْلِهِ 'it took away his mind,' with *bi-* indicating the object that is put in motion by the intransitive verb ذَهَبَ—see W II, 159C.

قابِل here 'next.'

أَخَذَ الحَيُّ مَضاجِعَهُمْ the tribe took to the places where they [used to] lie down, they went to bed.

يَهْتِفُ بِي here: calls out to me.

أَقْبِلِي the imperative can introduce a conditional sentence—i.e., "do this or that, [and if you do it] this or that shall happen." The construction is frequent in proverbs, e.g. أَسْلِمْ تَسْلَمْ, "become a Muslim and you shall be safe" (saved from hellfire), or عِشْ قَنِعًا تَكُنْ مَلِكًا—see W II, 37D-38A.

كَأَنَّهُ مِنْ رِجالِ الحَيِّ here: who looked like, seemed to be a man from the (our) tribe.

بَيْت here probably 'clan,' 'family.'

دَعِي (f. sg. imperative) from root و د ع

خُذِي في For the idiomatic use of أَخَذَ في see W II, 155A-C: في often indicates the subject of conversation, and, in a more general way, the goal of an activity (e.g., نَهَضَ فيه, 'he stood up to look after it,' 'he took care of it'). Very frequent is the use of في in booktitles to indicate their contents, كتاب

الواضح المُبين في ذِكر مَن اسْتُشْهِدَ مِن المُحِبّين , *The Clear and Eloquent [Book] Dealing with Those Who Suffered Martyrdom from among the Lovers,* (the book is based on a spurious tradition connected with the genre of the present story, stating that chaste lovers, suffering in silence, when dying from love sickness may be classified as martyrs, as well as other traditional views which count as martyrs all those who die a tragic death). Translate خُذي في here: 'discuss,' 'engage in,' 'ask about.' Cf. below, Index, s.v. *fī*.

There exists a more detailed version of part of the story in *Aghānī* VIII, 153-54: Feeling that his end is near, Jamīl offers his possessions, including his clothes, to a man (whose name is not mentioned) on condition that this man announce Jamīl's death to Buthayna. Putting on Jamīl's clothes presumably makes him appear as a member of the tribe. Standing on an elevation (*sharaf*) this man should recite one of Jamīl's poems; curiously, this poem is not the same as the poem that appears in our version.

أهَمُّ عَلَيْكِ The preposition على is hard to classify in this context. Perhaps it expresses obligation here (W II, 169A-B), "more important for you [being something you have to investigate]"; but cf. also W II, 168A-169A, and expressions such as سَهْلٌ عَلَيَّ 'easy for me.'

وإنَّ هذا لَمِمّا يَهُمُّني "but this is indeed something/still this is something that concerns me." Frequently the particle و has an adversative meaning; see Bro., p. 180: اللهُ أَعْلَمُ وأَنْتُمْ لا تَعْلَمُونَ , "God is all-knowing, but you do not know."

Notes to Page 132

المُنْشِدُ الأَبياتِ the participle can govern either the genitive (الأبياتِ) or the accusative (الأبياتَ)—see W II, 64B-C for the difference in meaning, and cf. XIII, 324.

وقد قَضَى نَحْبَهُ in a positive circumstantial clause (حال) we may find before a perfect وقد ; in a negative clause one may find وما —see Bro., p. 194; W II, 332A-D.

آذَنْتُ منها الحَيَّ 'as a result of which/by which I [should have/could easily have] reached the ear of/have alerted the tribe.' مِن may indicate the causal point of departure—see W II, 131B-C. It is not necessary to change مِنْها into بِها .

سَقَطْتُ لِوَجْهِي I fell on my face; see above, مَضَى لِسَبِيلِه (text, p. 131, note p. 135).

أُغْمِيَ عَلَيَّ (lit., covering was done over me), I lost consciousness; see W II, 167C, for similar expressions. The passive is used because the agent is not indicated; hence الجارِيَةُ المَغْشِيُّ عَلَيْها , and Koran I: 6 غَيْرِ المَغْضُوبِ عَلَيْهِمْ , etc.—see W II, 268A-C; *Admin.* p. 71. Cf. also Index, s.v. *al-muqaddam.*

فَكَأَنَّ and it was as though, it seemed, it appeared that...

بَقِيَ here: to remain in the same place.

رَفَعْتُ صَوْتِي بالعَوِيل I raised my voice wailing.

يَرْحَمُ اللهُ God will/God may have mercy. The imperfect is sometimes used in the sense of an optative; see Index.

أَسْعَدْنَنِي بالبُكاءِ they assisted me/joined me in weeping; see Dozy.

أَقامَ here has to be taken as one of the 'sisters of كان,' though it is not mentioned as such in Wright's Grammar; translate, "they continued like this," i.e., assisting me. Cf. the variant فَلَمْ نَزَلْ .

رَثَوْهُ "they commemorated him," or (more likely) "composed elegies/ditties on him [celebrating his career and his character]." *Rithā'* is the most common term for the elegy as a genre, and *marthiya* for a poem belonging to this genre. The genre was often practiced by the female relatives of a warrior; see *EI*2, s.v.

MARTHIYA.

اِكْتَحَلَ to put on كُحْل(kohl), a cosmetic (antimony, collyrium, or some other substance) used not only to give the eyelids a black color, but also considered a remedy for eye disease; see Martin Levey, *Early Arabic Pharmacology*, Leiden 1973, pp. 94-95; G. Jacob, *Altarabisches Bedouinenleben* (reprint Hildesheim, 1967), pp. 44, 148, 238, and index.

إِثْمِد see Jacob, p. 238, 'antimony.'

مخيط perhaps to be read مِخْيَط; if this is not another word for 'comb' (see next note), one could think of a cord or pin used to separate one's hair into two tresses; cf. Dozy and L. For women's hair-does, see A. Musil, *The Manners and Customs of the Rwala Bedouins*, New York 1928, pp. 118, 175, and index.

مُشْط comb.

دَهَنَ to use an ointment. Perhaps sesame oil, which L relates specifically to the term دُهْن 'ointment,' and which is mentioned in Martin Levey, *The Medical Formulary or* Aqrābādhīn *of al-Kindī*, Madison 1966, pp. 285-86, as a remedy for head pains.

مِنْ صُداع for the sake of/because of a headache. For the pattern *fu'āl* indicating "sickness or ailment" or "sound" see W I, 113C-D.

خافَ على . . . من to be afraid for (على) [the harm that might happen to] somebody/something as a result of (من). . . .

بَصَر eyesight; probably in reference to migraine, which can cause a temporary impairment of vision.

مَصْبُوغ dyed. See G. Jacob, *Altarabisches Beduinenleben*, reprint, Hildesheim 1967, p. 140.

ولا 'nor,' takes up a previous negation. لا may also coordinate two negations—e.g., لا صَدَّقَ ولا صَلَّى , "he neither believed [the truth of the revelation] nor performed the *salāh*," where one should not take the negation as an introduction to a negative optative such as لا رَحِمَهُ الله , "May God not have mercy on him"; see W II, 2B-D, 327A-C; Bro., p. 177.

إزار although frequently used in the sense of 'loincloth,' here clearly used for a garment covering most of the body; see art. LIBĀS in *EI*2, s.v. (pp. 732b-733a).

ولا أزال and I shall not cease.

الشِّعْرَ كُلَّهُ the whole poem. The term شِعْر 'poetry' may also be applied to a single poem.

وهذا الغناءُ بَعْضُهُ (perhaps one should read في بعضه) and this music (i.e., the music attributed to Mālik [b. Abī 'l-Samḥ] on p. 201) was set to part of it (i.e., part of these lines as quoted earlier in the biography of Jamīl on p. 130 of the same volume of the *Aghānī*). The *Aghānī* seems to be the only text where this poem is documented; the modern editions of the *Dīwān* of Jamīl (see *GAS* II, 406-8) do not give any further references.

ألا to be taken as an interjection: O! up! come! etc.—see W I, 294C.

مَنْ لِ who is there for. . ., 'who is ready to help. . .'—see Vagl. II, 264; *WKAS*, s.v., p. 14b.

مَلَّ to be bored; here in the sense of 'to lose interest in the beloved.'

فَيَذْهَلُ either a poetic licence (so that the two hemistichs of the first line of the poem may be made to rhyme), as فَ requires a subjunctive after a negation (W II, 30 C-D); or فَ is to be taken in the sense of 'thereupon.' For a similar phrase see *Ar. Syntax*, p. 462: لا أنتَ تَنْهَى القلبَ عنها فيَذْهَلَ.[9]

ذَهَلَ to dismiss something, put something out of one's mind.

أفاقَ to wake up, to wake up after a swoon; here: to come to one's senses after infatuation.

تَعَزَّى to endure patiently, seek consolation.

أَجْمَلُ elative of جَميلٌ often means 'becoming,' cf. W II, 263C-264A; cf. also Koran XII:18: فَصَبْرٌ جَميلٌ interpreted as فَصَبْرٌ جَميلٌ (أَجْمَلُ) , "and therefore (to show) becoming patience is more seemly."

The line could be translated as follows: "Who assists (can/will/shall assist) a heart that cannot forget and give up grieving? Come to your senses, [Jamīl,] for enduring the breach with (عَنْ , lit. 'away from') Buthayna is more becoming." Jamīl has created a scandal by showing his love for Butahayna, who is already married. He has been admonished by his father. In this line the poet speaks to his heart/mind (قلب) urging it to accept the inevitable.

A Note on Diptotes

بُثَيْنَةُ this name is diptote (مَمْنوعٌ من الصَرْفِ). Distinguishing diptotes and triptotes is essential when it comes to scanning poetry, even though the poet may violate the rules as a poetic license, and even though there is often disagreement on whether a proper name or a place name is diptote or triptote. For a detailed discussion of the question, see W I, 242C-247B (and cf.

---

9 *Aghānī* XXII, 130, 359 (see also VIII, 153). This line is in *Dīwān*, ed. F. Gabrieli, in *Rivista degli studi orientali*, XVII, Rome 1938, p. 158; idem., ed. Ḥ. Naṣṣār, Cairo 1967, p. 160.

I, 177D-183); Vagl. I, 57-58, and II, 30-32; shorter discussion in Bro., pp. 87-88. Some of the most important rules are the following:

Diptote are:

(1) all proper names that are either feminine or have the feminine ending, regardless of whether they are names of women or men, e.g. سُعادُ ، زَيْنَبُ ، فاطِمَةُ (women), طَلْحَةُ (man), مِصْرُ and مَكَّةُ (place names and therefore fem.), عَقْرَبُ (man's name, but derived from a fem. substantive, see W I, 180A; for names of tribes see W II, 292A and 296C).

(2) proper names that are not of Arabic origin, e.g. إبْراهِيمُ , except certain monosyllabic names, such as لُوطٌ , Lot.

(3) proper names ending in ان , e.g. عُثْمانُ , except when derived from common substantives, e.g. سِنانٌ from سِنان , 'spear head.'

(4) proper names of the type فُعَلُ , e.g. عُمَرُ .

(5) proper names resembling verbal forms, e.g. يَزِيدُ or شَمَّرُ (resembles verb شَمَّرَ).

(6) proper names that for some other reason would be diptote, e.g. زَكَرِيَّاءُ (the اءُ ending is diptote; the name would be diptote in any case because it is a name of foreign origin) and عادِياءُ . In the same category, according to the Arab grammarians, are indeclinable names such as يَحْيَى .

(7) adjectives of the form أَفْعَلُ , e.g. أَحْمَدُ (exceptions in W I, 240D).

(8) هِنْدُ / هِنْدٌ is an example of a proper name which can be diptote or triptote, "though the former is preferred" (W). Names of tribes may be diptote (Vagl., II, 32).

Names ending in *-i* such as قَطامِ are indeclinable.

XIII. Ibn Jubayr, *Riḥla*

The *Riḥla* of Ibn Jubayr, Muḥammad b. Aḥmad al-Kinānī (539 or 540–614), or, by its full title *Tadhkira bi 'l-akhbār 'an ittifāqāt al-asfār*, is perhaps the most famous travelogue in Arabic, judging by the number of translations it has seen. There was a partial edition and an Italian translation by the famous Sicilian nationalist, Michele Amari, in *Journal asiatique* VI–VII, 1845–46 (still not completely outdated), a second Italian translation by C. Schiaparelli in 1906, both now outdated; an English translation by R. J. C. Broadhurst (London 1952),[1] a French translation by M. Gaudefroy-Demombynes (Paris 1949–65),[2] and a German translation by Regina Günther ([Thienemann] Stuttgart 1985)—not counting the numerous partial translations, e.g., M. Fleischhammer, *Altarabische Prosa* ([Reklam Verlag] Leipzig 1991), pp. 192–97; U. Rizzitano, *Storia e cultura nella Sicilia Saracena* (Palermo 1975), pp. 305–17; F. Gabrieli, *Viaggi e viaggiatori arabi* ([Sansoni] Firenze 1975), pp. 84–87; and discussions in scholarly publications.[3] Shortly before I completed annotating this section on Sicily, I saw a Catalan translation by F. Maillo Salgado, *Ibn Yubayr, A través del Oriente* (Barcelona 1988).

Of great interest is Adelgisa De Simone, "Trapani, Marsala e Mazara in una compilazione araba del secolo XIV," in *Studi arabo-islamici in memoria di U. Rizzitano*, Liceo Ginnasio Gian Giacomo Adria di Mazara del Vallo (Trapani 1980), a translation of a certain Muḥammad b. 'Abd al-Mun'im al-Ḥimyarī, whose *al-Rawḍ al-mi'ṭār fī khabar al-aqṭār* (ed. I. 'Abbās, Beirut 1975) dating from the fourteenth century quotes Ibn Jubayr extensively.[4]

The text prepared by W. Wright and revised by M. J. de Goeje (Leiden 1907) was based on a late, poorly written manuscript in the Leyden University Library and a few quotations in books by later authors. However, this Leyden manuscript must have been based on a good original; the author of this reader found in handwritten catalogues in Rabat three more manuscripts. These manuscripts offered

[1] Apparently based on Schiaparelli's translation.

[2] The fourth volume, which contains indexes, was added in 1965. This volume also contains important additions and corrections by G. S. Colin.

[3] See the article IBN JUBAYR in *EI2*. An interesting study on Ibn Jubayr in Arabic is Ḥ. Mu'nis (Monès), *Ta'rīkh al-Ghughrāfiya wa 'l-ghughrāfiyyīn fī 'l-Andalus* (Madrid 1386/1967), pp. 425–52, and index.

[4] See pp. 45–46 for the much debated identity of the author.

variant readings,[5] but few of them were of real importance. I have in a few places referred to manuscripts of Ibn Jubayr's work, three of which were not known at the time de Goeje revised Wright's edition.[6] I did not undertake to correct de Goeje's text on the basis of these manuscripts, since the translations without exception follow this text and did not take any variants into consideration.

I have attempted to take note of all translations.[7] While keeping in mind that, in translating a text which has some difficult passages and, at times, a strange vocabulary, one may sometimes disagree, I nevertheless did not find many of the translations very satisfactory. The translation by Broadhurst follows the Italian by Schiaparelli, and the French translation contains several mistakes (in part corrected in the fourth volume). The translation of pp. 323–28 of the Arabic text in *Altarabische Prosa* was the only one I found mostly (but not invariably) accurate. For this reason and, still more, because the manuscripts are beautiful and legible, I have appended photographs of sections of the text from one manuscript. The third manuscript was, at the time I saw it, in a bad state of preservation and could not be photographed without risking severe damage.

Ibn Jubayr seems to have owed his fame chiefly to his skills as a poet and a secretary, writing what one must assume were stylish letters in rhymed prose. Lisānaddīn Ibn al-Khaṭīb (d. 776) one of his many biographers,[8] makes a distinction between his *naẓm*, his *nathr*, and his *kalām mursal*. In the section presented here, one finds both ordinary prose and rhymed prose. Unfortunately, his rhymed prose is not outstanding (though Lisānaddīn qualifies it as *badī'*, 'stylistically outstanding') and he often uses it in the *Riḥla* in 'purple passages,' where historians, as well as art historians, would have been pleased if for the sake of clarity he had avoided it and used clear ordinary prose instead. His *naẓm*,

---

[5] See S. A. Bonebakker, "Three manuscripts of Ibn Jubayr's Riḥla," in *Rivista degli studi orientali* XLVII, 235–45 (omits variants that are not considered important).

[6] A reader of this size does not allow a complete list of references to manuscript variants (*apparatus criticus*). Moreover, one manuscript had deteriorated so much that I could only consult it in a few places. Some of the readings I found I have indicated as "variant" or "one/two mss have," limiting myself to important cases, and without indicating (as required in an *apparatus criticus*) what, if anything, I found in other manuscripts. There seems to be a fourth manuscript from which some passages are quoted in the translation of Gaudefroy-Demombynes. I have disregarded these readings, since they mostly confirm the readings found elsewhere, and because the notes in the Gaudefroy-Demombynes edition may not be accurate and complete. A new edition of the complete text, not only the section on Sicily, would be desirable.

[7] The translation by Günther was not available to me.

[8] See p. 3 of the Arabic introduction to the ed. by Wright and de Goeje.

'poetry,' is of better quality. His *dīwān*, 'collected poems,' is said to have been voluminous. Ibn Jubayr is also said to have composed many elegies (*marāthī*) in memory of his wife, whose death made a deep impression on him.

The *Riḥla* deals with Ibn Jubayr's first journey in 585–87. The chief aim was the pilgrimage to Mecca. He made two more such pilgrimages. After the death of his wife, we see him moving from Granada to Malaga, to Ceuta, and to Fez. Were these moves the result of the death of his wife, which had made him depressed and restless? Or did he find it profitable to teach the many *ḥadīth* he had heard during his journeys in different places? In any case, he decided on a third pilgrimage, which ended with a stay in Alexandria, where, after a further period of teaching, he died. "Prayers at his grave are answered," adds one biographer.

The story goes that Ibn Jubayr, serving a member of the Almohad family in his capacity as a secretary, was invited by his employer to share seven goblets of wine with him. Seeing no way to escape from what he was told to do, he drank and was rewarded with seven goblets of *dīnārs*. He then vowed to use the money for a pilgrimage. He received further assistance from his employer, sold some property, and set out on his journey (Wright and de Goeje, introd., p. 28). Modern scholars have doubted the truth of the story, pointing to his inclination to Sufism (*taṣawwuf*); but his strong religious convictions, apparent on almost every page of the *Riḥla*, may well be a sufficient explanation. Another story (introd., p. 25) relates how he helped arrange a marriage between the daughter of a *qāḍī* and a man who had initially been refused. The marriage was no success, and the husband complained to Ibn Jubayr. The latter, holding himself responsible for what had happened, not only helped dissolve the marriage, but also offered the unfortunate husband to cover, from his own pocket, the expenses incurred for the wedding.

According to a certain Abū 'l-Ḥasan al-Shārī (introd., p. 6), the *Riḥla* was not put together by Ibn Jubayr himself, but by a pupil. I can find no good reason to take this isolated statement seriously. The descriptions of the journey and of Ibn Jubayr's reactions are far too vivid to be considered second-hand work; nor was al-Shārī's statement apparently taken seriously by Lisānaddīn, since he quotes it without any further comment.

For further information see, in addition to the references quoted above, Lisānaddīn Ibn al-Khaṭīb, *al-Iḥāṭa fī akhbār Gharnāṭa*, ed. M. 'A. 'Inān, Cairo 1393–94, II, 230–39; H. A. R. Gibb, Ibn Baṭṭūṭa, *Travels in Asia and Africa*, London 1957–, index; A. Gateau, "Quelques observations sur l'intérêt du voyage d'Ibn Jubayr," in *Hespéris* XXXVI:3–4 (1949), 289–312; and the chrestomathy of R. Blachère and H. Darmaun, *Géographes arabes*, Paris 1957, pp. 318–48. For the *riḥla* genre see the small but attractive collection of translations by F. Gabrieli, *Viaggi e viaggiatori arabi*, Florence (Sansoni) 1975. Marginally connected, but interesting is: *Giornata di Studio: Testimonianze degli arabi in Italia,* Roma, Accademia Nazionale dei Lincei, 1988.

Lisānaddīn Ibn al-Khaṭīb (d. 778/1375) offers in his *A'māl al-a'lām,* ed. A. M. al-'Abbādī under the title *Ta'rīkh al-Maghrib al-'Arabī fī 'l-'aṣr al-wasīṭ,* (Casablanca 1964) several quotations from Ibn Jubayr's *Riḥla* to which I have occasionally referred in the notes.

A most interesting work offering reconstructions of some of the buildings visited by Ibn Jubayr, as well as excellent photographs, quotations from Amari's translation of Ibn Jubayr, and indexes is G. Bellafiore, *Architettura in Sicilia nelle età islamica e normanna (827–1194)*, especially pp. 21–22, 26–27, 57–58, 126–28, 142–44, 147–49, and 169, note 2.

In the notes a few references have been made to Amari's *Storia dei Musulmani di Sicilia,* 2nd ed. in three volumes (Pampolini, Catania 1933–39). This monumental study is not easily available.

Of some interest is a passage in al-Marrākushī, Abū 'Abdallāh Muḥ. b. Muḥ., *al-Dhayl wa-'l-takmila,* ed. I. 'Abbās (Beirut 1965), vol. V, 2, pp. 689–93, where we find in brief outline a journey undertaken in 633, the main purpose of which was again the *ḥajj*. There is an involuntary stay in Sicily; the rest of the itinerary follows that of Ibn Jubayr roughly in the opposite direction, and the unfortunate traveler died in 635 on his way home to Egypt.

From: Ibn Jubayr, *Riḥla*, ed. W. Wright and M. J. de Goeje (Leiden 1907), pp. 323-37.

ذكر مدينة مسّينة من جزيرة صقلية اعادها الله تعالى

هذه المدينة موسم تجّار الكُفّار، ومقصد جواري البحر من جميع الاقطار،، كثيرة الارفاق برخاء الاسعار، مظلمة الآفاق بالكفر لا يقرّ فيها لمسلم قرار،، مشحونة بعَبَدة الصلبان تغصّ بقاطنيها، وتكاد تضيق ذرعاً بساكنيها،، مملوءة نَتْناً ورجسا، موحشة لا توجد لغريب انسا، اسواقها نافقة حفيله، وارزاقها واسعة بإرْغاد العيش كفيله،، لا تزال بها ليلَك ونهارَك في امان، وإن كنتَ غريب الوجه واليد واللسان،، مستندة الى جبال قد انتظمت حضيضها وخناديقها والبحر يعترض امامها في الجهة الجنوبيّة منها ومرساها اعجب مراسي البلاد البحريّة لان المراكب الكبار تدنو فيه من البرّ حتى تكاد تمسّه وتُنْصب منها الى البرّ خشبة يتصرّف عليها فالحمّال يصعد بحمله اليها ولا يحتاج لزواريق في وسقها ولا في تفريغها الا ما كان مرسيّا على البُعْد منها يسيرا فتراها مصطفّة مع البرّ كاصطفاف الجياد في مرابطها واصطبلاتها وذلك لإفْراط عمق البحر فيها وهو زقاق معترض بينها وبين الارض الكبيرة بمقدار ثلاثة اميال ويقابلها منه بلدة تعرف بريَّة وهي عمالة كبيرة، وهذه المدينة مسّينة راس جزيرة صقلية وهي كثيرة المدن والعمائر والضياع وتسمِيَتُها تطول وطول هذه الجزيرة صقلية سبعة ايّام وعرضها مسيرة خمسة ايّام وبها جبل البُرْكان المذكور وهو يأتزر بالسُحب لإفْراط سموّه ويعتمُّ بالثلج شتاءً وصيفا دائما، وخصبُ هذه الجزيرة اكثر من ان

يوصف وكفى بانها ابنة الاندلس في سعة العمارة وكثرة الخصب والرفاهة مشحونة بالأرزاق على اختلافها، مملوءة بانواع الفواكه واصنافها، لكنها معمورة بعَبَدة الصلبان يمشون في مناكبها ويرتعون في اكنافها،، والمسلمون معهم على املاكهم وضياعهم، قد حسّنوا السيرة في استعمالهم واصطناعهم،، وضربوا عليهم إتاوة في فصلين من العام يؤدّونها، وحالوا بينهم وبين سعة في الارض كانوا يجدونها،، والله عز وجل يُصْلِح احوالهم، ويجعل العقبى الجميلة مَآلهم،، بمنّه، وجبالها كلّها بساتين مثمرة بالتفّاح والشاه بلّوط والبندق وللإجّاص وغيرها من الفواكه وليس في مسّينة هذه من المسلمين الا نفر يسير من ذوي المِهَن ولذلك ما يستوحش بها المسلم الغريب، وأحسن مدنها قاعدة ملكها والمسلمون يعرفونها بالمدينة والنصارى يعرفونها ببَلاَرْمة وفيها سُكْنى الحَضَريّين من المسلمين ولهم فيها المساجد والاسواق المختصّة بهم في الارباض كثير وسائر المسلمين بضياعها وجميع قُراها وسائر مدنها كسَرْقُوسة وغيرها لكن المدينة الكبيرة التي هي مسكن ملكها غليام اكبرها واحفلها وبعدها مسّينة وبالمدينة ان شاء الله يكون مقامنا ومنها نؤمّل سفرنا الى حيث يقضي الله عز وجل من بلاد المغرب ان شاء الله، وشأن ملكهم هذا عجيب في حسن السيرة واستعمال المسلمين واتّخاذ الفتيان المجابيب وكلّهم او اكثرهم كاتم ايمانه متمسّك بشريعة الاسلام وهو كثير الثقة بالمسلمين وساكن اليهم في احواله والمهمّ من اشغاله حتى ان الناظر في مطبخته رجل من المسلمين وله جملة من العبيد السُود المسلمين وعليهم قائد منهم ووزراؤه

وحُجّابه الفتيان وله منهم جملة كبيرة هم اهل دولته والمرتسمون بخاصّته وعليهم يلوح رونق مملكته لانهم متّسعون في الملابس الفاخرة والمراكب الفارهة وما منهم الا مَنْ له الحاشية والخَوَل والاتباع ولهذا الملك القصور المشيَّدة والبساتين الانيقة ولا سيّما بحضرة ملكه المدينة المذكورة وله بمسّينة قصر ابيض كالحمامة مطلّ على ساحل البحر وهو كثير الاتّخاذ للفتيان والجواري وليس في ملوك النصارى اترف في الملك ولا انعم ولا ارفه منه وهو يتشبَّه في الانغماس في نعيم الملك وترتيب قوانينه ووضع اساليبه وتقسيم مراتب رجاله وتفخيم ابَّهة الملك وإظْهار زينته بملوك المسلمين وملكه عظيم جدّا وله الاطبّاء والمنجّمون وهو كثير الاعتناء بهم شديد الحرص عليهم حتى انه متى ذُكر له ان طبيبا او منجّما اجتاز ببلده امر بإمْساكه وادرّ له ارزاق معيشته حتى يُسْليه عن وطنه والله يعيذ المسلمين من الفتنة به بمنّه وسِنُّه نحو الثلاثين سنة كفى الله المسلمين عاديته وبسطته ومن عجيب شأنه المتحدَّث به انه يقرأ ويكتب بالعربيّة وعلامته على ما اعلمنا به احدُ خَدَمته المختصّين به الحمد لله حقّ حمده وكانت علامة ابيه الحمد لله شكرا لأنْعُمه، واما جواريه وحظاياه في قصره فمسلمات كلّهنّ ومن اعجب ما حدّثنا به خديمُه المذكور وهو يحيى بن فِتْيان الطرّاز وهو يطرّز بالذهب في طِراز الملك ان الافرنجيّة من النصرانيّات تقع في قصره فتعود مسلمة تعيدها الجواري المذكورات مسلمة وهنَّ على تكتُّم من ملكهنّ في ذلك كلّه ولهنّ في فعل الخير امور عجيبة وأُعْلِمنا انه كان في هذه الجزيرة زلازل مرجفة ذُعر

لها هذا المُشْرِك فكان يتطلّع في قصره فلا يسمع الا ذاكراً لله ولرسوله من نسائه وفتيانه وربّما لحقتْهم دهشة عند رؤيته فكان يقول لهم ليذكرْ كلُّ احد منكم معبودَه ومن يدين به تسكينا لهم، واما فتيانه الذين هم عيون دولته واهل عمالته في ملكه فهم مسلمون ما منهم الا من يصوم الاشهر تطوُّعا وتأجُّرا ويتصدَّق تقرُّبا الى الله وتزلُّفا ويفتكّ الاسرى ويربّي الاصاغر منهم ويزوّجهم ويحسن اليهم ويفعل الخير ما استطاع وهذا كلّه صُنْع من الله عز وجل لمُسلمي هذه الجزيرة وسرٌّ من اسرار اعتناء الله عز وجل بهم لقينا منهم بمسّينة فتى اسمه عبد المسيح من وجوههم وكبرائهم بعد تقدمة رغبة منه الينا في ذلك فاحتفل في كرامتنا وبرّنا واخرج الينا عن سرّه المكنون بعد مراقبة منه في مجلسه ازال لها كلَّ مَنْ كان حوله ممن يتّهمه من خُدّامه محافَظةً على نفسه فسألنا عن مكّة قدّسها الله وعن مشاهدها المعظّمة وعن مشاهد المدينة المقدّسة ومشاهد الشام فاخبرناه وهو يذوب شوقا وتحرُّقا واستهدى منّا بعض ما استصحبناه من الطُّرف المباركة من مكّة والمدينة قدّسهما الله ورغب في ان لا نبخل عليه بما امكن من ذلك وقال لنا انتم مُدْلون بإظْهار الاسلام فائزون بما قصدتم له رابحون ان شاء الله في متجركم ونحن كاتمون ايماننا خائفون على انفسنا متمسّكون بعبادة الله واداء فرائضه سرًّا معتقلون في ملكة كافر بالله قد وضع في اعناقنا ربقةَ الرقّ فغايتُنا التبرُّك بلقاء امثالكم من الحجّاج واستهداء أدْعيتهم والاغتباط بما نتلقّاه منهم من تُحَف تلك المشاهد المقدّسة لنتّخذها عُدّةً للايمان، وذخيرةً للاكفان،، فتفطّرت قلوبنا له إشْفاقا

ودعونا له بحسن الخاتمة واتحفناه ببعض ما كان عندنا مما رغب فيه وابلغ في مجازاتنا ومكافاتنا واستكتَمَنا سائرَ اخوانه من الفتيان ولهم في فعل الجميل اخبار ماثوره، وفي افتكاك الاسرى صنائع عند الله مشكوره،، وجميع خدمتهم على مثل احوالهم ومن عجيب شأن هؤلاء الفتيان انهم يحضرون عند مولاهم فيحين وقت الصلاة فيخرجون افذاذا من مجلسه فيقضون صلاتهم وربّما يكونون بموضع تلحقه عين ملكهم فيسترهم الله عز وجل فلا يزالون باعمالهم ونيّاتهم وبنصائحهم الباطنة للمسلمين في جهاد دائم والله ينفعهم ويجمل خلاصهم بمنّه، ولهذا الملك بمدينة مسّينة المذكورة دار صنعة (البحر) تحتوي من الاساطيل على ما لا يُحصى عددُ مراكبه وله بالمدينة مثل ذلك، فكان نزولنا في احد الفناديق واقمنا بها تسعة ايّام فلمّا كان ليلة الثلثاء الثاني عشر للشهر المبارك المذكور والثامن عشر لدجنبر ركبنا في زورف متوجّهين الى المدينة المتقدّم ذكرُها وصرنا قريبا من الساحل بحيث نبصره رايَ العين وارسل الله علينا ريحا شرقيّة رُخاءً طيّبة زجّت الزورق اهنأَ تزجية وسرنا نسرح اللحظ في عمائر وقرى متّصلة وحصون ومعاقل في قُنَن الجبال مشرفة وابصرنا عن يميننا في البحر تسع جزائر قد قامت جبالا مرتفعة على مقربة من برّ الجزيرة اثنتان منها تخرج منهما النار دائما وابصرنا الدخان صاعدا منهما ويظهر بالليل نارا حمراء ذات أَلْسُن تصعد في الجوّ وهو البُرْكان المشهور خبرُه وأعْلمنا ان خروجها من منافس في الجبلين المذكورين يصعد منها نفس ناريّ بقوّة شديدة تكون عنه النار وربّما

قُذِف فيها الحجر الكبير فتلقي به في الساعة الى الهواء لقوّة ذلك النفس وتمنعه من الاستقرار والانتهاء الى القعر وهذا من اعجب المسموعات الصحيحة، واما الجبل الشامخ الذي بالجزيرة المعروف بجبل النار فشأنه ايضا عجيب وذلك ان نارا تخرج منه في بعض السنين كالسيل العَرِم فلا تمرّ بشيء إلا احرقتْه حتى تنتهي الى البحر فتركب ثبجه على صفحه حتى تغوص فيه فسبحان المبدع في عجائب مخلوقاته لا اله سواه الى ان حللنا عشيَّ يوم الاربعاء بعد يوم الثلثاء المؤرَّخ مرسى شفلوذي وبينها وبين مسّينة مجرى ونصف مجرى.

ذكر مدينة شفلوذي من جزيرة صقلية اعادها الله

هي مدينة ساحليّة كثيرة الخصب واسعة المرافق منتظمة اشجار الاعناب وغيرها مرتَّبة الاسواق تسكنهم طائفة من المسلمين وعليها قُنّة جبل واسعة مستديرة فيها قلعة لم يُرَ امنع منها اتّخذوها عُدّةً لاسطول يفجؤهم من جهة البحر من جهة المسلمين نصرهم الله، وكان اقلاعنا منها نصفَ الليل فجئنا مدينة ثِرمة ضحوة يوم الخميس بسير رُوَيْد وبين المدينتين خمسة وعشرون ميلا فانتقلنا فيها من ذلك الزورق الى زورق ثانٍ اكتريناه لكون البحريّين [الذين] صحبونا فيه من اهلها.

ذكر مدينة ثرمة من الجزيرة المذكورة فتحها الله

هي احسن وضعا من التي تقدّم ذكرها وهي حصينة تركب البحر وتشرف عليه وللمسلسين فيها ربض كبير لهم فيه المساجد ولها قلعة سامية منيعة وفي اسفل البلدة

حمّة قد اغنَتْ اهلها عن اتّخاذ حمّام وهذه البلدة من الخصب وسعة الرزق على غاية والجزيرة بأسرها من اعجب بلاد الله في الخصب وسعة الارزاق، فاقمنا بها يوم الخميس الرابع عشر للشهر المذكور ونحن قد ارسينا في وادٍ باسفلها ويطلع فيه المَدُّ من البحر ثم ينحسر عنه وبتْنا بها ليلة الجمعة ثم انقلب الهواء غربيّا فلم نجدْ للاقلاع سبيلا وبيننا وبين المدينة المقصودة المعروفة عند النصارى ببلارمة خمسة وعشرون ميلا فخشينا طول المقام وحمدنا الله تعالى على ما انعم به من التسهيل في قطع المسافة في يومين وقد تلبث الزواريق في قطعها على ما أعْلمنا به العشرين يوما والثلاثين يوما ونيّفا على ذلك فاصبحنا يوم الجمعة منتصَف الشهر المبارك على نيّة من المسير في البرّ على أقْدامنا فنفذنا لطِيَّتنا وتحمّلنا بعض اسبابنا وخلّفنا بعض الاصحاب على الاسباب الباقية في الزورق وسرنا في طريق كانها السوق عمارةً وكثرةَ صادر ووارد وطوائف النصارى يتلقّوننا فيبادرون بالسلام علينا ويؤنسوننا فرأينا من سياستهم ولين مقصدهم مع المسلمين ما يوقع الفتنة في نفوس اهل الجهل عصم الله جميع امّة محمّد صلعم من الفتنة بهم بعزّته ومنّه فانتهينا الى قصر سعد وهو على فرسخ من المدينة وقد اخذ منّا الإعْياءُ فمِلْنا اليه وبِتْنا فيه وهذا القصر على ساحل البحر مشيَّد البناء عتيقه قديم الوضع من عهد ملكة المسلمين للجزيرة لم يزل ولا يزال بفضل الله مسكنا للعُبّاد منهم وحوله قبور كثيرة للمسلمين اهل الزهادة والورع وهو موصوف بالفضل والبركة مقصود من كلّ مكان وبازائه عين تعرف بعين المجنونة وله باب وثيق

من الحديد وداخله مساكن وعلاليّ مُشْرِفة وبيوت منتظمة وهو كامل مرافق السكنى وفي اعلاه مسجد من احسن مساجد الدنيا بهاءً مستطيل ذو حنايا مستطيلة مفروش بحُصُر نظيفة لم يُرَ احسن منها صنعةً وقد عُلِّق فيه نحو الاربعين قنديلا من انواع الصفر والزجاج وامامه شارع واسع يستدير باعلى القصر وفي اسفل القصر بئر عذبة فبتْنا في هذا المسجد احسنَ مبيت واطيبه وسمعنا الاذان وكُنّا قد طال عهدنا بسماعه واكرمنا القوم الساكنون فيه وله امام يصلّي بهم الفريضة والتراويح في هذا الشهر المبارك، وبمقربة من هذا القصر بنحو الميل الى جهة المدينة قصر آخر على صفته يعرف بقصر جعفر وداخله سقاية تفور بماء عذب، وابصرنا للنصارى في هذه الطريق كنائس مُعَدّة لمرضى النصارى ولهم في مدنهم مثل ذلك على صفة مارستانات المسلمين وابصرنا لهم بعكّة وبصُور مثل ذلك فعجبنا من اعتنائهم بهذا القدر، فلمّا صلّينا الصبح توجّهنا الى المدينة فجئنا لندخل فمُنِعنا وحُمِلنا الى الباب المتّصل بقصور الملك الافرنجيّ اراح الله المسلمين من ملكته وأدّينا الى المستخلف من قِبَله ليسألنا عن مقصدنا وكذلك فعلُهم بكلّ غريب فسُلِك بنا رحاب وابواب وساحات ملوكيّة وابصرنا من القصور المشرفة والميادين المنتظمة والبساتين والمراتب المتّخذة لاهل الخدمة ما راع ابصارنا، واذهل افكارنا،، وتذكّرنا قولَ الله عز وجل وَلَوْلَا أَنْ يَكُونَ ٱلنَّاسُ أُمَّةً وَاحِدَةً لَجَعَلْنَا لِمَنْ يَكْفُرُ بِٱلرَّحْمٰنِ لِبُيُوتِهِمْ سُقُفًا مِنْ فِضَّةٍ وَمَعَارِجَ عَلَيْهَا يَظْهَرُونَ وابصرنا فيما ابصرناه مجلسا في ساحة فسيحة قد احدق

بها بستان وانتظمت جوانبها بلاطات والمجلس قد اخذ استطالة تلك الساحة كلّها فعجبنا من طوله وإشْراف مناظره فأعْلمنا انه موضع غداءِ الملك مع اصحابه وتلك البلاطات والمراتب حيث تقعد حُكّامه واهل الخدمة والعمالة امامه فخرج الينا ذلك المستخلف يتهادى بين خديمين يحفّان به ويرفعان اذياله فابصرنا شيخا طويل السَبَلة أبيضها ذا ابّهة فسألَنا عن مقصدنا وعن بلدنا بكلام عربيّ ليّن فاعلمناه فاظهر الاشفاق علينا وامر بانصرافنا بعد ان احفى في السلام والدعاء فعجبنا من شأنه وكان اوّل سؤاله لنا عن خبر القسطنطينيّة العظمى وما عندنا منه فلم يكن عندنا ما نُعلمه به وقد نقيّد خبرها بعد هذا، وكان من اغرب ما شاهدناه من الامور الفتّانة ان احد مَنْ كان قاعدا عند باب القصر من النصارى قال لنا عند انصرافنا عن القصر المذكور تحفّظوا بما عندكم يا حجّاج من العُمّال الممكّسين لئلا يقعوا عليكم وظنّ ان عندنا تجارة تقتضي التمكيس فاستجاب له احد النصارى فقال ما اعجب امرك يدخلون حرم الملك ويخافون من شيء ما كنت اودُّ لهم الا آلافا من الرباعيّات اَنهضوا بسلام لا خوف عليكم فقضينا عجبا مما شاهدناه وسمعناه وخرجنا الى احد الفنادق فنزلنا فيه وذلك يوم السبت السادس عشر للشهر المبارك والثاني والعشرين لدجنبر وفي خروجنا من القصر المذكور سلكنا بلاطا متّصلا مشينا فيه مسافة طويلة وهو مسقّف حتى انتهينا الى كنيسة عظيمة البناء فأعْلمنا ان ذلك البلاط مَمْشى الملك الى هذه الكنيسة.

ذكر المدينة التي هي حضرة صقلية اعادها الله

هي بهذه الجزائر امّ الحضاره، والجامعة بين الحسنَيْن غضارة ونضاره،، فما شئتَ بها من جمال مخبر ومنظر، ومراد عيش يانع أخضر،، عتيقة انيقه، مشرقة مؤنقه،، تتطلّع بمراى فتّان، وتتخايَل بين ساحات وبسائط كلّها بستان،، فسيحة السكك والشوارع، تروق الابصار بحسن منظرها البارع،، عجيبة الشان، قُرْطُبيّة البنيان، مبانيها كلّها بمنحوت الحجر المعروف بالكَذّان،، يشقّها نهر معين، ويطّرد في جنباتها اربع عيون،، قد زخرفت فيها لملكها دنياه، فاتّخذها حضرةَ ملكه الافرنجيّ اباده الله،، تنتظم بلبّتها قصورُه انتظام العقود في نحور الكواعب، ويتقلّب من بساتينها وميادينها بين نزهة وملاعب،، فكم له فيها لا عُمِرت به من مقاصير ومصانع، ومناظر ومطالع،، وكم له بجهاتها من ديارات قد زخرف بنيانها، ورفه بالإقْطاعات الواسعة رُهْبانها، وكنائس قد صيغ من الذهب والفضّة صلبانها،، وعسى الله عن قريب ان يصلح لهذه الجزيرة الزمان، فيعيدها دار ايمان، وينقلها من الخوف للإمان،، بعزّته انه على ما يشاء قدير، وللمسلمين بهذه المدينة رسم باقٍ من الايمان يعمرون اكثر مساجدهم ويقيمون الصلاة باذان مسموع ولهم ارباض قد انفردوا فيها بسكناهم عن النصارى والاسواق المعمورة بهم وهم التجار فيها ولا جمعة لهم بسبب الخطبة المحظورة عليهم ويصلّون الاعياد بخطبة دعاءُهم فيها للعبّاسيّ ولهم بها قاضٍ يرتفعون اليه في احكامهم وجامع يجتمعون للصلاة فيه ويحتفلون في وقيده في هذا الشهر المبارك واما

المساجد فكثيرة لا تحصى واكثرها محاضر لمعلّمي القرآن وبالجملة فهم عزباء عن اخوانهم المسلمين تحت ذمّة الكفّار ولا امن لهم في اموالهم ولا في حريمهم ولا ابنائهم تلافاهم الله بصنع جميل بمنّه، ومن جملة شبه هذه المدينة بقرطبة والشيء قد تشبّه بالشيء من احدى جهاته ان لها مدينة قديمة تعرف بالقصر القديم هي في وسط المدينة الحديثة وعلى هذا المثال موضوع قرطبة حرسها الله وبهذا القصر القديم ديار كانّها القصور المشيّدة لها مناظر في الجوّ مظلمة تحار الابصار في حسنها، ومن اعجب ما شاهدناه بها من امور الكُفران كنيسة تعرف بكنيسة الأنْطاكيّ ابصرناها يوم الميلاد وهو يوم عيد لهم عظيم وقد احتفلوا لها رجالا ونساء فابصرنا من بنيانها مراى يعجز الوصف عنه ويقع القطع بانه اعجب مصانع الدنيا المزخرفة جُدرها الداخلة ذهب كلّها وفيها من الواح الرخام الملوّن ما لم يُرَ مثله قطُّ قد رُصّعت كلّها بفصوص الذهب وكُلّلت باشجار الفصوص الخُضْر ونُظِم اعلاها بالشمسيّات المذهَّبات من الزجاج فتخطف الابصار بساطع شعاعها وتُحدث في النفوس فتنة نعوذ بالله منها وأعْلمنا ان بانيها الذي تنسب اليه انفق فيها قناطير من الذهب وكان وزيرا لجدّ هذا الملك المشرك ولهذه الكنيسة صومعة قد قامت على اعمدة سوارٍ من الرخام ملوّنة وعلت قبّة على اخرى سوارٍ كلّها فتعرف بصومعة السواري وهي من اعجب ما يُبْصَر من البنيان، شرّفها الله عن قريب بالاذان،، بلطفه وكريم صنعه، وزيُّ النصرانيّات في هذه المدينة زيّ نساء المسلمين فصيحات الالسن ملتحفات منتقبات خرجن في هذا

العيدَ المذكور وقد لبسن ثيابَ الحرير المذهَّب والتحفن اللُحُف الرائقة وانتقبن بالنُقُب الملوَّنة وانتعلن الاخفاف المذهَّبة وبرزن لكنائسهنّ او كُنُسهنّ حاملات جميع زينة نساء المسلمين من التحلّي والتخضُّب والتعطُّر فتذكّرنا على جهة الدُعابة الادبيّة قولَ الشاعر

انّ مَنْ يدخل الكنيسة يوما   يلقَ فيها جآذرًا وظِباءا

ونعوذ بالله من وصف يدخل مدخل اللغو، ويؤدّي الى اباطيل اللهو،، ونعوذ به من تقييد، يؤدّي الى تفنيد،، انه سبحانه اهل التقوى واهل المغفرة، فكان مقامنا بهذه المدينة سبعة ايّام ونزلنا بها في احد فناديقها التي يسكنها المسلمون وخرجنا منها صبيحة يوم الجمعة الثاني والعشرين لهذا الشهر المبارك والثامن والعشرين لشهر دجنبر الى مدينة اطرابُنْش بسبب مركبين بها احدهما يتوجّه الى الاندلس والثاني الى سَبْتَة وكُنّا اقلعنا الى الاسكندريّة فيه وفيهما حجّاج وتجّار من المسلمين فسلكنا على قرى متّصلة وضياع متجاورة وابصرنا محارث ومزارع لم نَرَ مثل تربتها طيبا وكرما واتّساعا فشبّهناها بقَنْبانية قرطبة او هذه اطيب وامتن وبتْنا في الطريق ليلة واحدة في بلدة تعرف بعَلْقَمة وهي كبيرة متّسعة فيها السوق والمساجد وسكّانها وسكّان هذه الضياع التي في هذه الطريق كلّها مسلمون وقمنا منها سحر يوم السبت الثالث والعشرين لهذا الشهر المبارك والتاسع والعشرين لدجنبر فاجتزنا بمقربة منها على حصن يعرف بحصن الحمّة وهو بلد كبير فيه حمّامات كثيرة وقد فجرها الله ينابيع من

الارض واسالها عناصر لا يكاد البدن يحتملها لإفراط حرّها فاجزنا منها واحدة على الطريق فنزلنا اليها عن الدوابّ وارحنا الابدان بالاستحمام فيها ووصلنا الى اطرابنش عصر ذلك اليوم فنزلنا فيها في دار اكتريناها.

ذكر مدينة اطرابنش من جزيرة صقلية اعادها الله

هي مدينة صغيرة الساحه، غير كبيرة المساحه،، مسوَّرة بيضاء كالحمامة مرساها من احسن المراسي واوفقها للمراكب ولذلك ما يقصد الروم كثيرا اليها ولا سيّما المقلعون الى برّ العدوة فان بينها وبين تُونِس مسيرة يوم وليلة فالسفر منها اليها لا يتعطّل شتاءً ولا صيفا الا رَيْثَما لا تهبّ الريح الموافقة فمجراها في ذلك مجرى المجاز القريب وبهذه المدينة السوق والحمّام وجميع ما يحتاج اليه من مرافق المدن لكنها في لهوات البحر لإحاطته بها من ثلاث جهات واتّصال البرّ بها من جهة واحدة ضيّقة والبحر فاغرٌ فاهُ لها من سائر الجهات فاهلها يرون انه لا بدَّ له من الاستيلاء عليها وان تَرَاخَى مدى ايّامها ولا يعلم الغيب الا الله تعالى وهي مرفقة موافقة لرخاء السعر بها لانها عل محرث عظيم وسكّانها المسلمون والنصارى ولكلا الفريقين فيها المساجد والكنائس، وبرُكنها من جهة الشرق مائلا الى الشمال على مقربة منها جبل عظيم مفرط السموّ متّسع في اعلاه قُنّة تنقطع عنه وفيها معقل للروم وبينه وبين الجبل قنطرة ويتّصل به في الجبل للروم بلد كبير ويقال ان حريمه من احسن حريم هذه الجزيرة جعلها الله سبيا للمسلمين وبهذا الجبل الكروم والمزارع وأعْلمنا ان به نحو

اربعمائة عين متفجّرة وهو يعرف بجبل حامد والصعود اليه هيّن من احدى جهاته وهم يرون ان منه يكون فتح هذه الجزيرة ان شاء الله ولا سبيل ان يتركوا مسلما يصعد اليه ولذلك ما اعدّوا فيه ذلك المعقل الحصين فلو احسّوا بحادثة حصّلوا حريمهم فيه وقطعوا القنطرة واعترض بينهم وبين الذي في اعلاه متّصل به خندق كبير وشأن هذا البلد عجيب فمن العجب ان يكون فيه من العيون المتفجّرة ما تقدّم ذكره واطرابنش في هذا البسيط ولا ماء لها إلّا من بئر على البُعْد منها وفي ديارها آبار قصيرة الأرْشية ماؤها كلّها شريب لا يُساغ، وألفينا المركبين اللذين يرومان الإقْلاع الى المغرب بها ونحن ان شاء الله نؤمّل ركوب احدهما وهو القاصد الى برّ الاندلس والله بمعهود صنعه الجميل كفيل بمنّه، وفي غربيّ هذه البلدة اطرابنش المذكورة ثلاث جزائر في البحر على نحو فرسخين منها وهي صغار متجاورة احداها تعرف بمليطمة والاخرى بيابسة والثالثة تعرف بالراهب نُسِبت الى راهب يسكنها في بناء اعلاها كانه الحصن وهي مكمن للعدوّ والجزيرتان لا عمارة فيهما ولا يعمر الثالثة سوى الراهب المذكور.

شهر شوّال عرّفنا الله يمنه وبركته

استهلّ هلاله ليلة السبت الخامس من ينير بشهادة ثبتت عند حاكم اطرابنش المذكورة بانه ابصر هلال شهر رمضان ليلة الخميس ويوم الخميس كان صيام اهل مدينة صقلية المتقدّم ذكرُها فعيّد الناس على الكمال بحساب يوم الخميس المذكور وكان مصلانا في هذا العيد مالبارك باحد مساجد اطرابنش المذكورة مع قوم من اهلها

امتنعوا من الخروج الى المصلّى لعذر كان لهم فصلّينا صلاة الغرباء جبر الله كلّ غريب الى وطنه وخرج اهل البلد الى مصلاهم مع صاحب احكامهم وانصرفوا بالطبول والبوقات فعجبنا من ذلك ومن إغْضاء النصارى لهم عليه، ونحن قد اتّفق كراؤنا في المركب المتوجّه ان شاء الله الى برّ الاندلس ونظرنا في الزاد والله المتكفّل بالتيسير والتسهيل ووصل امرٌ من ملك صقلية بعقلة المراكب بجميع السواحل بجزيرته بسبب الاسطول الذي يعمّره ويعدّه فليس لمركب سبيل للسفر الى ان يسافر الاسطول المذكور خيّب الله سعيه ولا تمّم قصده فبادر الروم الجنويّون اصحاب المركبين المذكورين الى الصعود فيهما تحصُّنا من الوالي ثم امتدّ سبب الرشوة بينهم وبينه فاقاموا بمركبَيْهم ينتظرون هواء يُقْلِعون به.

* * *

Notes to Page 147

مَسِّينَة Messina.

أعادَها اللهُ may God restore it [to the Muslims].

مَوْسِم [favorite] meeting place; facility for trade.

جَوارٍ sing. جارِيَة ship.

أقْطار sing. قُطْر region.

كَثيرَةُ الإرْفاقِ much in profit; offering much profit.

مُظْلِمَةُ الآفاقِ 'darkened in its horizons', 'though its horizon is darkened.'

لا يَقِرُّ . . . قَرارٌ there is no rest, comfort, way of feeling at home.

عَبَدَة sing. عابِد servant, worshiper.

صُلْبان sing. صَليب cross (as a Christian symbol).

غَصَّ بِ to choke on.

ضاقَ ذَرْعاً بِ (lit., to be unable to hold in one's embrace) to have no room for.

مَمْلوءَةً نَتْناً The subject is مَدينة —i.e., مَدينةٌ مَمْلوءةٌ نَتْناً . The verb مَلأ is construed with a double accusative (W II, 47C-48AC) In the passive, one of the two accusatives becomes a nominative (W II, 52A-D), and the same is true when the verb is replaced by a verbal adjective, as in دَلْوٌ مَمْلوءةٌ ماءً , corresponding to مُلِئَتِ ٱلدَّلْوُ ماءً .

رِجْس dirt, impurity; cf. Koran 22:30: فٱجْتَنِبوا الرِّجْسَ مِنَ الأَوْثان .

أَوْجَدَ to allow, let obtain.

نافِقَة حَفيلَةٌ profitable, full of people (i.e., merchants).

بِإِرْغادِ العَيْشِ كَفيلةٌ guaranteeing ease, comfort.

لا تَزالُ. . . في أَمان [yet] one always [enjoys] safety.

يَد probably 'doings.'

اِسْتَنَدَ إلى to lean against, cover the slopes of.

اِنْتَظَمَتْ . . . وخَنادِيقَها i.e., the foothills reach as far as the moats, link up with the moats. See p. 152 below (منتظمة أشجار الاعناب) and notes, p. 182.

خَنادِيقُ sing. خَنْدَق . See W I, 229A-B.

اِعْتَرَضَ (lit., to stand in the way) to stand/stretch out in front.

فِي الجِهَةِ الجَنُوبِيَّة i.e., in the direction of Syracuse.

مِنْهَا in relation to it (the city).

مَرَاسٍ sing. مَرْسًى harbor, port.

فِيهِ i.e., in the harbor.

تَمَسُّهُ to touch (i.e., the shore). This reading, suggested by Fleischer (in the notes to this page in Ed. Wright-de Goeje), is confirmed by two manuscripts in Rabat not known at the time Wright and de Goeje prepared their editions.

يُتَصَرَّفُ عَلَيْهَا on which one can move back and forth.

اِحْتَاجَ لِ more common is احتاج إلى .

زَوَارِيقُ sing. زَوْرَق small boat.

فِي وَسْقِهَا when engaged in loading them (i.e., the ships).

إِلَّا ما كان مَرْسِيًّا except for those [ships] that are at anchor (see Dozy for مَرْسِيًّا, root *r-s-w*).

اِصْطَفَّ to be lined up in a row (صَفّ).

مَعَ along.

جِيَاد sing. جَوَاد good horse, steed.

مَرَابِط sing. مَرْبِط place where a horse is tied, kept ready (see *EI* 1, s.v. RIBĀṬ).

اِصْطَبْل stable (from Greek σταβλίον).

فِيهَا at this [particular] place.

زُقاق strait (Ibn J. means the Strait of Messina).

منهُ on it (i.e., on the زقاق).

تُعْرَفُ بِرِيَّة known as, called Reggio [di Calabria]. See W I, 10B for the ending o represented by *tā' marbūṭa.*

هي عِمالةٌ كبيرة it is [part of] a large province.

رَأْس beginning, top.

بَلْدَة town. The difference between بَلَد and بَلْدَة is not clear; see footnote 27, below.

عَمائِر sing. عِمارة cultivated land (also 'building').

ضِياع sing. ضَيْعَة settlement, domain.

تَسْمِيَتُها تَطُول mentioning them all would take too long. For the verbal noun pattern *taf'ila* see W I, 115B, 116C-D, 122C.

بُرْكان volcano.

اِئْتَزَر (lit., put on an إِزار , a garment fastened around the middle), here: to cover oneself.

Notes to Page 148

كَفَى بِ See *WKAS*, s.v; W II, 161A and D and compare:

كَفاهُ it was sufficient for him (one object).

كَفاهُ شَرَّ فُلانٍ he protected him against the evil of so and so—i.e., the danger of being attacked by so-and-so (two objects).

I. كَفَى بِالسَّلامَة داءً lit., being in good health is enough by way of illness—i.e., if one is healthy, one is still sick enough (because one is on one's way to death notwithstanding); cf. Latin, *senectus ipse est morbus.*

II. كَفَى بِالمَرْءِ فَضْلاً أَنْ تُعَدَّ مَعايِبُهُ When it comes to merit, it is enough for a man that his faults can be counted.

A way of remembering these two last constructions is that I could be expressed by كَفَتِ السلامةُ , and that II could also be expressed: كَفَى المَرْءَ فَضْلاً .

كَفَى بِأَنَّها "it is sufficient to keep in mind that it. . .," "just keep in mind that it. . . ."

سَعَة العِمارَة extent of cultivation.

رَفاهَة welfare.

على ٱخْتِلافِها "in their variety," "of [many] different kinds."

مَناكِب . . . أكناف (figurative) "the shoulders and flanks of it (the land),"—its mountains and plains (?).

أمْلاك sing. مِلْك [landed] property.

حَسَّنوا السِّيرَة they have a decent way.

اِسْتِعْمال employment.

اِصْطِناع probably: treatment, see Dozy.

ضَرَبَ على impose.

إِتاوة tribute, tax.

حالَ بَيْنَ to come between, interfere; here: rob of, deny.

كانوا يَجِدُونَها which they (the Muslims) once had at their disposal.

عُقْبَى outcome.

مَآل eventual destination; best translated, "[May God] eventually [grant them a good outcome]." Bl., p. 252, line 1, observes that the imperfect may be used in the sense of an optative. This may very well be the case in this sentence, even though Ibn Jubayr frequently uses the perfect also in the sense of an optative. An alternative would be: "One may/can hope that God will better their circumstances," or, "One may/can hope that God will eventually. . ."[9]

مَنّ favor.

شاه بَلُّوط chestnut.

بُنْدُق hazel nut.

إِجَّاس pear (in Spain), elsewhere 'plum'; see Dozy.

ذَوو المِهَنِ artisans, workers.

ولذلك ما يَسْتَوْحِشُ and it is for this (very) reason that [in that city a foreign Muslim] feels uncomfortable. ما is not, as one might think, a negation, but rather a corroborative particle as in: والتشبيه يَزيد المَعْنى وُضوحاً ويُكْسِبُهُ
تَأْكيداً ولهذا ما أطبَقَ جميعُ المتكلِّمون من العرب والعَجَم عليه, "The simile makes the concept [one intends to express] clearer and lends force to it; for that reason all people engaged in disputation among Arabs and non-Arabs apply it (i.e., use the simile)." For further examples see pp. 159 (l. 6) and 160

---

9   Cf. also sentences such as p. 340, lines 7-8 in the Ed. of Wright-de Goeje (not included in this Reader): والله . . . . يُيَمِّنُ مَقْصَدَنا "One may hope that God will grant us luck [in undertaking this journey]."

(l. 3) and notes ad loc.; W II, 264B; Dozy II, 563b; *Glossarium*, s.v. ما ; Th. Nöldeke, *Zur Grammatik des classischen Arabisch*, bearbeitet. . . von A. Spitaler, Darmstadt 1963, pp. 61-62.

قاعِدَة capital, important city; see Dozy.

ملك can be read مَلِك (king) or مُلْك (kingdom).

عَرَّفَهُ بِ to name.

بالَرْمَة Palermo.

سُكْنَى habitat.

حَضَرِيّ settled; here: city dweller (see Dozy, s.v.).

أَرْباض sing. رَبَض quarter, suburb.

ولَهُمْ فيها المَساجِدُ they have there (in Palermo) mosques and their own (lit. 'special to them') markets and suburbs. Two manuscripts in Rabat have respectively: (1) المساجد ولأسواق المختصة بهم والأرباض . . . ; *and* (2). . . من المساجد والأسواق المختصة بهم والأرباض The reading بالأرباض is supported by a third manuscript which, at the time I saw it, could hardly be consulted without causing severe damage. The reading of (1) is supported by Lisānaddīn, p. 103. Cf. also p. 156 (l. 14), below.

كثير not in the Rabat manuscripts and probably to be deleted; for *kathīr, qarīb*, etc. without fem. ending, see Vagl. II, 55; L, s.vv.

. . . بضِياعِها the pronouns refer to صقلية (Sicily).

سَرَقُوسَة Syracuse.

لكِنّ begins a new sentence, probably intended as a footnote to his description of Messina.

مُقام sojourn.

شَأْن (lit., affair) doings, behavior, circumstances, way of ruling, facts known about.

اتَّخَذَ to choose, adopt, employ [servants, officers]. The verb اتَّخَذَ has many different meanings; see Index.

مَجابيب sing. مَجْبُوب castrated.

كاتِمٌ إيمانِهِ hiding his beliefs, professing his belief in secret. Because كاتِم is being used in the sense of a present, one can also read كاتِمٌ إيمانَهُ, though this is not common; see Bro., p. 172; W II, 64B-65A; and cf. p. 150 (l. 14), below (ونحن كاتمون إيمانَنا).

تَمَسَّكَ بِ to hold on to, persevere in.

كَثيرُ الثقة having much confidence. ثقة (from وثِق) is also used as a substantive in the sense of 'reliable authority on Prophetic tradition.'

سَكَنَ إلى to rely upon.

أَحْوال (lit., circumstances, situations); here: day-to-day decisions (?).

حَتَّى أَنَّ to such an extent that. . . / and this goes so far that. . . . When a substantive precedes immediately, which is the case here, one does not use حَتَّى إنَّ, see *Ar. Syntax*, pp. 479-80.

ناظِر overseer.

قائِدٌ مِنْهُمْ a chief, leader [chosen] from among them.

Notes to Page 149

حُجَّابه الفِتْيان Fityān, pl. of فَتَى. In Spain the term *fityān* was used for officials, originally slaves (*ghilmān*, not necessarily castrated), who had been promoted to a high rank after having been freed. Since the term *ḥājib* came to be used for vizier, it is possible that the *fityān* mentioned here were the king's most trusted counselors, as also suggested by the context (cf. أَهْلُ دَوْلَتِهِ , 'the people of/pillars of his state').

اِرْتَسَمَ بِ to assume the title of (see Dozy); here: to enjoy the distinction of being/belonging to.

خاصَّة close associates, trusted counselors.

لاحَ to appear.

رَوْنَق splendor.

اِتَّسَعَ في to be able to allow themselves (see Dozy); Lisānaddīn reads متّسعون في الملابس .

وما مِنْهُمْ إلَّا مَنْ لَهُ not belong to them except those who have. . .; there is not anybody among them who does not have. . .

الحاشِيَةُ والخَوَلُ والأَتْباعُ the article indicates the whole category as in "the Englishman loves outdoor life" (see W I, 269B-C); the three terms are probably synonyms or near synonyms. One could translate: "a retinue, stewards, and an escort."

مُشَيَّد translate: "beautiful," "well-built."

حَضْرَة مُلْكِهِ seat of his government.

أَطَلَّ على to overlook.

اِتَّخَذَ to adopt [as slaves or servants]; cf. p. 148, l. 14 (اتّخاذ الفتيان المجابيب).

للفِتْيان one of the two manuscripts clearly reads للقِيان , and this reading is supported by Lisānaddīn, p. 104.

قَيْنَة plur. قِيان singing girl; etymology uncertain, see article ḲAYNA in *EI*2.

جارِيَة here: slave girl.

أَتْرَفُ في المُلْكِ (lit., more luxurious in his kingship), "displaying more luxury at his court."

أَنْعَمُ . . . أَرْفَهُ more pleasant, more comfortable.

اِنْغَمَسَ في to plunge into; here: to enjoy to the full extent.

يَتَشَبَّهُ في . . . بِمُلوكِ المُسْلِمِين in. . . he resembles (see Dozy), imitates the kings of the Muslims.

تَرْتِيب قوانِينِهِ in setting/establishing his statutes (?).

وَضْع أَسالِيبِهِ instituting his protocol(s); أَسالِيب , sing. أُسْلوب (root *s-l-b*).

تَقسيم مَراتِبِ رِجالِهِ making distinctions in rank between his officials, ranking his officials.

تَفْخِيم أُبَّهَةِ المُلْكِ وإِظْهار زِينَتِهِ enhancing the pomp of his kingdom and displaying its splendor.

مُلْكُهُ عَظِيمٌ جِدًّا possibly: the power/extent of his kingdom is very considerable; he exercises enormous power.

كَثِيرُ الاعْتِناء very much interested.

شَدِيدُ الحِرْصِ very eager.

أَدَرَّ له to make ample/plentiful

أَسْلَى عن to make forget.

أَعاذَهُ مِنْ to offer a refuge, to protect against.

عادِيَتَهُ وبَسْطَتَهُ take as a hendiadys: his evil [exercise of] power.

المُتَحَدَّثُ بِهِ which is being spoken about, which people tell each other.

عَلامَة formula corresponding to our "initialing" placed between the *basmalah* and the text of the document, usually a religious formula.

على ما according to what...

المُخْتَصِّينَ بِهِ those close to [the king]; cf. p. 148, l. 10, above (المساجد والأسواق المختصّة بهم).

حَقَّ حَمْدِهِ... شُكْراً لأَنْعُمِهِ as he is entitled to be praised... out of gratitude for his blessings. Respectively, absolute object and accusative indicating motive; see W II, 54A-B, and 121A-C. Two manuscripts have على أنعمه.

حَظايا plur. of حَظِيَّة (root *ḥ-ẓ-y*) favorite [of a ruler]; see W I, 222C.

بن فِتْيان reading uncertain. The *Ibn* in the name is supported by two manuscripts.[10]

طَرّاز embroiderer.

طِراز workplace where embroidery was done, often ornamented with Arabic characters; see *EI*2, s.v.

إفْرَنْجِيّ Western European; see *EI*2, s.v. IFRANDJ.

الإفرنجيّة a Western European girl; cf. the verse quoted below, p. 158.

وَقَعَ to end up; translate: "... when it so happens that she ends up in his castle."

---

10 The name *Fityān* is supported by Abū Bakr al-Mālikī, *K. Riyāḍ al-nufūs*, ed. Ḥ. Mu'nis (Cairo 1951), I, 476, and elsewhere. The poet Ibn Ḥayyūs (394-473) had the *kunya* Abū Fityān.

عادَ to become (one of the 'sisters of كان '; see W II, 102A and D).

على see W II, 169C-170B: على indicates a condition of any kind, cf. the proverb النّاسُ على دِينِ مُلوكِهِم , "people follow the religion of their kings."

تَكَتَّمَ to practice secrecy.

زَلازِل sing., زَلْزَلَة earthquake.

ذَعَرَ to frighten.

Notes to Page 150

لها refers to زلازل , see *Ar. Syntax*, p. 246: with verbs in the passive one may translate *li/la* 'because of,' 'by,'—e.g., حتى ما أُراعُ له , "till I am no longer frightened by him."

المُشْرِك acceptance of the Trinity makes one a 'polytheist.'

تَطَلَّعَ to inspect; see Dozy.

دَهْشَة embarassment, consternation.

عند رُؤْيَتِهِ when they saw him.

فكان يَقُولُ لَهُمْ but then. . . / but every time he would say to them. . . .

لِيَذْكُرْ let mention, let pray to; see W II, 35B-D: لِ with jussive can be used in the sense of a command, advice, or suggestion.

مَعْبُودَهُ his object of worship.

مَنْ يَدِينُ به the object of his religious conviction.

تَسْكِيناً لَهُمْ to put them at ease.

عُيُون one of several plurals of عَيْن ; see W I, 226B. According to the dictionaries, أَعْيان would mean 'the important people,' 'the notables,' and عيون 'the sources,' 'the fountains,' or 'the spies'; but one cannot be certain that the meanings listed for عيون in the dictionaries are exhaustive. Because Ibn Jubayr on p. 343, l. 1, of Ed. Wright-de Goeje uses أعيان for 'notables,' it is unlikely that عيون here should be translated the same way. One should rather think of 'overseers'—'sources' in the sense of those who as administrators or inspectors guarantee income from taxes.

عِمالة administration.

الأَشْهُر see art. ṢAWM in *EI*2: four additional months of fasting are recommended in addition to Ramaḍān.

تَطَوُّعاً وتَأَجُّراً voluntarily and to win [more] heavenly reward.

اِفْتَكَّ to ransom slaves.

أَسْرَى , sing. أَسِير see W I, 220 A-C, for this plural that denotes injuries and defects.

الأَصاغِر مِنْهُمْ the children among them.

ما اَسْتَطاعَ 'as much as he can'; see *Ar. Syntax*, pp. 435-36, and W I, 273B-C: ما should be taken as an apposition to الخَيْر (lit., [namely] that which he can).

صُنْعٌ مِن الله the work of God (i.e., without God's inspiring these good deeds they would not take place).

سِرٌّ مِن أَسْرار one of the secrets—i.e., one of the secret manifestations.

اِعْتِناء concern.

عَبْد المَسيح Possibly a pseudonym or a nickname acceptable to Muslims and Christians alike, the *Masīḥ* being mentioned in the Koran.[11]

بَعْدَ تَقْدِمَةِ رَغْبَةٍ مِنْهُ إلينا في ذلك after he had extended/advanced an invitation to us to that effect; or, after he, from his side, had conveyed his wishes to that effect (i.e., to see us).

اِحْتَفَلَ في كَرامَتِنا he went out of his way in showing respect to us (كرامة may have the meaning of إكْرام).

أَخْرَجَ إلينا عَنْ سِرِّهِ المَكْنُون "he disclosed to us his closely concealed secret" (Glossary).[12] Form IV can indicate moving to a place/into a situation, entering upon a period of time. See W I, 35B-C.

مُراقَبَة inspection, cautionary measure.

لها the pronoun refers to مراقبة. Translate: on account of it, as a result of it.

اِتَّهَمَ to suspect.

مُحافَظَةً على نَفْسِه to guard his own safety.

---

11 See *K. al-Jalīs* (above, IV, ed. I. 'Abbās), Vol. IV, 8; Ṭabarī, *Annales*, Index, p. 358; *Wāfī*, XIX, 148, no. 128 (with references). The 'Abd al-Masīḥ b. Muḥammad mentioned in Ibn al-Qāḍī, *Durrat al-ḥijāl*, ed. M. A. Abū 'l-Nur (Cairo/Tunis 1974), III, 171, no. 1144 (variant: al-Samīḥ for al-Masīḥ) was probably a Muslim. The question is discussed in G. Gabrieli, *Il nome proprio arabo-musulmano, Memoria preliminare* (Rome 1915), pp. 21, 22, note 2; 27 (39c).

12 Variants: أخرج الينا and خرج الينا عن.

مَشاهِد sing. مَشْهَد place that is an object of pilgrimage, holy place.

يَذُوبُ شَوْقاً وتَحَرُّقاً lit., "he was melting as a result of his passionate longing and burning [desire to visit these places]"—i.e., burning desire almost made him faint.

اِسْتَهْدَى to ask for a present.

اِسْتَصْحَبَ to take along [from the pilgrimage].

طُرْفَة probably: souvenir.

بِما أَمْكَنَ مِنْ ذلك with that which [we felt] we could [give away] of these souvenirs, bring ourselves to give away.

مُدْلُونَ بِإِظْهارِ الإسلام (root *d-l-w*) [in a position] to profess Islam openly.

فازَ to be fortunate.

رابِحُونَ . . . في مَتْجَرِكم probably intended figuratively; Koran 2:16 uses the expression فما رَبِحَتْ تِجارَتُهُم in speaking of those who do not accept God's Message.

كاتِمونَ إِيمانَنا hiding our religious belief. See W II, 64B-C, and Bro. 172-73: when the participle has the meaning of the imperfect tense, there are two possible constructions, قاتِلُ النّاسِ and قاتِلٌ النّاسَ e.g., Koran 3:185 كُلُّ نَفْسٍ ذائِقَةُ المَوْتِ or ذائِقَةٌ المَوْتَ, both acceptable. In this case, however, the choice of the first alternative is stylistically determined by the sequence of undetermined predicates preceding and following كاتمون.

أداء الفَرائِض fulfilling one's religious obligations; also used specifically for fixed shares in an estate; see *EI*2, s.v. FARĀ'IḌ and FARḌ.

مُعْتَقَلونَ في مِلْكَةِ كافِرٍ shackled by being in the possession of an unbeliever.

رِبْقة loop, rope tying up animals.

رِقّ slavery (note the alliteration in the *rā'*).

غايَتُنا all we can do, the most that we can do.

أَدْعِيَة sing. دُعاء prayer. Cf. دَعَا لَهُ بِ he called upon [God]/ prayed for him that [things would end well].[13]

اِغْتَبَطَ to rejoice, be thankful for a gift or a blessing received.

تَلَقَّى to receive.

تُحَف, sing. تُحْفَة precious object (cf. مَتْحَف, 'museum'); here probably 'souvenir.'

مَشْهَد sacred place, commemorative structure; see the art. MA<u>SH</u>HAD in *EI*2.

عُدَّة لِلْإِيمان "means of strengthening one's belief" (?).

ذَخيرة للأَكْفان "provisions for the shrouds." See Dozy who, among other translations, mentions *relique, provision.* I am not aware of a custom among Muslims to put souvenirs in the grave at burial; أكفان could be a metaphor for "death." Note that the use here of rhymed prose limits the choice of suitable terms.

أَشْفَق to show compassion, to be concerned [about somebody].

---

13 Variant: واستكتمنا امره وانصرفنا من مجلسه بعد وداعه وقد قضينا عجبا من شأنه وعلى مثل وتيرته وشأنه سائر (وتيرة = conduct'). Gaudefroy-Demombynes' translation makes no mention of the existence of this variant in the manuscript in Fès he examined (see p. 144, note 6, above).

Notes to Page 151

أَتْحَفَ to give as a present.

أَبْلَغَ to go to the utmost.

اِسْتَكْتَمَ (with double object) he asked us to keep secret [the identity of]. . . .

سائِر W II, 206D-207A: the remainder, the remaining, the other. The term is, very confusingly, also used in the sense of "all," especially in later writers.

مَأْثُورة memorable [deeds].

اِفْتِكاك الأَسْرَى ransoming prisoners.

عِنْدَ الله in the presence of God [on the Day of Resurrection].

خَدَمَتهم their servants—apparently the servants of these *fityān* of high rank.

يَحْضُرُونَ عِنْدَ مَوْلاهُم they may be occasionally, they may find themselves in the presence of their master (the Norman king).

فيَحِينُ وَقْتُ الصَّلاةِ "and then the time for, while the time for the *ṣalāt* arrives."

أَفْذاذ, sing. فَذّ single.

لَحِقَ to overtake, to reach.

سَتَرَ to hide (in the sense that, miraculously, he can see them performing their *ṣalāt* but does not notice).

نِيَّة here probably 'their intention(s) to do whatever they are doing in the name of Islam'—cf. الأعمال بالنيّات, "[the value of good] deeds depends on intentions."

نَصِيحة counsel, advice, help.

بَاطِن inner, hidden, secret.

جِهاد Holy War (probably not intended here as a kind of 'spiritual *jihād,*' but in the sense that living at an outpost of Islam, they struggle to keep Islam alive).

واللهُ يَنْفَعُهُمْ May God (or: 'God will,' cf. p. 148, l. 5, above) make them benefit from their pious work.

ويُجْمِلُ خَلاصَهُمْ and grant them a deserved delivery [from their present distress]. Other translations of خلاص, such as 'reward', 'outcome' may be considered.

دار صَنْعَة dockyard.

(البحر) both manuscripts read للإنشاء, 'for construction.'

أساطيل pl. of أُسْطول (from Greek στόλος), fleet.

مَراكِبِهِ the pronoun refers to ما, i.e., "comprising of fleets (intended as plural?) that which (or: that [concerning] which [we can say]) the number of its ships cannot be counted."

المدينة Palermo is intended.

فَنادِيق irregular pl. of فُنْدُق, 'hotel,' 'inn' (Greek πανδοχεῖον); see W I, 229A-B: دَراهِيم for دَراهِم from sing. دِرْهَم.

ليلةَ الثَلاثاء or الثُلاثاء the night of (preceding) Tuesday; the Muslim day begins at sundown; see for instance (there are several handbooks on the subject) M. Ocaña Jimenez, *Tablas de conversión*. . . (Madrid-Granada 1946), p. 12.

دَجَنْبِر or دُجَنْبِر December; الشهر المبارك stands for Dhū 'l-Ḥijja.

المدينةِ المُتَقَدِّمِ ذِكْرُها the aforementioned city (Palermo); cf. notes, p. 35, above, and Index, s.v. *al-muqaddam.*

وصِرْنا قريباً من الساحِل [while sailing] we came close / were close to the shore.

صار, though one of the 'sisters of كان,' can mean not only 'to become,' but also 'to attain,' 'to end up,' 'to arrive.'

بِحَيْثُ 'so that'; W I, 288B-C, omits this adverb from his list.

رَأْيَ العَيْنِ cf. Dozy: *en ma présence.* One would be inclined to believe that telescopes existed. Most likely he means that nobody had to point out to him which direction one had to take to reach the coast.

رُخاءً soft wind (here used in apposition to ريحاً). See W I, 178B-C: names of various types of winds are fem. by analogy with ريح .

سَرَّحَ to let [one's eyes] travel over, feast one's eyes upon; see Dozy and Wehr.

عَمائِر sing. عِمارَة either 'cultivated stretches of land' or 'habitations'; see Dozy.

قُرًى plur. of قَرْيَة (W I, 199D) 'village,' 'small town.'

مُتَّصِلة uninterrupted, one following the other.

مَعاقِل plur. of مَعْقِل stronghold.

أَشْرَفَ to overlook, to be high.

تِسْع جَزائِر the Aeolian Islands (Isole Eolie) are nowadays counted as seven in number. One should probably read سبع , keeping in mind that تسع and سبع are graphically close. In one of the two manuscripts the numeral is illegible; the other has تسع.

جِبالاً مُرْتَفِعَةً *ḥāl* (circumstantial accus.) 'like high mountains.'

اثنتان منها he probably refers to Stromboli and Volcano, but Stromboli is too far to the north to be visible. For Volcano, see *Sicilia*, pp. 465-68.

على مَقْرُبَةٍ مِنْ at a close distance from.

ويَظْهَرُ بالليل ناراً حَمْراءَ "and at night it appears like / looks like red fire" (the smoke lights up because the fire in the crater shines on it). This description is accurate as far as Stromboli is concerned.

ذاتَ أَلْسُنٍ with [fiery] tongues.

المَشْهورُ خَبَرُهُ see p. 147, l. 17, above.

خُرُوجَها the pronoun ها refers to نار.

مَنافِس plur. of مَنْفَس breathing hole; here obviously 'crater.'

منها the pronoun ها refers to مَنافِس.

نَفَسٌ نارِيٌّ a fiery stream of air (actually gas).

تكون عنه النارُ "which causes this fire" (or what looks like it).

Notes to Page 152

ورُبَّما قُذِفَ فيها الحَجَرُ الكبيرُ The passage is obscure: it is difficult to assume that anybody would venture to walk up to the rims of the craters (Volcano or Stromboli) to throw stones into them. Perhaps one should read منها, i.e., from the edges of the منافس? On the other hand, قذف does not appear in the dictionaries in the sense of 'to fall,' but it could conceivably mean 'is ripped off' [from the edges by one of the bursts of gas]. Still another solution would be منها, i.e., from the depths of the منافس. Schiaparelli read قذف منها الحجرُ الكبيرُ فتلقي به النارُ الى الهواء. The two manuscripts also read فيها, but have مُسَوَّداً, 'blackened' for في الساعة.

وتَمْنَعُهُ من الاسْتِقْرارِ والانْتِهاءِ إلى القَعْرِ "and keeps it from coming to rest [in the crater] and reaching the bottom.

المَسْمُوعات the things one hears; cf. p. 34 (note on مُجَلَّدات).

بالجزيرة on the island of Sicily [itself] (he means the notorious volcano Etna).

أمَّا . . . فَ See W I, 292B: فَ often introduces the main clause after أمَّا.

تَخْرُجُ fem. to agree with نار, which here must be understood in the sense of 'stream of lava.'

السَيْل العَرِم meaning uncertain; see Koran xxxiv:16: "But they turned away and we sent against them the Flood of the Dyke *(Sayl al-'Arim).*" Ibn Jubayr takes *al-'Arim* apparently as an adjective, perhaps preferring the interpretation, "[torrent of which the rush] is not to be withstood" for *'arim.*

فتَرْكَبُ ثَبَجَهُ على صَفحِهِ "it rides the high sea [floating on] its surface." What he has in mind is apparently lava turning into pumice stone. Three manuscripts I have seen have طائرة على صفحه.

فَسُبْحانَ see W II, 72D-73C: Arab grammarians take several expressions of command, praise, etc. as objects to a verb from the same root that has to be understood, i.e. (أُسَبِّحُ) سُبْحانَهُ 'I praise His (God's) glory,' and (اِصْبِرْ) صَبْراً 'be patient!'

المُبْدِع 'the Unique [Creator],' one of the "Most Beautiful Names [of God]" (الأسماء الحُسْنَى), traditionally considered to be ninety-nine in number; see *EI2*, s.v. AL-ASMĀ' AL-ḤUSNĀ, where the term is translated as 'the Absolute Creator of beings.' These names often appear in proper names, e.g., 'Abd al-Ghaffār.

في عَجائِبِ مَخْلوقاتِهِ concerning / with regard to the the marvels of His creation: "The Unique Creator of Marvels."

عَجائِب sing. عَجِيبة miraculous thing.

سِوَى see W II, 209C-210A: 'another' (besides so-and-so), a near synonym of غَيْر.
Cf. also below, XIV, first poem.

إلى أنْ حَلَلْنا to be connected with صِرْنا on line 6 of the preceding page: "[and we pursued our course, noting all these remarkable sights] till we arrived. . . حَلَّ means literally 'to loosen [the strings tying luggage],' 'to alight.'

عَشِيَّ يومِ الأَرْبِعاءِ (late) in the afternoon / in the early evening of Wednesday.

بعد يوم الثَلَثاءِ / الثُلَثاءِ المُؤَرَّخ after Tuesday [of which we have indicated the date earlier], i.e., not at the end of Tuesday, the Muslim day beginning at sundown.

شُفْلوذي Latin Cephalœdium, modern Cefalù. Spelling uncertain: one manuscript has Shaflūdhī, the other Shuflūdhī. See also *Sicilia*, pp. 453 ff.

مَجْرَى (lit. 'course') a distance of 100 nautical miles.

ساحِلِيٌّ situated on the coast.

مُنْتَظِمة [having] neatly arranged [rows of vines]; another possible translation would be '[a town] surrounded by [rows of vines],' 'in the midst [of vines], cf. p. 147, انْتَظَمَتْ خَناديقُها; p. 154, بُيوت مُنْتَظِمة and ميادين منتظمة ; p. 155, انْتَظَمَت ; p. 156, تَنْتَظِمُ; and Dozy, s.v.[14]

---

14 Ibn Jubayr's understanding of the terms اتَّصَلَ and انْتَظَمَ is not always clear. On p. 252, lines 9-10, of the Wright-de Goeje edition, he speaks of a *balad* as واسِعُ الأَسْواقِ كَبيرُها مُتَّصِلُ الانْتِظامِ, which means that the terms cannot be considered near synonyms. From p. 158 of this Reader (مُتَّصِلة) it appears that اتَّصَلَ is a near synonym of تَجاوَرَ. اتَّصَلَ may be translated 'to be joined,' 'to follow one another,' 'to be attached to'—see p. 213, lines 1, 6, 9, 10, 20 of the Wright-de Goeje edition,

أَشْجار الأَعْنابِ vines.

مُرَتَّبَةُ الأَسْواقِ with well-arranged/convenient markets.

وعَلَيْها قُنَّةُ جَبَلٍ and above it is a mountain top.

واسِع [flat and] wide.

أَمْنَع (elative of مَنِيع) less accessible, more easy to defend.

اتَّخَذَ here: to take, to choose.

عُدَّة cf. above, p. 150, last line; here: refuge.

أُسْطول see above, p. 151, l. 8.

يَفْجَؤُهُمْ could attack them by surprise (cf. below, p. 153, l. 12, ما يُوقِعُ and note ad loc.).

مِنْ جِهَةِ . . . مِنْ جِهَةِ coming from/from the direction of. . ., from the side of/undertaken by. . .

أَقْلَعَ to set sail.

ثِرْمَة Termini Imerese (Latin: Thermae Himerenses). See *Sicilia*, pp. 441-42.

---

and cf. Fagnan, s.v., 'durer, se poursuivre.' Limiting oneself to those passages in the Wright-de Goeje edition where the context is of some help, it appears likely that the various meanings of انْتَظَمَ correspond to those listed by Dozy. انْتَظَمَ apparently means 'to surround,' e.g., as a necklace (p. 156 of this Reader, تَنْتَظِمُ), 'to frame,' 'to be connected with, adjacent,' 'to follow, to touch,' 'to be regularly, orderly arranged.'

رُوَيْد calm, easy.

ثانٍ used in the sense of آخَر.

لِكَوْنِ . . . مِنْ أَهْلِها because the sailors who were with us belonged there (in Termini) [and stayed].

وَضْع position.

رَكِبَ to dominate (fortified town).

أَشْرَفَ على to overlook.

Notes to Page 153

حَمَّة hot spring.

أَغْنَى عَنْ 'to enable to dispense with'; عَنْ is often used after verbs meaning or implying 'doing without, avoiding', cf. رَغِبَ عَنْ 'to have a desire [to stay] away from,' 'to hate' (the opposite of رَغِبَ في 'to desire')—see W II, 141B.

سَعَة (root *w-s-'*) ampleness, abundance. See W I, 118C, for the loss of the initial root consonant.

أَرْسَى to anchor.

مَدّ high tide.

اِنْحَسَرَ to withdraw.

اِنْقَلَبَ الهَواءُ غَرْبِيًّا the wind turned west.

سَبِيل here: 'means, possibility.'

بَلَرْمَة Palermo.

طُولَ المُقامِ a long stay, a long delay.

وحَمِدْنا اللهَ . . . على ما أَنْعَمَ بِهِ مِنْ . . . "and we praised God . . . for what he granted us of . . . / for his blessing us by . . . .

في قَطْعِ المَسافَةِ in [granting us to] cover the distance.

في يَوْمَيْنِ i.e., Wednesday and Thursday—cf. pp. 151, ll. 9-10, and p. 152, ll. 6-7.

زَوارِيق irregular plural of زَوْرَق —see W I, 229A-B.

ونَيِّفاً على ذلك 'or somewhat more than that'—see W I, 258A.

مُنْتَصَف middle, 15th day of the month—see W II, 249A.

على نِيَّةٍ مِنَ ٱلمَسيرِ with the intention of getting under way.

على أَقْدامِنا on foot.

نَفَذْنا لِطِيَّتِنا we set out to our destination. See Dozy, s.v. نفذ.

تَحَمَّلَ carry [on one's own back].

أَسْباب possessions.[15]

خَلَّفْنا . . . على . . . we left . . . in charge [of] . . .

كَأَنَّها السوقُ عِمارةً as busy (lit. populous) as a market. Cf. p. 158, l. 14 (السوق والمساجد) and the note on the use of the article.

---

15 Two manuscripts read: أسبابنا على أعناقنا.

صادرٍ ووارِدٍ coming and going.[16]

النَّصارَى the Christians; plural of نَصْرانِيّ. A form نَصْران exists, which would justify a plural of the type *fa'ālā* (see W I, 221D), but W I, 223C, lists the plural as irregular. See also L, s.v., and art. NAṢĀRĀ in *EI*2.

بادَرَ بِ to haste in doing something ('before somebody else does so' may be implied). For Muslims, being the first to greet was a sign of politeness.

آنَسَ to make somebody feel at ease, show friendliness (opposite of أَوْحَشَ).

سِياسَة here: 'way of handling.'

لِينِ المَقْصَدِ leniency, tolerance.

ما يُوقِعُ 'such as would easily create/bring about' (the imperfect can indicate something that could possibly happen).

فِتْنَة temptation.

جَهْل here: ignorance [of Christian doctrine and its mistakes].

عَصَمَ اللهُ may God protect.

صلعم abbreviation for صَلَّى اللهُ عَلَيْهِ وَسَلَّمَ, the benediction customarily used after the name of the Prophet.

قَصْرِ سَعْد former Muslim stronghold on the Pizzo Cannita near Palermo.[17]

---

16 Cf. the proverbial line of poetry:

أَصْدِرْ هُمُومَكَ لا يَقْتُلْكَ وارِدُها فكلُّ وارِدَةٍ يَوْماً لَها صَدَرُ

"Drive out your worries! Let not those that come kill you!
For all things coming shall one day pass on."

17 See G. B. Pellegrini, "Terminologia geografica araba in Sicilia," in *Annali del'*

أَخَذَ مِنْ to affect, take its toll from.

مِلْنا from مالَ to turn aside, to halt.

عَتِيقَةُ قَدِيمُ الوَضْعِ (the pronoun refers to بناء) old [of construction] and founded in early times.

. . . مِنْ عَهْدِ dating from the period of. The root *'-h-d* has a variety of meanings that are often difficult to keep apart. The following are some of the most frequent: 'period,' 'time at which something happened,' e.g., عَهْدي بِهِ قَرِيبٌ *I met him only recently*; 'command,' e.g., عَهِدَ إِلَيْهِ بِ *he charged, enjoined him to do something,* وِلايَةُ العَهْدِ *succession by way of covenant* (hence: وَلِيُّ العَهْدِ *heir apparent*); 'promise,' 'oath,' e.g., عَلَيَّ عَهْدُ الله لا أَفْعَلَنَّ كذا *I charge myself with an oath sworn to God [that shall take effect when] I shall not do such a thing* (see W II, 172D, 339D-340A, and note), i.e., *I promise to do it*; 'memory,' 'acquaintance,' e.g., ما لي عَهْدٌ بكذا *I do not remember such a thing,* عَهْدي بالعَرَبِ لا تُباعُ *From what I know of the Arabs (the Arab character), they are not for sale (they are not willing to accept a bribe or a deal)*; لام العَهْدِ (W I, 269C) definite article indicating something already known.

مَلَكَة government, rule.

لا يَزالُ probably to be translated as an optative.

وَرَع pious fear, zeal in avoiding sin.

مَقْصود goal [of pilgrimage?] (note that مَوْصوف and مَقْصود and لَهُ (last line of page) all refer to the castle) .

Istituto Orientale di Napoli, sez. long. 3 (1961), p. 185 (with references). See also K. Baedeker, *Southern Italy and Sicily,* Leipzig 1908, p. 314.

عَيْن المَجْنونَة the Spring of the Crazy [Woman] (?).

Notes to Page 154

مَساكِنُ وعَلالِيٌّ (from عُلِّيَّة) living quarters and upstairs rooms (or perhaps balconies, see Dozy); root علو or علل, see L, p. 2147b, and W I, 222B.

بُيُوت مُنْتَظِمَة uninterrupted series of rooms.

مُسْتَطيل oblong.

كامِلُ مَرافِقِ السُّكْنَى perfect in its living conveniences, has perfect....

حَنايا plur. of حَنِيَّة arcade or arched window; see W I, 221B-C.

الأَرْبَعِينَ قِنْدِيلاً instead of the older الأربعين القنديلاً; see W II, 244B.

يَسْتَدِيرُ بِأَعْلَى running around the highest point of...

كُنَّا قد طالَ عَهْدُنا بـ... "it had been a long time since we..." (see above).

وأَطْيَبَهُ (the pronoun suffix refers to مَبِيت) "we spent the night in the most convenient and pleasant way possible."

لَهُ the pronoun must refer to the mosque.

التَّراويح non-obligatory *ṣalāts* held in Ramaḍān; see *EI* 1-2, s.v.

قَصْر جَعْفَر place name. The ruins are still in existence under the name of "la Favara" or "Castello di Mare Dolce." See Amari, Index, *Sicilia* (Milano 1968), p. 179.

سِقايَة water supply, water basin.

كَنائِس plur. of كَنِيسَة church. Perhaps to be understood here in the sense of monastery with a hospital.

مَرْضَى for the pattern *fa'lā*, see note on أَسْرَى, p. 173 above.

مارِسْتان short for Persian *bīmāristān*: substantives of foreign origin often have sound fem. plurals—see W I, 198B.

عكّة and صور (Acre and Tyre) are towns on the Syrian-Palestinean coast.

اِعْتِناء concern, foresight.

قَدْر degree, extent.

جِئْنا لِنَدْخُلَ "we came there with the intention of entering," "we were about to enter."

أُدِّينا we were conveyed, handed over.

مُسْتَخْلَف lieutenant.

مِنْ قِبَلِ from the side of..., on behalf of...; see W II, 189D.

سُلِكَ بِنا رِحابٌ وَأَبْوابٌ وَساحاتٌ we were taken along squares, gates, and courtyards.

مُلوكِيّ kingly, majestic.

مَيادِين plur. of مِيدان here probably 'open square,' i.e., not surrounded by buildings.

مُنْتَظِمَة "one following the other" (?).

مَراتِب plur. of مَرْتَبة Glossary: servants quarters.

اِتَّخَذَ see Index.

راعَ to frighten; to be imposing, to excite admiration.

قَوْلَ اللهِ the Word of God [in the Koran, 43:33].

وَلَوْلا . . . يَظْهَرُونَ "And were it not that mankind would have become one community [there being then no distinction between Believers and Unbelievers] We might well have appointed, for those who disbelieve in the Beneficent, roofs of silver for their houses and stairs (of silver?) whereby to mount." See also the translation in W II, 7B. Ibn Jubayr probably means to say that the splendor of the castle almost suggests that, after all, God had decided to build a castle for a nonbeliever; in other words, he is only reminded of the passage in the Koran by what he sees.

أَبْصَرْنا فيما أَبْصَرْناهُ we noticed among other things.

مَجْلِس here: audience room (?).

فَسيح spacious.

أَحْدَقَ بِ to surround.

Notes to Page 155

اِنْتَظَمَ here: 'to be connected/adjacent.'

بَلاط Glossary: portico, gallery. Cf. above, p. 96 (text) and p. 99 (notes).

أَخَذَ to occupy.

مَناظِرُ plur. of مَنْظَر. See L and Dozy: rooms or balconies from which one can look out (apparently rooms upstairs).

حُكّام plur. of حاكِم. police officers, magistrates—see Dozy.

عِمالة governmental administration.

أَمامَهُ in front of him; apparently, 'at a short distance from him.'

تَهادَى to stride; and (more likely here) to walk with an uncertain gait, totter.

يَحُفَّانِ '[were] at his sides'; here perhaps: 'supporting him from both sides.'

سَبَلَة mustache.

ذو أُبَّهة inspiring reverence, of majestic appearance, dignified.

بَلَد homeland.

لَيِّن smooth, fluent.

أَشْفَقَ على to show concern, pity, sympathy for.

أَمَرَ بِانْصِرافِنا he gave orders that we [be allowed to] leave.

أَحْفَى to be kind, polite.

دُعاء [pronouncing] blessings. Cf. above, p. 151, l. 1, ودَعَوْنا لَهُ.

القُسطَنْطِينِيَّة العُظْمَى Constantinople.[18]

ما عِنْدَنا مِنْهُ what [information خَبَر] we might have/could provide.

. . .وَقَدْ نُقَيِّدُ "and we expect to write down. . ." For قَدْ, see Index. Ibn Jubayr is referring to a story (not in this Reader) that occurs on pp. 337-40 of Ed. Wright-de Goeje.

فَتَّانَة really tempting (in the sense that they would move the travelers to give up their inimical feelings towards the Christian monarch).

تَحَفَّظَ بِ to watch carefully over.

---

18 Two manuscripts have القسطنطية.

العُمَّال المُمَكِّسِين officials collecting taxes. See articles ZAKĀT and MAKS in *EI* 1-2.

اسْتَجَابَ the difference between this and أَجَابَ, considered a synonym, may be that اسْتَجَابَ means 'felt himself called upon to answer.'

ما أَعْجَبَ أَمْرَكَ "how unusual are your doings!" "how strange that you think that way!"

يَدْخُلونَ . . . وَيَخافونَ (intended as a question) "would they enter. . . would they fear. . . ?"

حُرُم pl. of حَرِيم, private quarters.

ما كُنْتُ أَوَدُّ See W II, 266B-C: *kāna* preceded by a negation may have the sense of the present. The sense seems to be: "I do not expect them [to return home having gained in trade, *tijāra,* with] less than thousands of *rubā'īs* (Glossary: quarter *dīnārs*)." The Wright-de Goeje edition (footnote), apparently feels that *wadda* here must have the sense of 'hope': "I hope that they will get nothing but some thousands of *rubā'īs*. . . ." "I should not wish them/like them [to go home] without at least. . ." would also be possible, considering the reputation of generosity of William II (placed by Dante in Paradise), which is here echoed by his court official.

نَهَضَ here: to leave.

لا خَوْفَ عَلَيْكُمْ you have nothing to fear.

قَضَى to reach the end/the utmost; "we were utterly amazed."

مُتَّصِل continuous; see above, p. 154, l. 11 (text), and note.

عَظِيمَة البِناء of enormous proportions.

مَمْشَى place covered on foot.

Notes to Page 156

حَضْرَة residence, capital.

الجَزائِر Two manuscripts read الجزيرة, which is preferable.

أُمّ الحَضارَة the center (lit. mother) of civilization.

غَضارَة ونَضارَة prosperity and fertility.

فَما شِئْتَ بِها مِنْ . . . you have there/find there whatever you want of...

مَخْبَر ومَنْظَر "things to see and hear."

ومَراد عَيْشٍ يانِعٍ أَخْضَر lit. pasture ground for life (means of subsistence) ripe and green; "a place where the ripe and green make life delightful." See Dozy, s.v. مَراد.[19]

عَتيقَة probably: elegant, but cf. above, p. 153, l. 15.

مُشْرِفَة مُؤْنِقَة "lofty and admirable."

تَتَطَلَّعُ بِمَرْأًى فَتّانٍ "it appears before your eyes offering an alluring sight."

تَخايَلَ to walk with a proud gait, to behave proudly; "it rises proudly with courtyards and open spaces full of flowers."

فَسيحَةُ السِكَكِ والشَّوارِعِ with roomy alleys and streets.

عَجيبَةُ . . . البُنْيانِ "a city of amazing character, built in the manner of Cordova."

---

19 Lisānaddīn, p. 105, has موارد 'sources,' 'means.'

مَبانٍ plur. of مَبْنًى edifice; for the plural see W I, 227A-B; I, 247A; and cf. the conflicting pattern *fa'ālin* (220C-221A), where the ending *-in* is part of this type of plural, and not derived from the last radical of the root as in مَبانٍ and جَوارٍ.

كَذَّان Glossary: tufa.

مَعِين bringing water at all times.

ويَطَّرِدُ . . . عُيون four springs flow at the city's sides (surrounding areas?).

زُخْرِفَتْ . . . دُنْياهُ "in this city the earthly life of its king (Sicily's king/the king residing in Palermo) is adorned" (cf. Koran X:25).

اتَّخَذَ to adopt, to select.

انْتَظَمَ here clearly 'to be strung around' (=to surround); the reference, according to Amari, *Storia*, III, 817, is to the castles surrounding the old city: la Ziza, La Cuba, Maredolce, etc.

كاعِبَة woman with full breasts, beautiful woman.

يَتَقَلَّبُ . . . بَيْنَ (subject: the King) to enjoy at will—see L. s.v. For بَيْنَ . . . وَ 'both. . . and. . .' see W II, 180C-181A.

مِنْ here: 'in.' See W II, 138D, and Index.

نَزْهَة two of the manuscripts have نُزَه, which is a better parallel to مَلاعِب.

فيها refers to حَضْرة.

لا عُمِرَتْ بِهِ (optative in parenthesis).[20]

مقاصير . . . مَطالِع perhaps: pavilions, palaces, belvederes, and towers. Glossary: مَصْنَع 'structure of any kind.' See also Dozy.

جِهاتِها its surrounding areas.

دِيارات plur. of the plur. of دَيْر. See W I, 231C-232D.

رفه one of the manuscripts reads رَفَّة or رُفَّة

إِقْطاع "fief." So in Christian terms; in an Islamic context this translation would not be correct—see *EI*2, s.v.

رُهْبان and صُلْبان plurals of the type *fuʿlān;* see W I, 218A-B.

عَسَى. . . أنْ followed by subjunctive—see W II, 108A-B.

زَمان time; here: fate, fortune; "[improve] its (the island's) lot," "[reverse] its fortune."

دار إِيمان abode of belief, country where Islam is professed.

ولِلْمُسْلِمِينَ . . . الإِيمان "the Muslims preserve on this island traces of their belief."

---

[20] Cf. the parenthesis in the following line of poetry:

إِنَّ الثَّمانينَ وبُلِّغْتَها قد أَحْوَجَتْ سَمْعي إلى تَرْجُمانِ

"The[se] eighty years [of mine]—and may you be made to reach them [too]—
Have put my hearing in need of an interpreter
(=somebody repeating these words)."

عَمَّرَ or عَمَرَ to frequent, keep up, keep in use.

أَقَامَ translate "observe their *ṣalāt* [and announce it]." Most likely, Ibn Jubayr has in mind أقام الصلاة in the sense of أَدامَ فِعْلَها, not the technical إقامة (verbal noun of أقام) which immediately precedes prayer and consists of a repetition of the أذان followed by the words قَد قامَتِ الصَّلاة. See L and art. IḴĀMA in *EI2*.

مَسْمُوع [clearly] audible.

اِنْفَرَدَ . . . عَنْ to be separated from.

النَّصارَى . . . بِسُكْناهُمْ Lisānaddīn, p. 106, reads بِأَسْمائِهِمْ وسكناهُم "where they live by themselves, bearing their [Muslim] names (?)," i.e., not disguising their Muslim identity.

وهم التُّجَّارُ فيها and they are the merchants there ('the merchants par excellence'?), or, 'they themselves work there.'

الخُطْبَة المَحْظُورَة عليهم the *khuṭba* [on Friday] which is forbidden to them.

الأَعْيادَ on the [Muslim] festival days (often celebrated outside the city walls and therefore allowed?). See p. 160, l. 16 (عَيَّدَ), and note ad loc.

دُعاء prayer/blessing for the recognized Muslim ruler traditionally pronounced as part of the Friday Sermon.

العَبَّاسِيّ the Abbasid [caliph].

اِرْتَفَعَ إلى to have recourse to.

جامع strictly speaking a Friday Mosque (which it may well be here), but also used in the general sense of 'mosque.'

يَحْتَفِلُونَ في وَقِيدِه which they take care to illuminate properly (as part of Muslim custom during Ramaḍān; see *EI*2, VI, 658b, s.v. MASDJID).

Notes to Page 157

مَحاضِر Glossary: schools.

عَزِيب عَنْ (plur. عُزَباء) far away from.

ذِمَّة [official] protection (usually protection accorded by Muslims to Christians, Jews, and Sabians).

لا أَمْنَ لَهُمْ في . . . they do not find safety for. . . In two manuscripts لا أمل لهم "they have no hope for/do not expect [security] for. . . ."

حَرِيم women's quarters, women; see p. 342 of Wright-de Goeje's text, ll. 8-13.

تَلافَى to better [somebody's condition].

شَبَه similarity.

والشَّيْءُ قَدْ تَشَبَّهَ . . . جِهاتِهِ (parenthesis) "and a thing may well assume the likeness of another in one respect only."

قُرْطُبَة Córdoba.

على هذا المِثال according to this (the same) pattern.

مَوْضُوع layout, urban plan.

في الجَوِّ مُظْلِمَة Ed. Wright-de Goeje suggested مُطِلَّة, 'reaching high into the air,' and this is confirmed by three manuscripts.

في "when seeing"; literally: '[when] dealing with,' '[when] engaged in'—cf. W II, 155A-D; *Ar. Syntax*, p. 244, lines 7-9.

كُفْران unbelief.

الأَنْطاكيّ Georges of Antioch, admiral of Roger II (1130-54). The church is known as "la Martorana."[21]

يَوْم المِيلادِ Day of the Birth of Christ, Christmas (cf. مَوْلِد for the Prophet Muḥammad's birthday).

اِحْتَفَلَ لِ to visit in great numbers, to flock to.

مِنْ بُنْيانِها See Index, s.v. *min*.

عَجَزَ عَنْ... to be incapable of...

ويَقَعُ القَطْعُ بِأَنَّهُ ... and which one would decidedly consider to be...

مَصانِع sing. مَصْنَع, see above, p. 156, l. 9 (مَقاصِير); notes, p. 195.

جُدُرُها (plur. of جِدار) begins a new sentence explaining مَصانِعِ الدُّنْيا المُزَخْرَفَةِ, and as such needs no conjunctive particle.

رُصِّعَتْ كلُّها بِفُصُوصِ الذَّهَبِ [ornamented] with inserted gems of gold (تَرْصِيع = *intarsio*, which may well be derived from this Arabic term).

كُلِّلَتْ crowned. Ibn Jubayr does not mention the mosaics in the Martorana which he must have noticed.

نَظَمَ to surround.

بِالشَّمْسِيّاتِ المُذَهَّباتِ مِنَ الزُّجاجِ 'gilded windows of glass,' 'windows gilded with glass.' He probably means that the windows have been ornamented with mosaics of gilt glass.

بِساطِعِ شُعاعِها for بِشُعاعِها السّاطِعِ the brilliance of its rays. See W II, 220D.

---

21 See *Sicilia*, pp. 128-30.

أَحْدَثَ bring about, generate.

نَسَبَهُ إلى to attribute something to somebody, to connect somebody's name with something.

قَنَاطِير plur. of قِنْطَار quintal.

مُشْرِك cf. the same term, p. 150, l. 1; notes, p. 172.

صَوْمَعَة tower.

قَدْ قامَتْ على أَعْمِدَةٍ سَوارٍ standing on mast-like (i.e., thin) columns. The two upper stories of the tower have open galleries one above the other supported by thin columns. The two lower stories show large open windows with columns. In 1726 the upper cupola collapsed. The reading أعمدة سوار (and أخرى سوار), tentatively accepted by Wright and de Goeje, is confirmed by two manuscripts and should be taken as a *badal*, "permutative." See W II, 230A-B, e.g, بُرْدٌ خَلَقٌ, 'an old tattered garment.' See also *Ar. Syntax*, p. 68.

مُلَوَّنَة 'colored' refers to أَعْمِدَة.

عَلَتْ قُبَّةٌ على أُخْرَى سَوارٍ كلّها (root of عَلَتْ is *'-l-w*) one cupola resting on another [likewise] entirely consisting of "masts."[22]

عُرِفَ بِ to be known as; see Index, s.v. *al-ma'rūf bi-* .

شَرَّفَها . . . بِالأَذانِ (Ibn Jubayr hopes that it will soon be used as a minaret).

---

22 See al-'Udhrī, Aḥmad b. 'Umar, *Fragmentos Geográfico-Históricos*, ed. 'A. al-Ahwānī, Madrid 1965, p. 96 (Sevilla): على عمد الرخام في كل ركن من الصومعة سارية على سارية الى اعلى الصومعة...

فَصِيحاتٌ [they are] eloquent.

مُلْتَحِفاتٌ مُنْتَقِباتٌ covered by cloaks and veils. Two manuscripts have مُنَقَّباتٌ. See Dozy, s.v. نَقَّبَ.

Notes to Page 158

مُذَهَّب probably: embroidered with gold.

لُحُف plur. of لِحاف, probably a large cloak covering the entire frame.

أَخْفاف plur. of خُفّ, boot, sandal.

لِ here: to, towards. See W II, 147D-148A.

كَنائِس plur. of كنيسة.

كُنُس plur. of كِناس 'hiding place of gazelles and antelopes' (with whom women are often compared). Ibn Jubayr plays on the identity of the roots of كُنُس and كَنيسة in the Arabic dictionary. For this play, called *tajnīs*, see *EI*1-2, s.v. TADJNĪS.[23]

مِنْ specifies زِينَة, 'finery.'

حَمَلَ to put on, use.

تَحَلَّى from حِلْيَة, 'ornaments,' 'jewelry.'

على جِهَةِ الدُّعابةِ الأَدَبِيَّة following the [common] way of jesting with [quotations from] literature, "as a literary jest."

---

[23] There is a voluminous literature in Arabic as well as in European languages on this device; see for example A. F. M. [von] Mehren, *Die Rhetorik der Araber*, reprint Hildesheim 1970, pp. 154-61.

الشاعِر *a* poet, i.e., somebody belonging to the genus of poets. See below, p. 158, l. 14 (السوق والمساجد); W I, 269B-C; Bro, p. 158; and cf. هو مثلُ الحمار, 'he is like *a* donkey.'[24]

يَلْقَ root *l-q-y*. مَنْ, 'he who,' often introduces a conditional sentence, because it may be equivalent to 'if there is somebody who.' See W II, 14B-C, 23C-24A.

جآذِر plur. of جُؤْذَر, calf of a wild cow. جآذِرا for جآذِر is a poetic license. See W II, 387C-D.

ظِباء plur. of ظَبْي antelope. A line of poetry may not end with a short vowel or nunation (*tanwīn*); a *sukūn* or long vowel is substituted (this long vowel must always be indicated in the case of the *ā*). See W II, 369B-C, and cf. below, XIV, Arabic Metrics.

نَعُوذُ . . . وَصْفٍ يَدْخُلُ مَدْخَلَ اللَّغْوِ a description that would be in the category of an idle joke. Ibn Jubayr, though a poet himself, apologizes, or pretends to apologize, for quoting an erotic line of poetry.[25]

أباطِيل اللَّهْوِ idle [and therefore sinful] pastime. أُبْطولة, plur. أباطِيل is a synonym of باطِل. See *EI*2, s.v. FĀSID.

قَيَّدَ see above, p. 155, l. 7 (وقد نُقَيِّدُ); notes p. 191.

تَفْنيد here: being considered silly, frivolous.

---

[24] The following line has been attributed to al-Akhṭal. Medieval scholars looked for it in Akhṭal's *Dīwān* but did not find it there. It is quoted by Ibn Rashīq, *al-'Umda*, ed. M. Qarqazān, Beirut 1408/1988, (II), 1026. See also the interesting notes in al-Baghdādī, 'Abdalqādir, *Khizānat al-adab*, ed. 'A. M. Hārūn, Cairo 1387/1967-1406/1986, I, 457-59 ff. Metre *khafīf*—see W II, 368A.

[25] The subject is discussed in almost every medieval handbook on literary theory. Early examples in S. A. Bonebakker, "Religious Prejudice against Poetry in Early Islam," *Medievalia et Humanistica*, NS 7, Cambridge 1976, pp. 77-99.

سُبْحانَهُ understood as short for أُسَبِّحُ سُبْحانَهُ. See W II, 72D-73D, and cf. سَمْعاً وطاعةً.

أَهْلُ ٱلتَّقْوَى وَأَهْلُ ٱلْمَغْفِرَةِ quoted from Koran 74:56; dictionaries under *t-q-y* or *w-q-y*. Cf. تَتْرَى from *w-t-r*.

أَطْرابُنْش Trapani.[26]

بِسَبَبِ مَرْكَبَيْنِ بِها because of two ships there (in Trapani), because there were two ships in Trapani.

سَبْتَة Ceuta.

فِيهِ apparently referring to the second ship. Cf. however the reading وكانا أقلعا من الاسكندرية وفيهما. . . for . . . وكُنّا. . . فيهما in three manuscripts.

قُرًى plur. of قَرْيَة —see W I, 199D.

تُرْبَة soil.

طِيباً وكَرَماً واتِّساعاً "in respect of richness, fertility, and extensiveness," "as rich. . . ."

قَنْبانِيَة Campaña.

أَمْتَنُ more solid/more reliable in its yield.

بَلْدَة تُعْرَفُ بِعَلْقَمَة a town known as. . . . The difference between بَلَد and بَلْدَة is not clear.[27]

---

26 See Adelgisa De Simone (above, Intro. to Ibn Jubayr), pp. 51-53.

27 M. Amari, *Storia dei Musulmani di Sicilia* (2nd edition by C. A. Nallino, Catania, 1931-39), II, 494, translates بلدة as 'terra,' 'town,' 'village'; Veccia Vaglieri,

عَلْقَمَة Alcamo. See *Sicilia*, pp. 268 ff.

قُمْنا مِن we departed from.

السوق والمساجد a market and mosques. The article ال here is used to indicate a single item or several items from a category; cf. هو مِثْلُ الحمارِ, "he is like a donkey"; and see W I 269B-C; Bro., p. 158; *Ar. Syntax*, pp. 180-84; *Admin.*, pp. 15-16 (nos. 128-135).

حِصْن الحَمَّة Terme Segestane (?).[28]

فَجَّرَها اللهُ يَنابيعَ cf. Koran 54:12: فَجَّرْنا مِنَ الأَرْضِ عُيُونًا, "We made the earth gush forth in springs."

Notes to Page 159

مِنَ الأَرْض three manuscripts read في الأَرْض, on the surface of the earth.

أسالَها عَناصِرَ (عَناصِر plur. of عُنْصُر) "[He] makes them (i.e., these natural hot springs) flow [bringing forth] 'pure elements,' i.e., mineral waters."

لا يَكادُ nearly not, hardly (note syntax of كادَ, literally: "not nearly"). Cf. Koran

---

II, 348, translates بلد, 'regio,' بلدة 'paese.' It is possible that Ibn Jubayr does not differentiate between the two terms; on p. 169, lines 20-21 of the Wright-de Goeje edition, he calls Mecca first a بلد and then a بلدة. See p. 147 (بلدة تعرف بريّة), p. 159 (l. 16), and p. 160 (l. 9), where Ibn Jubayr refers to Alcamo as a بلدة كبيرة and to Trapani, which he has earlier described as a مدينة صغيرة, as a بلدة. On p. 158, l. 17, بلد may mean 'region.'

28 Amari, *Storia* II, 48; Pellegrini, "Terminologia," p. 170 (with references). See also *Sicilia*, p. 217, which indicates that in this locality there are *"tre sorgenti sulfureo-termali a 44 e 46 gradi C."* The locality is indicated in the *Atlante Stradale d'Italia: Sud* of the Touring Club Italiano, Milano 1980, p. 38.

24:40: إِذا أَخْرَجَ يَدَهُ لَمْ يَكَدْ يَراها , "When he stretches out his hand he can hardly see it."

أَجَزْنا مِنْها واحِدَةً we passed by one of these springs.

دَوابّ plur of دابّة , riding animal (apparently they are no longer traveling on foot).

أَراحَ to give rest, cause to relax.

صَغِيرَةُ السّاحَةِ [offering] little room, small in size.

مِساحَة dimensions, territory.

أَوْفَق most convenient.

ولذلك ما. . . and for this very reason. . . See above, p. 148, l. 8, ولذلك ما يَسْتَوْحِشُ ; notes, p. 166.

الرُّوم In Ibn Jubayr's terminology probably 'Italians' or 'Christians,' but cf. *EI*1, s.v., and Dozy, s.v. رومي .

إِلَيْها to that [town, i.e., Trapani].

لا سِيَّما especially, in particular—see W II, 344A-D.

بَرّ العَدْوَة Dozy: the Coast of Africa.

بَيْنَها وبَيْنَ. . . because the first بين is attached to a pronoun, a second بين must follow; see W II, 180C.

تَعَطَّلَ Dozy: to be interrupted.

رَيْثَما as long as—see W I, 289B.

فَمَجْراها . . . القَرِيبِ and their (the ships') trip in this [direction] is [considered] a brief trajectory.[29]

السُّوقُ والحَمَّامُ Cf. above, p. 158, l. 14 (السوق والمساجد); notes, p. 203; and Index, s.v. article.

لَهَوات plur. of لَهَاة soft part of the palate, uvula; furthest or innermost part (of the mouth).

مِنْ جِهَةٍ واحِدَةٍ ضَيِّقَةٍ from one narrow direction (there is only a narrow isthmus connecting it with the mainland).

فاغِرٌ فاهُ لَها opening its mouth widely to [swallow up] the city.

رَأَى to see, to hold an opinion; here: to expect.

الاسْتِيلاء عَلَيْها [the sea's] gaining mastery over it (the town).[30]

وإنْ تَراخَى مَدَى أيَّامِها even though the stretch of days allotted to it [the city] is still ample.

رَخاء السِّعْرِ low price(s).

لِكِلا الفَرِيقَيْنِ both groups; كِلْتان / كِلان are inflected only when followed by a pronoun—e.g., مَرَرْتُ بِفاطِمَةَ وزَيْنَبَ كِلْتَيْهِما. See W II, 212D-214A.

بِرُكْنِها two manuscripts read يركبها (note the similarity in ductus), which would mean 'to sit on top of,' 'to overlook' [the city]; see Dozy, s.v.

---

29 مَجْرَى in the sense of 100 miles hardly fits in this context.

30 Looking down on Trapani from Erice one cannot escape the impression that Trapani is about to be be submerged.

مِنْ جِهَةِ الشَّرْقِ مائِلاً إلى الشَّمالِ in the northeastern direction.

سُمُوّ height.

اِتَّسَعَ to be wide, spacious. Cf. واسِع in the description of Cefalù, p. 152, l. 9.

قُنَّةٌ تَنْقَطِعُ عَنْهُ a mountain peak standing free from it (the mountain), i.e., not connected with it through a slope.

ويَتَّصِلُ بِهِ and adjacent to it, i.e., the fortress.

بَلَدٌ كَبِيرٌ subject of يَتَّصِلُ. For بَلَد see p. 158 and footnote 27. *Sicilia*, p. 235 (second half) confirms the importance of this town (present day Érice) in the Middle Ages.

حَرِيم here collective for 'women.'

سَبْي collective for 'captives.' One can also use the plur. سُبِيٌّ —see L and W I, 205B-C.

كُرُوم plur. of كَرْم, vine.

Notes to Page 160

جَبَل حامِد Monte San Giuliano. Cf. Pellegrini (see footnote 17, above), p. 165.

هَيِّن easy; root *h-w-n* —see W I, 146A-C.

مِنْهُ refers to جَبَل or to بَلَد.

يَكُونُ فَتْحٌ [a] conquest [of the island] could take place.

لا سَبِيلَ أَنْ يَتْرُكُوا there is no way/it is impossible that they would/could allow.[31]

لِذلك ما see p. 148, l. 8 (ولذلك ما يستوحش); notes, p. 166.

ولَوْ أَحَسُّوا بِحادِثَةٍ If they should be aware of/should notice something happening.

حَصَّلَ to bring over.

One manuscript reads for الذي . . . به of our text: البلد الذي في أعلاه ; another: البلد الذي في أعلاه متصلا به . This last reading seems preferable: "and then there would be between them (i.e., whoever might be in the fortress) and the town at the highest point of Jabal Ḥāmid adjacent to it. . . ."

هذا البَسِيط this flat stretch of land [between Jabal Ḥāmid and the sea].

آبار plur. of بِئْر—see W I, 211A-B, and Bro., p. 19.

قَصِيرَةُ الأَرْشِيَة i.e., because the [ground] water table is high. أَرْشِيَة plur. of رِشاء, 'bucket rope.' For the plur. *af'ila* see W I, 212B-C.

شَرِيب ، شِرِّيب ، شَرُوب brackish, hard to drink.

رامَ here: to plan.

بِها the pronoun refers to Trapani.

---

31 The words سبيلَ ان are missing from *Rawḍ*, pp. 28b and 390b, where this as well as some other sections from Ibn Jubayr are quoted. On both pages we find ولا يتركون مسلماً . I prefer the above interpretation to "it is unavoidable that they would [have to] let. . . ."

بَرّ الأَنْدَلُس the mainland of Spain (to be distinguished from culturally and politically important Spanish islands such as Majorca).

بِمَعْهُودِ صُنْعِه see above, p. 153, l. 15, and note on عَهْد, p. 187.

كَفِيلٌ بِ responsible/answerable for; here: "can be trusted to continue."

غَرْبِيّ west side, area west of...

فَرْسَخ parasang: almost 6 km.; see *EI*2, s.v.

مَليطَمَة ، يابِسَة ، الرّاهِب identified by Amari, *Biblioteca arabo-sicula. Versione italiana*, Torino 1881-89, p. 167, as Marettimo, Yābisa as Levanzo. Levanzo has a mountain called Pico del Monaco. See also Pellegrini, p. 166.[32]

نُسِبَتْ إلى traced back, named after.

راهِب Christian monk; see *EI*1-2, s.v.

أَعْلاها interpret as an accusative of place: 'at its [the island's] highest point.'

مَكْمَنٌ لِلْعَدُوّ [possible] hiding place for the [Muslim?] enemy.[33]

أُسْتُهِلّ هِلالُهُ its new moon became visible, the month began. See W II, 249C-D.

ثَبَتَتْ عِنْدَ حاكِمِ أَطْرابُنْش "stood firm/was accepted as a fact in the opinion of..." —see *EI*2, s.v. HILĀL (pp. 379a-381b).

حاكِم here officer guiding the Muslims in Sicily in judicial matters and possibly also responsible for their behavior.[34]

---

32 The spelling of the names of these islands is supported by *Rawḍ*, p. 390b.

33 A confusion is possible: There is a similar statement in *Rawḍ*, p. 486a, with regard to Pantelleria: وهي مكمن للغزاة من المسلمين والروم.

34 See Amari, *Storia*, III, 323.

أُبْصِرَ had been observed.

لَيْلَةَ الخَمِيسِ i.e., the night before Thursday (which is the beginning of Thursday according to the Muslim calendar).

المُتَقَدِّمِ ذِكْرُها i.e., Palermo.

عَيَّدَ to celebrate [the end of Ramaḍān].

عَلَى الكَمالِ by completing thirty days. They had not seen the new moon on the night before the first day of Ramaḍān and, relying on testimony and the date adopted as the beginning of the Fast in Palermo, counted the maximum of thirty days (بِحِسابِ يَوْمِ الخَمِيسِ) before assuming that the month of Ramaḍān had ended. See again art. HILĀL.

مُصَلًّى place where one performs the صلاة . On festival days the *ṣalāt* was performed by the whole community outside a city or town because an ordinary mosque could not hold all worshippers. Such places were called مُصَلًّى . Being a traveler, Ibn Jubayr was allowed to adopt a mosque as his مصلى . Cf. *EI*1, Supplement, s.v.; *EI*2, s.v.

Notes to Page 161

إِمْتَنَعَ مِنْ to be unable to—see Dozy, s.v.

صَلاةَ الغُرَباءِ either intended as a synonym for صلاة المُسافِرِ (see *EI*1, IV, 102a) or "the [nostalgic] *ṣalāt* of the traveler" far from home on a feast day.

جَبَرَ اللهُ . . . إلى to restore to. . ., bring back to—see Dozy, s.v.

بَلَد perhaps read بَلْدَة . See footnote 27, above.

صاحِب أَحْكامِهِمْ most likely the حاكم mentioned above.

اِنْصَرَفَ here: to return.

بُوقات plur. of بُوق, trumpet.

إغْضاء . . . لَهُمْ عَلَيْهِ closing their eyes [practising tolerance] towards them (i.e., the Muslims) for it.

ونَحْنُ قَدِ اتَّفَقَ كِراؤُنا في المَرْكَبِ "as for us, we had already had the opportunity of hiring a place in the ship/we had managed to obtain room in the ship." Cf. above p. 158, l. 10: نَحْنُ is the subject of the sentence as a whole, and قَد . . . المَرْكَب, which is a sentence by itself, is the predicate of نَحْنُ. See W II, 256A-B.

نَظَرَ في to look after, take care of.

زاد provisions [for the journey].

مُتَكَفِّل cf. note on كَفيل, p. 208.

وَصَلَ أَمْرٌ . . . بِ see p. 96 (وكُتِبَ . . . بذلك); notes, p. 102.

عُقْلَة blockade [of outgoing traffic]. See Dozy, s.v.

بِسَبَبِ الأُسْطولِ with a view to the fleet [the existence of which had to remain a secret].

عَمَّرَ to build, prepare; variant: يُنْشِئُهُ in two manuscripts.

أَعَدَّ to equip; (يُعَمِّرُهُ ويُعِدُّهُ is probably to be taken as a hendiadys: "which he was making ready").

إلى أَنْ until, before.

تَمَّمَ قَصْدَهُ two manuscripts have يَمَّنَ (favor, look favorably upon) قَصْدَهُ.

بادَرَ . . . إِلَى to hasten/hurry in [doing something].

الرُّومُ الجَنَوِيُّونَ the Rūm from Genoa; see above, p. 159, l. 6; notes, p. 204.[35]

تَحَصُّناً مِنَ الوالِي [thus] protecting themselves against the governor.[36]

اِمْتَدَّ سَبَبُ الرِّشْوَةِ the rope of bribery was extended:

---

[35] Ibn Jubayr had also started out on his journey on a ship from Genoa, see p. 35, 3 of Ed. Wright-de Goeje.

[36] From various manuscripts one can derive the following variants . . . وتحصُّنا بينهما وبينه . . . بمركبيهما. This would mean that one has a new sentence, "the captains of the two ships" (possibly accompanied by their crews) becoming the subject of وتحصُّنا.

XIV. Three Poems

Ibn Qanbar

The following poem is a satire by a minor Abbasid poet, al-Ḥakam Ibn Qanbar (2nd/8th century), on the famous poet Muslim b. al-Walīd (born between 130–40/747–57; d. 208/823). A short biography of Ibn Qanbar appears in *EI2* III, 73; see also *EI2*, s.v. MUSLIM B. AL-WALĪD. It mentions that Ibn Qanbar traced back his lineage to the Companions of the Prophet who had emigrated with him to Medina, and that Muslim traced back his origin to the 'Helpers' *(Anṣār)*, who joined the Prophet in Medina. The poem is therefore a typical example of a rivalry carried on through the centuries.

Ibn Qanbar makes the following points:

1. Your father is not your real father.
2. Poetry may be compared to weaving; see Goldziher, *Abhandlungen zur arabischen Philologie* (Leiden 1896), pp. 129–34, especially pp. 131–32.
3. Artisans, including weavers, belong to an inferior class of people; see I. Goldziher, "Die Handwerke bei den Arabern," *Gesammelte Schriften*, ed. J. de Somogyi, Hildesheim 1967–73, III, pp. 316–18; G. Jacob, *Altarabisches Beduinenleben*, reprint Hildesheim 1967, pp. 151–52, 154; and *EI2*, s.v. ḤĀ'IK.

Ibn Qanbar uses the well-known rhetorical trick of conceding a point to his imaginary opponent(s) only to turn the argument around to argue that, even so, his contempt for Ibn al-Walīd is justified.

* * *

From: M. J. de Goeje, *Diwan poëtae Abu-'l-Walid Moslim ibno-'l-Walid...* Lugduni Batavorum (Leiden) 1875, pp. 161–62; *Aghānī* XIX, 71.

لَسْتُ أَنْفِيكَ إِنْ سِوايَ نَفَاكا   عَنْ أَبِيكَ ٱلَّذِي لَهُ مُنْتَماكا
وَلِماذا أَنْفِيكَ يا ٱبْنَ ٱلْوَلِيدِ   مِنْ أَبٍ إِنْ ذَكَرْتُهُ أَخْزاكا
وَلَوَ ٱنِّي طَلَبْتُ أَلْأَمَ مِنْهُ   لَمْ أَجِدْهُ إِنْ لَمْ تَكُنْ أَنْتَ ذاكا
لَوْ سِواهُ أَبُوكَ كانَ جَعَلْنا   هُ إِذا ٱلنَّاسُ طاوَعُونا أَباكا
حاكَ دَهْراً بِغَيْرِ حِذْقٍ لِبُرْدٍ   وَتَحُوكُ ٱلْأَشْعارَ أَنْتَ كَذاكا

Notes:

نَفاهُ عَنْ to remove something from; the context makes it clear that the verb here means 'to deny paternity to.'

سِوايَ from سِوَى, see below.

إِنْ if; here: 'granted that,' 'although,' for which وَإِنْ is commonly used.

مُنْتَماكَ from مُنْتَمًى, a passive participle used as a noun of time or place, or as verbal noun (see W I, 129B-130A); from اِنْتَمَى إلى 'to trace one's lineage to.' For اِنْتَمَى لِ see Dozy, s.v.

ـكا the vowel at the end of a line of poetry is either dropped or lengthened. See Arabic Metrics, below.

لِماذا somewhat more emphatic than لِما or لِمَ: 'why then?'

نَفاهُ مِنْ cf. Dozy: to deny paternity to somebody,[1] e.g., نُفِيتُ مِنَ العَبَّاسِ.

أَخْزَى root (*kh-z-y*), 'to disgrace.'

---

1 So also E. Fagnan, *Additions aux dictionnaires arabes*, reprint Beirut, p. 175b.

وَلَوَ انّي read *wa-lawannī*, poetic license for *wa-law 'annī*—see W II, 375A.

لَئيم base, vile, stingy.

إِنْ لَمْ تَكُنْ أَنْتَ ذاكا "unless you are that person [who is more vile than his father]."

سِواهُ predicate of كانَ; i.e., "if your father were somebody else"—i.e., not the father from whom you claim descent. For سِواهُ as a near synonym of غَيْرُهُ, see 209D-210A.

جَعَلْناهُ. . . أَباكا "we should [nevertheless] make him your father." Classical poems usually divide lines into hemistichs. In case in a line of poetry a word has to be split between hemistichs, a space is left open—as we see here—or, in cases where letters are connected, the line joining the letters is stretched, e.g. لَـــــهُ.

إِذا النّاسُ طاوَعُونا (parenthesis) "if people would go along with us."

حاكَ to weave.

دَهْراً for a long time, "for ages."

بِغَيْرِ حِذْقٍ without skill.

لِ used instead of the accusative—see *Ar. Synt.*, pp. 247-48.

بُرْدٌ striped cloth used for cloaks; also, a garment made from this material. See *EI*2, V, s.v. LIBĀS (p. 734a).

The following translation may be helpful:

I do not deny you, though others may do so, your claim to descend from the father to whom you trace yourself back.

Why should I, O Ibn al-Walīd, deny you a father whom to mention can only bring you disgrace?

Were I to look for [a man] more despicable than he was, I should not find one, unless it were you yourself.

And even if someone else were your [real] father, I would [still] make him (the one you name yourself) your father, if people would go along with us.

[Since] for many years he inexpertly wove cloaks; in the same [clumsy] way you weave poems.

Bahā'addīn Zuhayr

The following poem is by Bahā'addīn Zuhayr (581/1186–656/1258), a comparatively late poet from the Ayyūbid period, about whose biography little can be said. Born in the Ḥijāz, he settled in Egypt at a young age. He served the Ayyūbid ruler al-Malik al-Ṣāliḥ (629/1232–636/1239). Ultimately he fell into disgrace and died in solitude and poverty. For further details see *EI2*, s.v., and the references quoted there, especially Ibn Kallikān, *Wafayāt al-a'yān*, ed. I. 'Abbās, Beirut 1968–71, II, 332–38, no. 247, and J. Rikabi, *La poésie profane sous les Ayyûbides,* Paris 1949, p. 121 and Index. The classical edition and translation of the Dīwān are by E. H. Palmer, Cambridge 1876–77, 2 vols.; there are also contemporary editions.

What makes this poem interesting is the use of old and well-known imagery applied in a new style, as well as the striking simplicity of diction which at first sight almost hides the poet's virtuosity; or, as Rikabi puts it in the *EI2* article mentioned above: "Without rejecting the poetics of his time or its rhetoric with its numerous figures, the poet in him scarcely allows a glimpse of the rhetorician"; or, in the words of Ibn Khallikān (p. 336): "His poetry equals what is commonly called *al-sahl al-mumtani',* the simple yet difficult [to equal in its eloquence]." The poet turns the girl's handicap into an asset, bringing in the already pre-Islamic theme of the misery of hoariness which young girls find distasteful; yet in this case the beginning of old age will not be discovered. The eyes of a beautiful girl are compared to dangerous weapons wounding the lover, but here they wound though kept in their scabbards. Roses bloom on her face, but the narcissus, often an image for the eye, is still closed. To remind us of one more common theme, he compares, in a daring simile, the body of the girl and her eyes forever closed to a safe meeting place. Pre-Islamic poets speak of the fear of spies reporting secret meetings to the relatives of the girl. In an urban setting, they may fear the keeper of a garden who could disturb them, neither of which could happen in her case.

* * *

From: Behà-ed-Dìn Zoheir (Bahā'addīn Zuhayr) of Egypt, *The Poetical Works,* Ar. Text, Metrical English tr.... by E. H. Palmer, 2 vols. (reprint Amsterdam 1971), I. 42; anonymous Beirut ed. (Dār Ṣādir 1383/1964), p. 71.

قالوا تَعَشَّقْتَها عَمْياءَ قُلْتُ لَهُمْ   ما شانَها ذاكَ في عَيْنِي وَلا قَدَحا

بَلْ زادَ وَجْدِيَ فيها أَنَّها أَبَداً   لا تُبْصِرُ ٱلشَّيْبَ في فَوْدِي إذا وَضَحا

إِنْ يَجْرَحِ ٱلسَّيْفُ مَسْلُولاً فَلا عَجَبٌ   وَإِنَّما عَجَبِي مِنْ مُغْمَدٍ جَرَحا

كَأَنَّما هِيَ بُسْتانٌ خَلَوْتُ بِهِ   وَنامَ ناطُورُهُ سَكْرانَ قَدْ طَفَحا

تَفَتَّحَ ٱلْوَرْدُ فِيهِ مِنْ كَمائِمِهِ   وَٱلنَّرْجِسُ ٱلْغَضُّ فِيهِ بَعْدُ ما ٱنْفَتَحا

Notes:

تَعَشَّقَ to love, fall in love with.

عَمْياءَ (circumstantial accusative—*ḥāl*) being blind, though she is blind.

شانَ (ش ي ن) to disfigure.

قَدَحَ (for the *ā* of قَدَحا see above, first poem); lit. 'to make a hole in'; here, to impair, make less attractive.

زادَ to increase.

وَجْد any kind of emotion; frequently erotic, but also used for religious ecstasy.[2] وَجْدِيَ is a poetic form for وَجْدِي, used here to fit the metre—see W I, 101D.

لا تُبْصِرُ أَبَداً for أَبَداً لا تُبْصِرُ.

وَضَحَ to be clear, to shine.

مَسْلُولاً while it is drawn.

---

2 See R. Hartmann, *Al-Ḳuschairîs Darstellung des Ṣûfîtums*, Berlin 1914, pp. 87-89, 135, 138-39, 212.

لا عَجَبٌ poetic license for لا عَجَبَ—see W II, 388A.

مُغْمَدٌ while it is sheathed.

كَأَنَّمَا (particle followed by a verbal or a nominal sentence) 'it is as though'—see *WKAS*, s.v. (p. 5a-b); Vagl., II, 181; *Ar. Synt.*, p. 395.

خَلا بِ to be alone in a place.

ناظِر The Palmer edition reads ناطور (term derived from Syriac) 'watchman, overseer (especially of a garden of vines or palm trees).' The Beirut edition reads ناظِر 'overseer.'

سَكْرانَ while being drunk. For the pattern *fa'lānu*, indicating apparently a transitory, often unfavorable, state, see W I, 135C.

طَفَحَ to be full to overflowing; here: to be full of wine.

تَفَتَّحَ and اِنْفَتَحَ to open up, to burst open.

كَمائِمُ plur. of كِمامَة calyx.

غَضّ fresh.

بَعْدُ ما أنْفَتَحَ for ما أنْفَتَحَ بَعْدُ.

The following translation may be helpful:

They say: You love her though she is blind. I say: In my eyes this does not make her ugly, nor does it hurt her charm.

But it makes my love grow stronger; for she cannot ever see the gray hair shining on my temples.

When a drawn sword wounds, no wonder; but I wonder how, when sheathed, it can still inflict a wound.

She is, as it were, a garden where I am alone; its keeper sleeps, drunk, full of wine.

In that garden, the rose has sprung forth from its calyx; but the narcissus, still fresh, has its eyelids closed.

Ibn al-Ḥalāwī

The following three lines were taken from a curious passage in a long poem quoted in volume VIII, 108, of *al-Wāfī bi-'l-wafayāt,* the voluminous biographical dictionary by al-Ṣafadī, Ṣalāḥaddīn Khalīl b. Aybak (born 696 or 697, d. 764/1363), now in the course of being published by a group of scholars.[3]

Little is known about the biography of Ibn al-Ḥalāwī, Sharafaddīn Abū 'l-Ṭayyib Aḥmad b. Muḥammad b. Abī 'l-Wafā' b. al-Khaṭṭāb b. Muḥammad b. al-Hizabr al-Raba'ī al-Mawṣilī al-Jundī (born 603, died 656) beyond his being a man of letters (*adīb*) known for his subtlety and wit (displayed in his poetry), his sociability, and his sense of humor (*luṭf, ẓarf, ḥusn 'ishra, khiffat rūḥ*). At some time in his career he apparently became a boon companion to Badraddīn Lu'lu', the vizier of the Zangid ruler Nāṣiraddīn Maḥmūd, the Atabeg of Mosul (*EI*2, IV, 80b; *Isl. Dyn.*, p. 121) who usurped power in 619/1222. He accompanied his patron to a meeting with Hūlāgū, but fell ill and died during the journey.

Ibn al-Ḥalāwī's *nisba* probably derives from *ḥalāwā,* pl. of *ḥalwā,* 'sweetmeat.' For the *nisba* ending *ī* replacing *ā,* see W I, 151D–152C.

---

3 *Bibliotheca Islamica,* 6. Volume VIII was edited by M. Y. Najm, Wiesbaden 1971 (see Abbreviations).

وَلِلْمَلاهِي بِهِ ضَجِيجٌ   وَلِلرَّاوَاوِيقِ وَٱلْمَقالِي

فَالدُّفُّ دُفْ دُفْ دُدُفْ دُدُفْ دُفْ   وَٱلزَّمْرُ تَلّى تَلَلْ تَلالِي

وَٱلْجَنْكُ دَنْ دَنْ دَدَنْ دَدَنْ دَنْ   تُصْلِحُهُ رَبَّةُ ٱلْحِجالِ

Notes:

مَلاهٍ pl. of مِلْهًى (root ل ه و) musical instrument—see *EI*2, s.v. MALĀHĪ.

ضَجِيج noise.

رَواوِيق plur. of راووق or راؤُوق strainer, wine cup. The plural is not indicated in Lane, but would be of the type *fa'ālīl*—see W I, 229A. According to Lane, راووق means 'strainer' for wine and other beverages. L quotes one authority who believes it means 'cup.' In a line in the Dīwān of al-Nabigha al-Ja'dī, ed. M. Nallino, *Le poesie di an-Nābiġa al-Ğadī*, Roma 1953, we find on p. 10:

وصَهْباءَ لا تُخْفِي القَذَى وَهْيَ دونَهُ   تُصَفَّقُ في راؤوقِها ثُمَّ تُقْطَبُ

This is translated on p. 13 as follows:

"E quanto [vino] dal color giallo, il quale [per la sua limpidezza] non potrebbe lasciare occulto [neppure] un bruscolo,—e quel vino ne era privo—versato nella coppa e poi mescolato [io ho bevuto. . .]."

According to this translation the term means *coppa*, 'cup,' but *coppa* could also indicate some larger receptacle, and this may be intended here.[4]

"And how oft [did I drink] yellow colored wine, [wine so limpid that] it would not hide any particle of dirt [in it], * [wine] poured into a *rāwūq* and

4 See P. Heine, *Weinstudien: Untersuchungen zu Anbau, Produktion und Konsum des Weins im arabisch-islamischen Mittelalter*, Wiesbaden 1982, pp. 80-82. One could also suggest that the pronoun in *dūnahū* refers to *qadhan*, i.e., a particle of

then mixed."

In Ibn al-'Adīm, *al-Wuṣla ilā 'l-ḥabīb fī waṣfi 'l-ṭayyibāt wa-'l-ṭīb*, ed. S. Maḥjūb and D. al-Khaṭīb, Beirut (?) 1406/1986, II, 811, the editors translate the term as "débourbeur," "cleanser."

مَقَالِ pl. of مِقْلَى frying pan (root ق ل ي or ق ل و).

جَنْكْ type of harp, the precise construction of which is not known.[5]

أَصْلَحَ possibly 'to tune'; cf. Dozy: صَلَّحَ 'accorder [un instrument].' More likely it means 'to take care of.'

رَبَّةُ الحِجَالِ "the mistress of the tent(s)," common expression for a woman.

The following translation may be useful:

There [at the feast] one hears the noise of instruments, wine vessels, and frying pans.

The tambourine says *duf duf duduf duduf duf;* the flutes go *tallā talal talālī.*

The jank makes *dan dan dadan dadan dan* in the hands of the mistress of the canopy (i.e., singing girl).

---

dust which is close to the wine.

5 See H. G. Farmer, *A History of Arabian Music*, London 1929, p. 210, and index; but cf. Bla., s.v. (790b).

Arabic Metrics

The Arabic system of prosody distinguishes feet, not individual syllables. See Wright II, 358C-359A, and 359-361.

It is based on the length of the syllables in these feet—that is, there are:

-short syllables

-long syllables

-overlong syllables, which are counted as long.

In order to be able to use the paradigms of Wright II, 362-368, indicating the postion of the long and the short syllables in each particular metre, we cannot use the Arabic system (described by Wright II, 358D), but have to work with the short/long system, the system that distinguishes individual short and long syllables. It is basically the same as the Arabic system, but much simpler.

Other grammars use the same system as Wright.

In this Reader I shall discuss only the question of determining short and long syllables and the special forms assumed by words at the end of each line to facilitate rhyme (Wright II, 368-73). The student is advised to go directly to Wright on the more complex subjects of the Arabic metres (Wright II, 358-68), the structure of the rhyme (Wright 350-58), and the principal metrical licenses الضرورات الشعرية (Wright II, 373-90).

When reading poetry, always try to determine the metre, as this may significantly facilitate interpretation, avoid errors, and suggest alternative readings, e.g. سَيِر for سَيْر.

Short and Long Syllables

The Shape of the Syllable:

Syllables always begin with a consonant.

Syllables can never end in more than one consonant—e.g., *bring-ing* is not possible; *bed-rid-den* is possible.

Syllables cannot begin with two consonants—e.g. *bring* is not possible; Plato becomes *Aflāṭūn.*

The Length of Syllables:

Short are: consonant+short vowel—e.g., ضَرَبَ *ḍa-ra-ba* (˘ ˘ ˘)

Long are:

a) consonant+vowel+consonant—e.g., لَمْ يَضْرِبْ *lam yaḍ-rib* (¯ ¯ ¯)
فَرَّ *far-ra* (¯ ˘)

b) consonant+long vowel—e.g., *mā* in سَمَاءٌ *sa-mā-'un* (˘ ¯ ¯)

c) consonant+long vowel+consonant ("overlong")—e.g., فارٌّ *fār-run* (¯ ¯).

Syllables in *waṣlah* and syllables ending in *tanwīn* are considered long:

بَيْتٌ *bay-tun* (¯ ¯)

بَيْتٌ ٱلْمالِ *bay-tul-mā-li* (¯ ¯ ¯ ˘).

The *wāw* and *yā'* in diphthongs are considered consonants; therefore دَنَوْا *da-naw* is (˘ ¯).

The following syllables are sometimes counted as long, sometimes as short:

a) the pronominal suffix هُ ه

b) the second syllable of أَنا (Wright I, 54C-D): أنا = (˘ ˘) or (˘ ¯)

c) the syllable *mu* which results from reading:

-kumu or *-humu* for هُمْ كُمْ (˘ ¯) or (˘ ˘)

antumu for أَنْتُمْ (¯ ˘ ¯) or (¯ ˘ ˘)

-tumu for تُمْ (˘ ¯) or (˘ ˘)

(This syllable *mu* we also find in prose:

-in *waṣlah:* قَتَلْتُمُ ٱلرَّجُلَ *qataltumu_r-rajula*

-before a pronominal suffix: قَتَلْتُمُوهُ قَتَلْتُمُونِي)

Short in spite of the spelling is the initial *u* in:

أُولاكَ (˘ ¯ ˘) and أُولائِكَ (˘ ¯ ˘ ˘) Wright I, 265B, 267

أُولو ، أُولي (˘ ¯) used as plural of ذو Wright I, 196A, 266A.

Long, regardless of the spelling, is any vowel that ends a verse.

Thus, every verse ends either in a consonant (i.e., a letter marked with *sukūn*) or in a long vowel. This long vowel may be:

a) a vowel naturally long

b) a long vowel replacing what in prose would be a short vowel + *tanwīn*. Thus, in rhyme one may either suppress *tanwīn* entirely, as in the so-called "pause" forms of prose, or suppress only the *nūn* of *tanwīn*, lengthening the short vowel that precedes. If the latter is done, the resulting *ū* or *ī* is normally not written with و or ي ; however, a resulting *ā* retains the ا of the *alif-tanwīn*.

c) a long vowel resulting from the lengthening of a normally short vowel by poetic license for metrical purposes; in this case, only the vowel *ā* is written in Arabic script with ا .

d) an *ī* added to a syllable that in prose normally ends in *sukūn;* this is done to allow the word to be used in a rhyme-scheme that requires a terminal long vowel. The jussive of the verb is frequently treated in this way.

A Selective Index of Entries Dealing with Difficult Idioms and Technical Terminology

This index takes the place of cross references, which are often cumbersome. The numerals refer to the page numbers in this Reader. The page number is followed by an indication of the term in question or the term under which the information is found. Bold type has been used to mark principal references; thus:

'ahd, ma'hūd **187 min 'ahdī**; 208 bi-ma'hūdi ṣun'ihī

means that the term *'ahd* is discussed in some detail in the notes (or footnotes) on page 187 and that an interesting derivation of the root *'-h-d* appears on page 208 of the notes. In a few cases the symbols ( ) and [ ] have been used to facilitate identification of the term discussed: [ ] indicates the term under which the idiom will be found in cases where this idiom is not part of the text, e.g., on page 23 under *'alā*: ***['alā] al-nāsu 'alā dīni mulūkihim***; ( ) is used in some cases to help in locating the context of an idiom on the page, e.g., *qad* on page 197: *(wa-'l-shay'u) qad (tashabbaha 'l-shay'a... jihātihī)*.

It would be technically impossible to list in this index all places where grammatical questions have been discussed. We have therefore limited ourselves to places which would normally be indicated by cross references (e.g., *ankara* and *ittakhadha,* which, depending on the context, should be translated in different ways) or forms which frequently present etymological difficulties (e.g., broken plurals with the sequence *a-ā-i/ī* or ending in *in,* of which there exist a rich variety). Only in a few cases have questions been listed which have been discussed only once in this reader.

hal min mawḍi'in see min.

ḥaṣala, ḥaṣṣala, taḥṣīl 36 *taḥṣīl*; **92 *ḥaṣala***; 92 *ḥaṣṣala ḥaṣala li*; 207 *ḥaṣṣala.*

ḥattā 87 *[fa-mā waqaftu ḥīnan] ḥattā*; **88 *(ṭaraḥtu) ḥattā idhā... ṭaraḥtu,*** and see *idhā*; **123 *ḥattā atat*; 168 *ḥattā anna/ḥattā inna*.**

ḥusbānāt see Plurals (feminine)

ḥusna... wa-ḥusna... see Accusative (adverbial) expressing determination/specification.

idh see idhā.

idhā, idh, idhā bi, fa-idhā, ḥattā idhā 38 *fa-idhā*; **42 *idh***; 42 *fa-idhā*; **84 *idhā bi-dayrin*; 88 *(ṭaraḥtu) ḥattā idhā... ṭaraḥtu***; 85 *wa-idhā bāriyyatun maṭrūḥatun*; 91 *wa-idhā tilka 'ādatu 'l-rāhibi kānat ma'a...*; 89 *idh*; 112 *idh*; 133 *idhā anā bi...*

ilā 62 *(aḥabbu) ilayhi.*

Imperative introducing conditional sentence **136 *aqbilī***; see also *man* below.

Imperfect as optative (?) 138 *yarḥamu 'llāhu*; **166 *(ma'āl) yuṣliḥu... yaj'alu***; 173 *a'ādhahū min (wa-'llāhu yu'īdhu 'l-Muslimīna)*; 178 *wa-'llāhu yanfa'uhum*; 187 *lā yazālu.*

Impersonal expressions see maghshiyyan 'alayhā, ughmiya 'alayya.

'inda **58 *'indaka***; 108 *istatara 'indī*; 112 *'indī*; **115 *wa-'indahū***; 191 *mā 'indanā minhu.*

innamā 23 *innamā.*

intaẓama, ittaṣala 162 *intaẓamat... khanādīquhā*; **182–83 *muntaẓima* and note**; 194 *intaẓama.*

ista'arati 'l-dunyā nāran see Accusative (adverbial) expressing determination/specification.

ittakhadha 56 *fa-'ttakhidhhā li-rijlika*; for further examples of the various meanings of *ittakhadha*, see 99; 168; 169; 177; 183 (2); 189; 194.

ittaṣala, intaẓama, see **182–83 *muntaẓima* below and note.**

ja'ala **52 *wa-ja'ala***; 57 *ja'ala.*

jawārin see Plurals (broken) of the type *jawārin, nawāḥin.*

jawālīq, jawāliq see Plurals (broken) with the sequence *a-ā-i/ī.*

kafā, kafāhu, kafā bi **164 *kafā bi annahā.***

kāna (sisters of) see zāla below.

kātama, māna'a, dākhala 51 *yukātimu*; **60 *māna'a***; 62 *māna'a*; 62 *[in] dākhalanī 'l-shayṭān.*

kātimu īmānihī, kātimūna īmānahum see *al-munshidu 'l-abyāti/a* below.

164 *minhu*; 173 *ṣun'un mina 'llāhī*; 174 *(ba'da taqdimati raghbatin) minhu ilaynā fī dhālika*; 185 *(ḥamidnā 'llāha 'alā mā an'ama bihī) min*; 187 *akhadha min*; **194 *min*;** 198 *min bunyānihā*; 169 *wa-mā minhum illā man*; **200 *min*;** 206 *min jihati... 'l-samāli*; **213 first poem *min abin*.**

min bayni see bayna.

mujalladāt see Plurals (sound feminine).

mukātabāt see Plurals (sound feminine).

al-munshidu 'l-abyāti/a, kātimu īmānihi, kātimun īmānahū, etc. **203 *al-munshidu 'l-abyāti/a*;** **168 *kātimu/n īmānihī/ahū*; 175 *kātimūna īmāna-nā*.**

muntaẓim, muttaṣil **182–83 *muntaẓima* and note.**

al-muqaddam/al-mutaqaddim dhikruhū, al-mashhūr khabaruhū, al-mutaḥaddath bihī **35 *al-muqaddam dhikruhū*; 138 *(ughmiya 'alayya) al-magḍūbi 'alayhim*;** 171 *al-mutaḥaddath bihī*; 178 *al-madīna al-mutaqaddim dhikruhā*; 180 *al-mashhūr khabaruhū*; 209 *al-mataqaddim dhikruhā*.

al-mutaḥaddath bihī see preceding entry.

muttaṣil see 179 *muttaṣila*; 192 *muttaṣil*; and cf. **182–83 *muntaẓima* and note.**

al-Naṣārā see next entry.

al-Naṣrānī, al-Naṣrāniyya, al-Naṣārā 106 *al-Naṣrānī*; 120 *al-Naṣārā*; **124 *al-Naṣrāniyya*; 186 *al-Naṣārā*;** 196 *(bi-suknāhum...) al-Naṣārā*.

nawāḥin see Plurals (broken) of the type jawārin.

Negations 51 *lā yamna'uhū ... illā...*; 53 *lan*; 59 *lam yash'ur illā bi*; **62 *lā... wa-lā...*;** 62 *mā kuntu li...*; **65 *mā ra'aytu lahā wajhan illā 'indaka*;** 110 *mā sha'ara... illā*; ***laysa lahū hammun illā imra'atu/ahū*; 135, *kallā*; 140 *wa-lā*** (coordinating negations); 192 *mā kuntu awaddu*; **203 *lā yakādu*; 218 second poem *lā 'ajabun*.** See also lā, laysa.

nisbatan see Accusative (adverbial) expressing determination/specification.

nublan wa-nuskan see Accusative (adverbial) expressing determination/specification.

Object see Active participle.

Object (double) in the passive 39 *wa-qad ruziqa 'l-shahādata*; **162 *[madīna] mamlū'atun natnan*.**

Optative see Imperfect as optative (?).

Participle (active) **87 *tālifun*.**

Participle (active) with object see al-munshidu 'l-abyāti/a, kātimu/n īmānihi/ahū, kātimun/kātimūna īmānahum.

Participle with subject see al-muqaddam, al-mataqaddim dhikruh.
Passive see Impersonal expressions.
Plurals (broken) with the sequence *a-ā-i /ī* or ending in *ā'u* **50 *mashāyikh*** (irregular plural; see also 98 *mashāyikh al-da'wa*); 54 *dawābb*; 87, *barābikh*; **92 *jawālīq/jawāliq***; 109 *taḍā'īf*; 111 *'ajā'ib*; 112 *mashāhīr*; 124 *asāqifa*; 125 *qasāwisa*; **162 *khanādīq***; 163 *zawārīq*; 163 *marābiṭ*; 164 *'amā'ir*; 170 *(waḍ') asālībihī*; 170 *(taqsīm) marātib (rijālih)*; 172 *zalāzil*; 172 *aṣāghir*; 175 *mashāhid*; 176 *naṣā'iḥ*; 178 *asāṭīl*; 178 *marākibihī*; 179 *'amā'ir*; 179 *ma'āqil*; 180 *manāfis*; 181 *(fī) ajā'ib (makhlūqātihī)*; 185 *zawārīq*; 188 *masākinu wa-'alāliyyu*; 188 *al-tarāwīḥ*; 188 *kanā'is*; 189 *mayādīn*; 189 *marātib*; 190 *manāẓir*; 193 *jazā'ir*; 195 *maqāṣīr... maṭāli*; 195 *maṭāli*; 197 *maḥāḍir*; 197 *'uzabā'*; 198 *maṣāni'*; 199 *qanāṭīr*; 200 *kanā'is*; 201 *ja'ādhir*; 201 *abāṭīl al-lahw*; 303 *(fajjarahā) yanābī'*; 203 *(asālahā)'anāṣir*; 204 *dawābb*; 220–21 *rawāwīq*; 218 *kamā'im*.
Plurals (broken) of the type jawārin, nawāḥin, etc.—i.e., last radical *w/y* (W I, 214C-D, 247A-B; this plural should not be confused with the type *fa'ālin*, W I, 220 C-221B; see **discussion 194 *mabānin***; and cf. 122 *shawānin*); **50 *jawārin***; 97 *nawāḥin*; 111 *aydin* (from hypothetical *ayduyun*); 161 *jawārin*; 163 *marāsin*; 177 *naṣā'iḥ*; **194 *mabānin***; 220 third poem *malāhin*; 221 third poem *maqālin*.
Plurals (broken) of the type *fa'ālā/fa'lā* 171 *ḥaẓāyā*; **177 *asrā***; 189 *marḍā*.
Plurals (broken) ending in an 202 *quran*.
Plurals (sound feminine) plurals in mujalladāt, ḥusbānāt, ṣawāḥibāt, etc. **34 *mujalladāt*; 74 *mujalladāt***; 109 *mukātabāt*; 109 *ḥusbānāt*; **135 *ṣawāḥibātī***; 181 *masmū'āt*; 181 *[fī 'ajā'ibi] makhlūqātihī*; 189 *maristānāt*; 195 *diyārāt*.
Poetic licenses **18 *'alayka ghayriya*; 19 *tunjīnī*; 141 *fa-yadhhalu***; **141 *Buthayna*** (note on diptotes); 201 *ja'ādhiran*; 217 second poem *(wajd) wajdiya*; 218, second poem, *fa-lā 'ajabun*.
Poetry see 222–24, Arabic Metrics and **18 *'alayka ghayriya***; **217 2nd poem *(wajd) wajdiya*.**
qad **37 *qad waḍa'a***; 37 *wa-qad ruziqa 'l-shahādata*; 58 *qad*; 59 *qad wāfā bihī*; 63 *wa-qad ṣirta lī*; 64 *fa-innī qad radadtuki 'alayhi*; **71 *fa-qad*; 73 *qad nāma***; 98 *wa-qad mashā huwa*; 138 *qad qaḍā naḥbahū*; 184 *qad aghnat*; 197 *(wa-'l-shay'u) qad tashabbaha... jihātihī*; 199 *qad qāmat 'alā a'midatin sawārin*; 201 *(qayyada) wa-qad nuqayyidu*; 210 *(wa-naḥnu) qadi 'ttafaqa kirā'unā fī 'l-markabi*.

Addenda

to p. 5, n. 7 — Wolfdietrich Fischer, *A Grammar of Classical Arabic*, 3rd rev. ed., translated from German by Jonathan Rodgers (New Haven: Yale University Press, 2002).

to p. 6, n. 8 — Kees Versteegh, *The Arabic Language* (Edinburgh: Edinburgh University Press, 1997).

to p. 7 — Wheeler Thackston, *An Introduction to Koranic and Classical Arabic* (Bethesda, MD: Ibex Publishers, 2000 [1994]).

to p. 9 — C. E. Bosworth, *The New Islamic Dynasties Arabic: A Chronological and Genealogical Manual*, enlarged and updated (Edinburgh: Edinburgh University Press, 1996).

to p. 28, n. 2 — Michael Cooperson, "Biographical Literature," in *The New Cambridge History of Islam*, Vol. IV: *Islamic Cultures and Cocieties to the End of the Eighteenth Century*, edited by Robert Irwin (Cambridge: Cambridge University Press, 2010), pp. 458–473.

to p. 79 — Julia Bray, "Al-Tanūkhī's *al-Faraj ba'd al-Shidda* as a Literary Source," in *Arabicus Felix: Luminosus Britannicus. Essays in Honour of A. F. L. Beeston on His Eightieth Birthday*, edited by Alan Jones (Reading: Ithaca Press, 1991), pp. 108–128.

to p. 128 — Hilary Kilpatrick, *Making the Great Book of Songs: Compilation and the Author's Craft in Abū l-Faraj al-Iṣbahānī's* Kitāb al-Aghānī (London: RoutledgeCurzon, 2003), esp. pp. 1–33.

Corrigenda

Page	*Present Reading*	*Corrected Reading*
p. 4, l. 29	Denonmbynes	Demombynes
p. 16, l. 8	مغترراً	مُغْتَرِرًا
p. 18, l. 1	[of the dangers].	[of the dangers]. For the uncontracted form مُغْتَرِرًا instead of مُغْتَرًّا , see W I, 69A-B; II, 378B-D.
p. 7, l. 21	*Arabisch*	*Arabisch: Wörterverzeichnis*
p. 8, l. 3	*dictionnnaires*	*dictionnaires*
p. 9, l. 10	H. Blachère: Gaudefroy-Demonbynes	R. Blachère and M. Gaudefroy-Demombynes
p. 50, l. 18	سما يه	سما به
p. 77, l. 15	*elimnatio*	*eliminatio*
p. 89, l. 7	مَأْشوم	مَشْؤُوم
p. 91, l. 14	p. 390	p. 87
p. 96, l. 16	فمن مُتعجِّبٍ	فمن بين مُتعجِّبٍ
p. 100, last line	is late!	misses the introduction to the *ṣalāt*, though he may still be in time for the *ṣalāt* proper; see *EI* 2, s.v. ṢALĀT (VIII, p. 929a).
p. 105, l. 12	إراهيم	إبراهيم

p. 111, ll, 4, 5	*madhab*	*madhhab*
p. 125, l. 1	قَساوِسة 'priests,' may be plur. of قِسِّيس.	قِسِّيسِينَ plur. of قِسِّيس 'priest.' Note also the broken plur. قَساوِسة, cf. W I, 230A-B.
p. 133, l. 9	sexual organs	vulva
p. 141, l. 1	negation	question
p. 144, l. 13ff.	"For this reason … one manuscript."	*[Delete sentence]*
p. 150, l. 1	بتطلّع	يتطلّع
p. 160, last line	مالبارك	المبارك
p. 216, l. 6	Kallikān	Khallikān
p. 217, l. 2	زاذَ	زادَ

CPSIA information can be obtained at www.ICGtesting.com
Printed in the USA
LVOW111956080312
272253LV00002B/6/P

9 781937 040031